Praise for *The Ar*

"Sharply written, exhaustively reported."
—Nick Gillespie, *The New York Times Book Review*

"[Matt Bai's] unsparing, incisive, and altogether engaging book is a must-read for anyone unaware of the seismic shift that's afoot among the Democrats. . . . A layered, colorful portrait of a party in transition . . . an energetic and timely narrative." —Jose Antonio Vargas, *The Washington Post*

"Whether writing in the first person or the more traditional reportorial third person, [Bai] is a superb stylist and a skilled selector of telling, sometimes humorous, anecdotes." —Steve Weinberg, *The Boston Globe*

"Bai's storytelling abilities are so deft and the tale he tells is so important that you don't have to be a political junkie to enjoy this book."
—*The Connecticut Post*

"Bai is an excellent writer and reporter with a deft touch for revealing character and a reliable gift for crafting memorable phrases. . . . This book underscores his emergence as an important new voice in the political dialogue."
—Ronald Brownstein, *The American Prospect*

"Matt Bai combines the jaded eye of a gossip column with the arc of a Greek tragedy in this incisive tale of Democratic soul-searching. . . . Bai has deep access to Democratic chieftains and a knack for the polemical vignette. . . . Bai succeeds as a sly observer of the left's parlor talk, conferencespeak, and off-the-cuff confessions." —*Mother Jones*

"Matt Bai's *The Argument* is the most significant book to date on the upcoming 2008 elections. . . . Bai has a novelist's eye for the details of the two-way flow between politics and personality, and his extraordinary book is an exposé of sorts, revealing the emotional underpinnings of the new wave of liberal activism that's reshaping the Democratic Party. . . . The new left-wing activists are a subject so rich in fraught personalities as to be a treasure trove for a novelist. Until that novel comes along, though, the uncanny characters that Bai has brought to life will do very nicely." —Fred Siegel, *City Journal*

"Matt Bai has written a slice of history in progress. It is a fun read and will no doubt spark all sorts of debates and disagreements." —Don Hazen, *AlterNet*

ABOUT THE AUTHOR

Matt Bai writes on national politics for *The New York Times Magazine*, where his work has twice been featured in "The Best American Political Writing." Previously, he was a reporter for *The Boston Globe* and a national correspondent for *Newsweek*. He has also been a fellow at Harvard's Kennedy School of Government. He lives with his family in Washington, D.C.

For more information, please visit www.mattbai.com.

The Argument

Inside the Battle to Remake

Democratic Politics

MATT BAI

PENGUIN BOOKS

PENGUIN BOOKS

Published by the Penguin Group

Penguin Group (USA) Inc., 375 Hudson Street, New York, New York 10014, U.S.A.
Penguin Group (Canada), 90 Eglinton Avenue East, Suite 700, Toronto,
Ontario, Canada M4P 2Y3 (a division of Pearson Penguin Canada Inc.)
Penguin Books Ltd, 80 Strand, London WC2R 0RL, England
Penguin Ireland, 25 St Stephen's Green, Dublin 2, Ireland (a division of Penguin Books Ltd)
. Penguin Group (Australia), 250 Camberwell Road, Camberwell,
Victoria 3124, Australia (a division of Pearson Australia Group Pty Ltd)
Penguin Books India Pvt Ltd, 11 Community Centre,
Panchsheel Park, New Delhi – 110 017, India
Penguin Group (NZ), 67 Apollo Drive, Rosedale, North Shore 0632,
New Zealand (a division of Pearson New Zealand Ltd)
Penguin Books (South Africa) (Pty) Ltd, 24 Sturdee Avenue,
Rosebank, Johannesburg 2196, South Africa

Penguin Books Ltd, Registered Offices:
80 Strand, London WC2R 0RL, England

First published in the United States of America by The Penguin Press,
a member of Penguin Group (USA) Inc. 2007
Published in Penguin Books 2008

1 3 5 7 9 10 8 6 4 2

THE LIBRARY OF CONGRESS HAS CATALOGUED THE
HARDCOVER EDITION AS FOLLOWS:
Bai, Matt.
The argument : billionaires, bloggers, and the battle to remake
Democratic politics / Matt Bai.
p. cm.
Includes index.
ISBN 978-1-59420-133-2 (hc.)
ISBN 978-0-14-311417-8 (pbk.)
1. Democratic party (U.S.) 2. United States—Politics and government—2001–
3. Progressivism (United States politics) I. Title.
JK2316.B335 2007
324.2736—dc22   2007018536

Printed in the United States of America
Designed by Claire Vaccaro

This book is for all those voters

who have generously shared with me

life's rarest commodities:

their time and their wisdom.

May you have the government you deserve.

"Too often in the recent past, we have succumbed
to the temptation of believing that more money,
more slogans, more evasion of confrontation, more
sophisticated media advisors, more access to
television, more courtship of lobbyists and interest
groups would satisfy the emptiness in our souls.
It was never to be. There is no political salvation
down that path. All the money in the world, the
cleverest media manipulators, the pollsters and
focus-group experts cannot provide one thing: the
soul of a party."

● GARY HART, *The Courage of Our Convictions*

Contents

Preface

When I think back on it now, I suppose this book began—as so many of the most important things in life do, really—while rumbling in a van through the soybean fields of eastern Iowa. It was April 2003, and I was on assignment for the *New York Times Magazine,* traveling with Howard Dean, who was just then becoming a serious contender for the presidential nomination of the Democratic Party. I found Dean interesting, but what interested me more were his crowds. I had seen my share of standard political rallies, but I was completely unprepared for the depth of partisan passion and fury that swelled within the gymnasiums and community centers on our route. "I'm Howard Dean, and I represent the Democratic wing of the Democratic Party!" the candidate would thunder, hitting his signature line, and long-suffering liberals found themselves literally moved to tears.

In Washington, Dean's campaign was written off as the latest of the party's quadrennial children's crusades, an antiwar juggernaut fueled by the same college kids whose parents had screamed for Gene McCarthy. But when you saw it up close, you knew it was more than that; not only were those kids at the Dean rallies, along with their

hippie parents, but so were housewives and middle-aged labor guys
and a lot of people who didn't even call thcmselves Democrats.
Having endured eight years of Clintonian centrism, an election they
believed was stolen, and then, finally, their party's own capitulation
on the war in Iraq, Iowa liberals had had enough—not just of George
W. Bush and conservative Washington, but of what they saw as their
own party's ineffectual pragmatism. Dean, the former Vermont governor with the hard, gravelly voice, had tapped into a well of resentment that Democrats back in Washington, and those of us who
covered them, simply didn't understand.

Something was happening under the surface of Democratic politics, and it had nothing to do with the usual politicians or consultants.
What I had glimpsed in Iowa was the emergence of the first political
movement of the Internet age.

And so, in the months and years after I first traveled with Dean, I
set out across the country to find the places where this nascent movement was coalescing and to trace its arc. My initial investigation led
me to a cadre of elite financiers, led by George Soros, the Hungarian-
born billionaire, who had begun to meet in secret, pulled together
by a mysterious and closely guarded set of PowerPoint slides. This
weird discovery was followed by others that led me on a meandering
odyssey to every part of the continental United States (and Alaska)—
from the Hollywood mansion of the television producer Norman
Lear to a hotel overlooking the Vegas strip with sparkling chocolate
fountains. I walked the streets of Columbus with door knockers and
drove the California coast with celebrity bloggers. I sat with former
president Bill Clinton, who, forced to defend his legacy against this
liberal insurrection, had lost his cool in front of a clandestine gathering of millionaires in Texas. And I met lesser-known politicians like
Mark Warner and Ned Lamont, whose early forays into this new
movement foreshadowed challenges that now confront the party's
2008 presidential candidates.

Returning to Washington after these trips, I would encounter colleagues and party leaders who remained, as ever, fixated on the deal making in Congress, on who was up and who was down in the midterm elections, and on the early jostling for the 2008 campaign. I'd hear about how elected Democrats like Nancy Pelosi and Harry Reid, the party's leaders in the House and Senate, were supposedly determining the direction of the party. And I began to suspect that all of us who followed Democratic politics had been missing the story. The real reinvention of the party was happening not in Washington, but in New York and San Francisco and Denver and, yes, even in Alaska. More than at any time since the 1960s, the party and its leading politicians were being forced to respond and adapt to a popular movement beyond their control—a widespread uprising led by baby boom liberals, wealthy investors, and defiant bloggers whose faith in party and country had been severely shaken by twelve years of Republican rule.

These outsiders called themselves "progressives," hearkening back to the good-government reformers of the last century. The people they most emulated, however, were the movement conservatives of the Goldwater era, who had not only overthrown the leadership of their party, but who had managed, in an incredibly short time, to wrest control of the national agenda. The leaders of this progressive movement were a disparate group of activists, many of whom were barely known in Washington. Most had money (often more than they knew what to do with), or they had power, or they had neither but understood, intuitively, the potential of new technologies to change political fortunes. Some were motivated purely by ideology, others by anger, and still others by personal torment or a desire for glory. They shared a contempt for the culture of Washington and a belief that the moribund Democratic Party and its traditional interest groups were quickly losing power to a band of political neophytes who hadn't been corrupted by all those years of governing—and who were, therefore, better suited to the politics of the information age.

For two years, from John Kerry's devastating loss in 2004 through the Democratic triumph of 2006, I followed the trail of these new progressives, and I came to like and admire many of them. They were revolutionaries, and the revolt they had started was redefining the Democratic Party. They found creative ways to democratize Democratic politics and to engage a legion of new volunteers. They set out to drive conservatives from Washington and challenge their own party's jaded establishment. And yet they knew, on some level, that a political movement had to be about more than building lists and fighting the power, and they struggled openly to articulate the larger meaning of their cause. I was surprised to discover, as I tried to understand the progressive revolt, that most of its leaders were trying to understand it too. What they were still searching for in these early days of the movement was an argument, some compelling case for the future of American government. They aspired to win—but to what end? If the progressives ultimately triumphed, what would their victory mean?

This remains a critically important question, not just to the Democratic Party and all those who care about it, but to the country as a whole. As I write this, the rigid conservative ideology that has transformed Washington over the past twenty-five years has been soundly discredited. The elections of 2006 marked an emphatic rejection of George W. Bush, both of his failed foreign policy and of his general contempt for dissent and debate. But they also exposed a deeper fatigue with a conservative doctrine that now seems, on so many levels, to be incompatible with the realities of governing. The same ideologues who railed against the profligacy of liberal government ended up running federal deficits that would have been unimaginable to Jimmy Carter. The same reformers who ran against machine-era corruption found themselves shamed by scandal. The same conservatives who denounced "nation building" somehow plunged the country into a bloody experiment in remaking the Arab world. Some version of Goldwater-Reagan conservatism will surely persist through this dark period, but several of its most cherished dogmas—the reflexive disdain of multilateralism, the belief in the superiority of pure markets—have likely lost the shine that made them so tantalizing to voters in the last years of the twentieth century.

At the same time, the Republican defeat in the 2006 elections signified just that—a Republican defeat. There's not much reason to think that the Democratic Party has suddenly overcome its confusion about the passing of the industrial economy and the cold war, events that left the party, over the last few decades, groping for some new philosophical framework. As Chuck Schumer, the architect of the party's successful campaign to win back the Senate, put it in a book published just after the elections, "Unless we are able to answer the question that Democrats are always asked—'What does the Democratic Party stand for?'—voters will go right back to voting for the Republican Party they have been supporting for the last 25 years. Our victory was well deserved, but the Democratic Party still needs a new paradigm." Until they find that governing paradigm, something more contemporary than merely defending programs of the New Deal and espousing the social justice rhetoric of the 1960s, it will be hard for Democrats to establish themselves as anything other than a slightly dated alternative to the mess that is modern conservatism. This would seem to be the main challenge for a rising progressive movement.

There is now, at the core of our politics, a hole waiting to be filled. Writing on Daily Kos just hours after the midterm elections, Simon Rosenberg, one of the early visionaries of the progressive movement, summed it up this way: "Like two heavyweight boxers stumbling into the 15th round of a championship fight, the two great ideologies of the 20th century stumble, exhausted, tattered and weakened, into a very dynamic and challenging 21st century." Americans seem to sense, perhaps better than their aging leaders do, that the solutions of the last century are wholly inadequate to the unprecedented threats of global terror and a global economy. A kind of lingering unease shadows the land, and the movement that dominates the next generation of American politics will be the one not that exploits this emotion, nor that tries to soothe it away, but that articulates some new and persuasive argument for how we meet the future.

I offer this book, then, not just as the story of an oddly heroic group of activists who somehow seized control of their party, but also as a series of questions about the new progressive movement and the future of American politics. How do we, as a nation, move beyond the tired doctrines of a receding era? Who will explain the difficult truths of our new reality? What will the next version of American government look like?

Whose argument will carry the day?

CHAPTER ONE

Election Day

For a certain crowd of influential Democrats in the nation's capital, it was an unspoken rule: If you found yourself in Washington on election day, you made your way over to the Palm. The ritual had started in 1994, the year that saw six decades of Democratic hegemony wiped out in the space of a few hours. On that afternoon, before the disastrous results had come in, Mike Berman had treated seven of his closest friends to lunch in the back room of the steakhouse on Nineteenth Street. The circle of attendees, every two years since, had rapidly grown to include scores of lobbyists, lawyers, elected officials, and interest group leaders, but Berman, a round and gregarious man who was one of the city's most prominent Democratic lobbyists, still picked up the check. He was one of those Washington icons unknown to most ordinary Americans. He had hit his ceiling in government as a deputy chief of staff for Vice President Walter Mondale, but by the time Bill Clinton was president, Berman was on a short list of insiders who could simply walk into the White House any time he pleased. His biennial lunch was one of the few events in Washington where Democrats still drank heavily during daylight hours, guzzling house wine from crystal goblets that were constantly refreshed by waiters in ash gray aprons.

Over the years, the walls of the Palm had been covered from chair rail to ceiling with likenesses of the most powerful politicos who lunched there regularly, so that the whole place had come to feel like some kind of museum exhibit, a fresco unearthed among the ruins of the twentieth-century American empire. A lot of Berman's guests on this first Tuesday of November 2004 were immortalized somewhere on those walls. Madeleine Albright, the former secretary of state. Carol Browner, who had run the Environmental Protection Agency. Tom Downey, the former congressman. Bob Barnett, the elite Washington lawyer. Hilary Rosen, the onetime superlobbyist for the music industry, who was there with her domestic partner, Elizabeth Birch, former president of the Human Rights Campaign. So exclusive was the guest list that a former party chairman from the 1980s hovered pathetically in the front of the restaurant, hoping in vain for a last-minute invite.

At every table one could detect the dissonance between the high-minded ideals of the 1960s, which had inspired most of the guests to seek a life in public service, and the money-for-influence culture of the 1990s, which had eventually swallowed them whole. Anne Wexler, a policy aide to Carter, was now one of Washington's premier corporate lobbyists, fronting for such clients as General Motors and American Airlines. Susan Brophy, who had been Clinton's liaison to states and cities, was the chief lobbyist for Time Warner. Steve Morrissey and Marcia Hale, two other Clinton administration officials, now lobbied for United Airlines and the chemical giant Monsanto, respectively.

Old friends playfully cheated off one another as they filled out Berman's election day ballot, which asked them to predict whether President Bush or John Kerry would win the presidential election, along with the winners of all the key congressional races. The winner always got a nice bottle of wine, and, some years, a weekend in San Francisco at a hotel owned by one of Berman's friends. This year's entries reflected overwhelming confidence. Handheld Black-Berrys vibrated loudly on tabletops, carrying news of the latest polling from around the country. Cell phones were answered and snapped shut. Elated laughter rose above the din of the dining room.

The crowd at the Palm was just now getting word of the first wave of exit poll numbers. The exit polls were the exclusive province of the newspapers and networks that hired the pollsters, and they weren't supposed to leak out before all the votes were counted; it would have been like letting the viewers rip open the envelope for Best Picture halfway through the Oscars. But the insiders at the Palm had friends at the newspapers and networks—that's what made them insiders, after all—and so, via furtive phone calls and e-mails, they always got to know who had won long before the rest of the country heard the news. Secrecy applied only to those outside the club.

This year's exit polls showed Kerry thumping Bush in the Electoral College; he was said to be up by 4 points in Ohio, 3 in Florida, and 10 in Pennsylvania, all fiercely contested swing states. What's more, early word had it that Tom Daschle, the Senate minority leader and a close friend of many at the Palm (his wife, Linda, was a lobbyist for the airline industry), was on course to pull out a narrow victory in South Dakota. If races in Florida, Colorado, Kentucky, and Louisiana followed that trend, Democrats might hold their ground in the Senate or, just maybe, they might even erase the Republicans' slim two-seat advantage and regain control.

The Democrats at the Palm detested everything about George W. Bush: the way he sputtered when he talked and swaggered when he walked, his sense of entitlement and spiritual superiority, his unrelenting contempt for all things coastal, academic, and intellectual, not to mention his imperious policies at home and abroad. But at the

Palm, this election was about more than ideology. This crowd constituted a kind of government-in-waiting, and its restoration would
have practical implications. If Kerry won, some in the room would
likely become cabinet secretaries or high-ranking officials, while
others could expect to take up residence abroad as foreign ambassa-
dors. Democratic lobbyists, who had become increasingly irrelevant
in Republican Washington, would be able to return, at last, to the
West Wing, where they felt they belonged. These were men and
women who had known, at a young age, great power and influence,
and they wanted it back. Throughout their twelve years in exile, they
had almost believed that the next campaign would make everything
right; they needed only to raise a little more cash, to find a better
slogan or a more charismatic leader. Forget all this talk about the
Democratic Party lacking a compelling vision or having abandoned
its principles. There was nothing wrong with their party that a
postelection transition team couldn't fix.

And so, as initial reports filtered in from Ohio and Florida and
Pennsylvania, the restaurant could barely contain the pent-up eupho-
ria. Near the front entrance, Tom Nides, a veteran operative who had
become Morgan Stanley's chief administrative officer, ran into Rosa
DeLauro, one of the party's congressional leaders. Giddily, they
exchanged kisses on the cheek and broke into the old Democratic
tune from the days of FDR:

> *"Happy days are here again,*
> *the skies above are clear again. . . ."*

The insiders at the Palm didn't know, as they ate and drank and
filled out their ballots, that they were no longer the only ones
who had access to the media's precious exit polls. In a small apartment
some four hundred miles away in Burlington, Vermont, Jerome

Armstrong was staring at two side-by-side computer screens on the desk in his living room. Few people at the Palm had ever heard of Jerome, but in the Democratic Party's new and growing universe of online activists, he was, at forty, already a legend, the man who had pioneered the political blog and spawned a movement of liberal imitators. Online, where respect was hard to come by, they sometimes called him "Blogfather." Early in 2004, Jerome had moved to Burlington to work for Howard Dean, drawn by his assault on the party's equivocating Washington establishment. Jerome had invented, as he went along, the brand new business of online politics.

Now, as his wife, Shashi, and his four-year-old son, Taj, played on the floor nearby, Jerome heard the sound of an instant message alert, and a bunch of numbers popped up on his screen. The executives at MSNBC, in their endless quest to be cool, had hired a few young, unknown bloggers to provide online commentary as election day unfolded. Those bloggers had been sitting in the network's Secaucus, New Jersey, studio when the first wave of secret exit polls rolled in. And, of course, one of them had quickly sent the data to the Blogfather in Burlington.

Jerome groped for a pen and started copying down the numbers. He smiled. *Fuck yeah* was his first response. Then he looked closer. Kerry was leading by 18 points in Minnesota and 9 points in Wisconsin. That was insane. The polling had to be off. On the blogs, though, you didn't stop to evaluate information—you passed it on and corrected it later. Jerome did a quick cut-and-paste, added a few lines of context, and hit the send key.

He grabbed the cell phone and called Markos Moulitsas Zúniga, known throughout the blogosphere as "Kos," and Duncan Black, who went by the name "Atrios." Seconds later, they added links to Jerome's blog, MyDD.com, on their sites. Laughing, Jerome watched the spike in traffic as a thousand blog followers flocked to his site. Yahoo News soon posted a story announcing that Jerome had somehow gotten hold of the numbers, adding its own link. Within an hour, a hundred thousand visitors were pounding at Jerome's virtual door, overwhelming the rented set of servers that powered his site from the safety of a cooled room in upstate New York. The blog crashed and went dark. It took hours to restore the servers, but it hardly mattered; by then, it seemed that any American with a computer and more than a passing interest in politics had pulled down the detailed data that had been, in every previous election, the property of a select few. The club had just gotten a whole lot bigger.

J ohn Podesta never ate lunch—as a meal, he found it overrated— and so he just picked absently at the Palm's creamed spinach. He was always jumpy on election day, and the truth was that he could think of nowhere else useful to be. Here, at least, Podesta was among family. (Literally, in fact, since his more garrulous brother Tony, a longtime party lobbyist, was also lunching at the Palm.) Having served as Bill Clinton's last chief of staff, Podesta had held a measure of political power that most of Berman's guests had spent their lives dreaming about. The restaurant was full of people who had done his bidding at the White House or who had sought his counsel or business over the years. And yet, even to them, Podesta remained somewhat inscrutable.

Lanky and hawklike, with round spectacles that slid down to the edge of his nose, Podesta's ascetic nature made him an enigmatic figure in a city where people generally advertised their power, whether or not they actually possessed it. At fifty-five, he still lived in the same modest house in Northwest Washington that he had owned for decades, still attended weekly mass at his local Catholic church, and, most mornings, rose before dawn to train for marathons. Election day with Berman's group was the only day of the year when Podesta allowed himself some wine at lunch. He had, in fact, won the last election day contest at the Palm, but he had never bothered to collect his prize.

Unlike most of the friends seated around him, however, Podesta didn't believe that electing Kerry was going to magically cure all that was ailing his party. He had, after all, been down this road before. In 1992, Democrats had rejoiced at finally winning back the White House for the first time since Watergate, only to lose their decades-long hold on Congress two years later. They had celebrated again when Clinton easily won reelection, then watched helplessly as the country, at every other level of politics, took an even harder turn to the right—and as the party lost control, in 2000, of everything in Washington for the first time since a brief interlude during the Eisenhower administration. Their hope had been rekindled when they regained control of the Senate by happenstance in 2001 (after James Jeffords, a Republican senator, defected from his party), but that victory, too, had been quickly wiped out, when Democrats got pounded in the ensuing midterm elections. By this time, the party resembled nothing so much as a hollow-eyed, stubble-faced craps player in the early hours of morning, hoping against hope that each lucky seven would change his fortunes for good, only to fall ever deeper into the abyss.

The booming nineties had, in fact, been the party's worst decade since the roaring twenties. Despite Clinton's two electoral triumphs, Democratic influence at the state and local levels had declined precipitously. Since Lyndon Johnson's time, one in six Democrats had walked out of the party, obliterating what had once been a substantial advantage in voter registrations. The hard truth was that these baby boomer Democrats celebrating at the Palm had inherited from their parents and grandparents the vessel of a dominant political party, a great party whose legislative ingenuity had fueled the greatest period of national prosperity in the history of the world, and in a few short decades, they had managed to run it aground on the shoals of neglect.

The questions that vexed Podesta that afternoon were more profound than whether Democrats could pick up a few congressional seats, or even whether they could recapture the White House. They were the questions that few guests at the Palm wanted to think about, especially when they were on the doorstep of a revival. What had happened to the once-great Democratic Party? What was its argument—its reason for being—now that the era of big government was supposed to have passed? And who was going to rebuild it?

These were the questions that Podesta was supposed to be probing at his sleek new think tank, the Center for American Progress. With a projected budget of $10 million a year, CAP was to be the advance guard of a new liberal movement, a strategic and intellectual counterweight, eventually, to conservative behemoths like the Heritage Foundation. Podesta had intended to retire, or as much as his constitution would allow, after he left the White House—teach law at Georgetown, sharpen his cooking skills—but he had agreed to help write the business plan for this new think tank, and before he knew it, he had been pressured into running it. The pressure—and the money—came from a triumvirate of wealthy liberal families whom he hadn't known in the White House: the Soroses of New York (George and his son, Jonathan); the Lewises of Cleveland (Peter and his son, also named Jonathan); and the Sandlers of San Francisco (Herb and Marion, their daughter, Susan, and their son-in-law, Steven Phillips).

Podesta, like everyone else at the Palm, was firmly ensconced in the 1990s Democratic establishment. But, since getting to know these new donors, he had become a bridge between this old world of Democratic politics and the new citizen-led movement that was just now emerging on the fringes of the party—an outsider movement populated not just by Dean disciples and online pioneers, but also by a group of ideological millionaires who had bonded over a mysterious set of PowerPoint slides. These outsiders always called themselves "progressives," mostly because the word "liberal" had become so tainted in the public mind, but also, presumably, to invoke the populist spirit of the Roosevelt era. As the rare insider trusted by outsiders, Podesta could see that this movement of bloggers and business tycoons wasn't some fleeting political fad. Fueled by an endless supply of money and the transformative technology of the Web, it had the potential to overrun the party.

Election day would be a critical moment for this nascent movement, one way or the other. In the short term, the progressive millionaires wanted desperately to unseat a president who they did not believe had really been elected in the first place. Kerry, a stalwart of the party establishment, didn't excite the new progressives, but they thought a coconut would be a better president than Bush. Empowered by complex but important changes in the way campaign money could be raised and spent, the three families had bankrolled a venture called America Coming Together (ACT for short), which, in the months leading up to the 2004 election, had assembled its own army of door knockers and its own database of Democratic voters—setting up, for the first time ever, an alternative structure to the Democratic Party's voter turnout machine. George Soros and Peter Lewis had each kicked in an astounding $20 million to ACT and a sister organization called the Media Fund, while their sons, the two young Jonathans, had traveled around the country raising money from other rich guys with liberal leanings. In all of American history, no small group of partisans had ever invested so much money to win a single campaign.

And yet some of these progressives quietly wondered if their movement would really be better served, in the long term, by a Kerry victory. They believed—and had often learned from experience—that simply putting a Democrat in the White House wouldn't right the party, and might in fact make the job harder. If anything, a lot of wealthy donors, driven by their contempt for Bush, might decide that movement building was President Kerry's job, not theirs. Painful as another loss would be, it was possible that Democrats needed to hit rock bottom before they could really change.

The unofficial election night party of the movement would be an exclusive gathering at George Soros's tastefully opulent apartment on Manhattan's Upper East Side. Normally, Podesta, who had been working Democratic campaigns his entire life, would have stayed in Washington to watch the results, giving some live interviews to the cable channels and hanging out with friends from the Palm. This election day, though, he could feel the energy and power in Democratic politics shifting away from the familiar world he had long inhabited. And so, on what was also the eve of their twenty-sixth wedding anniversary, John Podesta and his wife, Mary, hopped aboard a three P.M. shuttle and flew to New York.

All three families of the progressive money triumvirate had gathered in New York, along with several dozen buoyant friends and Democratic activists. Like John Podesta and Jerome Armstrong, they had been hearing the rumors of a landslide. It was, for them, like taking a new business public, the moment when you find out if a particularly risky investment is going to be a wild success or a calamitous disappointment.

Aside from a few politicians, such as Hillary Clinton, just about all the liberals nibbling on miniature grilled cheese sandwiches in Soros's home fell into one of two groups: business entrepreneurs who had made tons of money, and political entrepreneurs who were trying to get their hands on it. Among those in the latter group was a longtime but little-known party operative named Rob Stein, who had become a kind of spiritual adviser to the new progressives. As he and his wife, Ellen, mingled with all the millionaires, Rob was feeling increasingly nervous. This wouldn't have surprised anyone who knew him well. Fit and deliberate, with soothing blue eyes and crisply pressed shirts,

Rob exuded a kind of thoughtful serenity, but just under the surface, he was a chronic worrier who feared the unexpected. The latest exit polls had shown the race tightening to within a few points in critical states, and, unlike most of the donors and some of the younger activists in the room, Rob had been around campaigns long enough to see more than a few victory parties quickly turn to funerals.

Briefly, in the early nineties, Rob had been chief of staff at the Commerce Department. A few times he had even sat in a room with the president of the United States. But, in accordance with the harsh natural law of Washington hierarchy, he had been a minor figure in the Democratic ecosystem. Now that was about to change. Among the crowd at the Soros party, he was considered a visionary, the man with the PowerPoint business plan for the progressive movement. Thanks to the rebellion brewing in the Democratic Party, Rob Stein, in his sixtieth year, was on the verge of becoming one of the most powerful men in Democratic politics.

In the living room, a wide-screen TV and camera had been set up, linking the Soros party, via satellite conferencing, to a hotel suite in Washington where the leaders of the service employees' union, one of the largest and most powerful in the country, had set up their command post for the night. The idea had been to create something akin to the White House Situation Room: The union's president, Andy Stern, who had donated significant money and manpower to ACT, would sit in front of a camera with ACT's top officials in Washington, and from there they would hold periodic conversations throughout the night with the philanthropists in Manhattan. In theory, it should have provided a nice contrast to the industrial age feel of most party headquarters on election night. In practice, it made for a painfully awkward social situation. The billionaire families in New York were desperate for up-to-the-minute intelligence; the Washington hands—seeing as they were in a hotel suite in Washington, and not in Ohio or Florida—had nothing for them that wasn't already on CNN. The two groups sat blinking at each other and exchanging niceties, like alien species who had finally managed to communicate across physical boundaries, only to find that they had nothing to say. At one point, Harold Ickes, a legendary party strategist who was taking part from Washington, appeared to fall asleep.

Even through the filter of a video screen, you could read the anxiety in the faces of Stern and the other experienced campaign operatives as the clock passed ten. Kerry took Pennsylvania, as expected, but Bush appeared to have Florida and smaller swing states such as New Mexico and Iowa. Morose organizers on the ground in Ohio, the last great hope for Kerry, reported that heavy downpours had tested the resolve of urban black voters stuck in impossibly long voting lines. The victory that had seemed inevitable during the afternoon suddenly seemed less assured. Even after the conferees in New York and Washington mercifully decided to return to their respective vigils and reconvene later, the giant screen in Soros's apartment continued to carry the live feed of an empty hotel couch. It was as if all the Democrats in Washington had spontaneously combusted.

At about the same time, Terry McAuliffe was standing near the outdoor stage in front of Kerry headquarters in downtown Boston, draping his elastic arms around the likes of Lance Armstrong and Sheryl Crow. "The Macker," as even close aides liked to call him (as in "The Macker has landed!" or "You need a few minutes with the Macker?"), was operating on just a few hours' sleep, having spent the last week in a blur of several cities a day, rallying troops in outdoor malls and airport hangars. Even so, he remained his characteristic self—which is to say, affirmatively, almost alarmingly, cheerful. When Bill Clinton, his close friend and golfing buddy, had made McAuliffe chairman of the Democratic National Committee four years earlier, the former investment banker had vowed that the party would not be outspent in the next election. Never again, or at least not on his watch, would it have to pull out of states early because the cash well was running dry. He had kept that promise. He had proven himself to be the greatest, most prolific, most brazen fund-raiser in his party's history, if not in the history of American politics. In a few weeks, assuming the exit polls held up, he expected President Kerry to name him the next secretary of commerce. Selling American ingenuity abroad, downing beers with foreign friends in strange lands—there could be no better assignment for a man who couldn't set foot in a Washington restaurant without slapping the backs of half the patrons, his booming voice heralding the Macker's arrival.

One of the party's top young thinkers and speechwriters, Andrei Cherny, had written two speeches for McAuliffe to carry around that night. Cherny was sure McAuliffe wouldn't need a concession speech, but it was a speechwriters' tradition, and one that Cherny always observed, to respect the hand of fate by writing one anyway. The real speech, the festive one that the Macker was to deliver that night to a crowd of local supporters who had just finished celebrating their first World Series title in eighty-five years, began like this: "From the Red Sox sweep to a sea of Blue States, tonight, Boston, you're not just the cradle of liberty. You're the cradle of victory!" It went on:

> I'd like to say a personal word tonight to Democrats across the country. Since the day you chose me as your chairman nearly four years ago, there have been many times that people told us this day would never come. But in the darkest hours, you never gave up on your faith in this party, in this nation, in this democracy. You worked and believed and worked and planned and worked some more. You built a Democratic Party ready for the 21st century. And tonight this victory is yours!

McAuliffe had balked when Cherny and Jano Cabrera, his communications director, brought the speech to him in his hotel suite that afternoon. "Don't you think we should tone it down?" he had asked. "I mean, the polls will still be open in some states." It was the first time in his long career, beginning with his stint as Jimmy Carter's finance director in 1976, that McAuliffe could ever remember scolding someone *else* for excessive optimism; it had always been the other way around. Cherny and Cabrera had made the speech more ambiguous, just to be cautious. By eight o'clock, though, the Republican spokesmen had stopped doing TV interviews, which indicated to McAuliffe that they knew they were through. His BlackBerry buzzed with giddy e-mails. Staff members told him that friends in the Republican White House had begun sending them notes of congratulations.

And so, now, he was standing, at last, in the biting cold (a native of upstate New York, McAuliffe claimed he didn't even own a coat), preparing to introduce the Black Eyed Peas. Suddenly, McAuliffe's personal aide pulled him aside. He led him back to the hotel across the street, where the DNC had a "boiler room" on the second floor. There they gave him the news: Florida had gone to Bush, and Ohio was fading. McAuliffe had trouble processing this. Were they sure? How could this be? When he reemerged outside, he didn't seem like the Macker anymore. The week's insanity appeared to have descended on him all at once, leaving his face a sickly gray. His wife, Dorothy, asked him what had happened. "It's not looking good," was all he could whisper before rediscovering his smile and bounding onstage.

As far as McAuliffe was concerned, the Democratic Party had done everything possible to elect John Kerry. He had given Kerry's people all the money and organization they needed, and they had squandered it with a campaign that was timid and erratic. This defeat belonged to them, not to him. So after hearing from John Sasso, one of Kerry's top strategists, that Bush had won, McAuliffe slipped out of the crowd and back to his hotel, where he finally crashed. At two in the morning, the phone rang. It was Lou Sussman, the campaign's top fund-raiser; Kerry's team was going to need McAuliffe's help finding money for a recount. McAuliffe's head reeled for a moment. Then he hung up the phone and went back to sleep.

I hadn't been invited to the Soros soiree, and I hadn't been able to bear the thought of standing outside in Boston on a frigid November night. And so, instead, I had returned that election week to the place where I had spent a large chunk of that campaign year: Columbus, Ohio, the ideological dead center of the country. Ohio was expected to be one the decisive theaters of engagement between Bush and Kerry, and Soros and his brethren had spent some $18 million on ACT operations in that state alone, making it their single biggest gamble. If the winner of the 2004 campaign was going to be determined by the state that had given us no less than eight American presidents (not to mention Wendy's hamburgers and the chocolate buckeye), then I wanted to be there to see it.

ACT's election night celebration in Ohio was to be held in what looked like an old warehouse on Main Street in Columbus. The event space had brick walls, exposed copper piping, and a sad little mirrored ball hanging from the ceiling. It was the kind of place where they might hold speed dating or senior bingo. By the time I wandered in at around eight P.M., hundreds of volunteer door knockers, many from California and New York, had shed their waterproof ponchos and gathered to watch the victory unfold on a jumbo TV. They gasped when Florida fell, cheered when Pennsylvania went blue, and then fell still as Tom Brokaw showed the world a map of Ohio and proclaimed that the Buckeye State would almost certainly determine the next president of the United States.

In the back of the ballroom, several of the more tech-savvy volunteers huddled over laptops and watched as the Ohio secretary of state's office posted the results in real time. Until recently, these precinct-by-precinct numbers had always been the restricted domain of campaign professionals, who breathlessly awaited updates from callers at the key precincts. This year, though, like seemingly everything else about the political process, the data had become fully democratized, so that anyone with a T1 line could get the raw numbers instantaneously. Which was great, except that none of us had any idea what we were looking at.

As the clock passed midnight, 77 percent of the state's precincts had reported, with Bush leading Kerry by fewer than 150,000 votes. The outstanding precincts, however, were largely in Cuyahoga County, the state's largest—a county so heavily Democratic that in the 2000 election there were entire precincts in which Bush garnered not a single vote. So it seemed reasonable to assume that Kerry would close the gap; the only question was whether there were enough votes still out there to propel him into the lead. But then 80 percent of the precincts had reported, and then 86—and still Bush's margin held steady. What a real pro would have known, from a single glance at the data coming in, was that the precincts in downtown Cleveland had long ago reported their results; the votes that remained to be counted were in outlying areas of the county that were decidedly mixed in their political proclivities. In other words, what the volunteers were watching on their computer screens was not, in fact, the dramatic comeback they thought they were watching, but a tragic end playing itself out, the vital organs of the Kerry for President campaign shutting down, one by one.

It was around one in the morning when Brokaw at last painted Ohio red. "It is now hard to see," he said solemnly, "how George W. Bush is not reelected president of the United States." The little ballroom went still, save for the intermittent sob, the creak of a folding chair, the ringing of a cell phone. "This is the end of the United States of America," one man said as he donned his coat and walked out. The volunteers in the back, however, were still staring at their screens, which showed a margin of 100,000 votes, and they were incredulous. After a quick huddle, they decided this was, in fact, not the end of the campaign at all, but a Brokaw-led conspiracy to throw the election. The other anchors weren't yet projecting Bush as the winner in Ohio. And so they did what a lot of people do when they don't like what they're watching: They changed the channel. This created a minor uproar among the dispirited volunteers, who for some reason seemed strongly to prefer Brokaw to Dan Rather and who had suffered enough for one night. Sensing a revolt, one of the techie volunteers then marched out from behind his laptop and pleaded with the crowd. "Folks, the reason we changed the channel is because NBC is the only network that called it!" he shouted hoarsely, trying to breathe hope back into the room.

I was standing in a corner with Steve Bouchard, the field expert whose job it had been to run ACT's operation in Ohio. He watched this scene unfold with a kind of morose detachment, as if he were looking down on us all from some far better place. Changing channels struck him as pointless. "I hear the PAX network hasn't called it either," he muttered sardonically. "Maybe we should put *that* on."

If anyone should have been despondent by the time the network anchors signed off for the night, it was George Soros. The renowned currency speculator, recognizable by his perpetual bed head and thick Hungarian accent, had written a book and taken to the lecture circuit to convince his fellow Americans that Bush represented the greatest threat yet to American democracy. He had spent almost $30 million of his own fortune to unseat the president. And yet, as he consoled the guests staggering out of his building into the cold Manhattan night, Soros remained remarkably composed. The Lewises, father and son, had retreated into a side room and closed the door when it became apparent that the election was out of reach. Soros, on the other hand, seemed philosophical and resilient. "We had to do what we did," he told his guests. "We took our best shot."

You didn't make billions the way Soros did—by speculating in the world's most tumultuous markets—without learning how to lose. He had gambled and lost hundreds of millions of dollars, famously, on Russian telecommunications, the fortunes of the yen, the boom and bust of Silicon Valley. In the long run, you never appraised your losses in isolation, but rather as part of a larger strategy. Yes, he had squandered $30 million, but this was a modest sum when compared with the $450 million his foundation spent every year to foster democracy in other parts of the world. And his investment had not been without some return. It had enabled him to make a well-publicized case against Bush and to bring thousands of new volunteers into the process. And it had inspired other wealthy ideologues to invest their money in independent political ventures too—a ripple effect that would have serious consequences for Democratic politics in the months ahead. Soros took solace in these things. He was nothing if not an optimist.

It wasn't until the sun came up over New York that Soros and his friends would begin to understand the deeper nature of their defeat. When all the votes were counted—and this time, unlike four years earlier, all but the most hardened conspiracists would come to accept that all the votes, had, in fact, been counted—the election of 2004 would stand as a stinging rejection of the Democratic Party. It wasn't the margin of Bush's victory that made it so profound; his four-point edge in the popular vote hardly qualified as a landslide, and, as Kerry would never tire of pointing out in the months to come, 75,000 switched votes in Ohio would have sent the president packing. Rather, it was the peculiar circumstances that made the outcome so historically remarkable. Having assumed the presidency under conditions that undermined his legitimacy, Bush had campaigned for reelection with an approval rating that hovered just above 50 percent; no president in modern history had won a second term with such tepid support. He had, in his first term, presided over a hemorrhaging of good jobs and an alarming increase in the national debt. Though he had rallied Americans in the wake of a scarring terrorist attack, he had failed to capture the culprit and had instead led the country, on false suppositions, into a war that now seemed grossly ill advised. His presidency—reminiscent in many ways of that of another Southern governor, Jimmy Carter—was increasingly hobbled by a growing sense of chaos and mismanagement, of events spiraling beyond anyone's control.

Against this backdrop, Democrats had pulled together and mounted a ferocious assault. They had stuffed Kerry's pockets with a record $200 million and donated another $150 million to outside groups like ACT. Hollywood celebrities, New York financiers, the country's leading editorial pages and magazine editors, the best-known novelists and scientists, rock stars as diverse and influential as Bruce Springsteen and Eminem—all the leading arbiters of American culture had been united in their determination to "re-defeat Bush," as the bumper stickers put it. They had rejoiced when Kerry stomped Bush in three of the most watched and most lopsided debates since the advent of television. But somehow, incredibly, in defiance of all historic markers, they had come up short again. And it wasn't just the presidency that had eluded them. Daschle was gone too, making him the first Senate leader of either party to be unseated in half a century. The party had lost every Senate race in the South and all but one in the West, widening the Republican majority from two seats to ten. There had been some state-level successes—in Colorado, a well-organized Democratic resistance had taken back the state legislature—but the national picture was bleaker than ever.

Twenty-four hours after they had marched to the polls with such enthusiasm, Democrats awoke Wednesday to find themselves not only deeper in the minority but, for the first time in a generation, without any genuine leadership or the slightest sense of direction. The familiar figures who had dominated Democratic politics throughout the '90s and into the new millennium were suddenly gone, having either left politics altogether or decided to retreat into the shadows for a while. At just fifty-four, Bill Clinton had retired to Harlem, where he spent his time attacking such crises as African AIDS and childhood obesity. His wife, Hillary, now ensconced in the Senate and nursing her own presidential ambitions, was biding her time quietly. Al Gore, still bitter from his 2000 defeat, was back in Tennessee. Daschle and Dick Gephardt, the House leader who had failed in his second and final bid for the White House, were packing up their boxes and preparing to leave the Capitol. Kerry stayed in Washington, but he seemed to have tapped out what little reservoir of personal loyalty existed for him.

Into this vacuum, entrepreneurs from outside the ruling establishment—people from Wall Street and Hollywood and cyber-space, political neophytes who were already amassing in clandestine meetings and on well-trafficked websites—were about to come rushing. In the months ahead, it would sometimes seem that every liberal with confidence and a computer had some bright new plan to reinvent Democratic politics. The power was moving away from the party elite and toward a group of progressives whose goal was to build a movement every bit as vibrant and consequential as the one that grassroots conservatives had unleashed on the country thirty years earlier.

All of this, however, seemed remote on that November morning after yet another devastating defeat. For John Podesta, the day held more trauma still. Unable to spare time during the campaign season, he had put off some painful and necessary dental work until the first available moment. And so, having returned to Washington first thing in the morning, he lay back in the dentist's recliner and tried to focus his mind on the uncertainty that lay ahead. What he would remember later, after most of the unpleasant experience had dissipated in the haze of the anesthetic, was the sound of a man's voice reading the news on the dentist's radio. "George W. Bush will be sworn in for a second term as president on January twentieth," the voice said, as Podesta felt the drill push down deep into his bone.

CHAPTER TWO

The Killer Slide Show

"You are about to become the third person in Washington to have a copy of this," Rob Stein said solemnly. He plunked a metal loose-leaf binder onto the table and patted it softly. This was back in May of 2004, six months before John Kerry's defeat, and we were sitting on the sun-splashed patio of a Starbucks on New Mexico Avenue, a block from his home in Northwest Washington. Rob studied me pensively, awaiting some reaction. With his curly gray hair and bemused expression, Rob looked remarkably like the actor Albert Brooks—even his grown-up children couldn't watch *Broadcast News* without laughing about it. He wore a silk shirt and khaki shorts. I looked down at the binder on the table as Rob dramatically flipped open the cover to reveal a collection of some forty PowerPoint slides, all with white lettering on a deep blue background. I glanced quickly at the title page: "The Conservative Message Machine's Money Matrix." In the lower corner, in smaller lettering, was the only sign of ownership. It said, cryptically, "The Phoenix Group."

By the time I met Rob that spring, he estimated that some seven hundred people had already seen his presentation. So many

Democrats now wanted to see the slide show, which required them to take an oath of confidentiality, that it simply wasn't possible for Rob to keep up with demand. The whole phenomenon reminded me, for some reason, of the old Monty Python sketch about the "killer joke," in which everyone who hears the joke—purported to be the world's funniest—instantly laughs themselves to death. But those Democrats who saw Rob's slide show didn't die; they were reborn. Wealthy contributors on both coasts told me that Rob's slides had awakened them, at last, to the truth of what was happening in American politics. They stumbled back onto Wall Street or Wilshire Boulevard or the Embarcadero blinking into the sunlight, as if having witnessed a revelation.

Naturally, I was eager to be transformed too. And so, for the next half hour or so, as we sipped our iced coffees, Rob flipped briskly through his slides, which he had reproduced on paper, with the practiced cadence of one who had done so, using the exact same words, a hundred times before. He began with a history of the modern conservative movement, which he dated back to 1971. That's when Lewis F. Powell, the future Supreme Court justice, wrote a confidential memorandum to business leaders warning that America's economic system was under attack by powerful liberals. A coordinated counterattack was needed. "Survival of what we call the free enterprise system," Powell said ominously, lay in "careful long-range planning and implementation, in consistency of action over an indefinite period of years, in the scale of financing available only through joint effort, and in the political power available only through united action and national organizations."

Heeding Powell's advice, a group of conservative philanthropists, disciples of the conservative icon Barry Goldwater, systematically financed a concerted movement to change virtually every aspect of American life. Their investments yielded an agenda for economic, social, and geopolitical change—lower taxes, deregulation, welfare

reform, school vouchers, preemptive military action—that would
have been considered extreme at the time Lewis penned his
memo, but that had, over time, become core tenets of the nation's
mainstream political debate. How had a few largely unknown, hard-
core conservatives managed to pull off such a momentous feat?

Rob had an answer. Conservatives had erected a ruthlessly efficient, $300 million "message machine," which Rob now diagrammed
in little teal boxes connected by a series of intersecting lines. They
were pouring $180 million a year into think tanks (the Heritage
Foundation, the American Enterprise Institute, the Cato Institute,
the Hoover Institution) that had spent the last thirty years developing
and promoting a new generation of policy ideas to support their central argument—that a meddling federal government had trampled
American liberties and weakened a great country. Along with
religious groups, philanthropic foundations, legal centers, and policy
journals, these think tanks housed the "message makers"—the
people who determined the conservative agenda and figured out how
to market it. This message machine sent out talking points to more
than a dozen major conservative broadcast outlets and newspapers,
from Rush Limbaugh and Fox News to the *Weekly Standard,* which
disseminated them to the grass roots. Here Rob's diagram looked like
the classic hub-and-spoke assembly, with the message machine, a
large circle in the middle, shooting out lines in every direction.

"This is perhaps the most potent, independent, institutionalized
apparatus ever assembled in a democracy to promote one belief
system," Rob told me, choosing his words deliberately. He wanted
me to know that he was not accusing conservatives of subterfuge or
fraud. They were simply investing in the capacity to make their argument as forcefully as they could. "What you need to understand
about me is that I try to be respectful and objective about this. Not
only is it a legitimate exercise in democracy, but I think they came up
with some extraordinary ideas."

The main point of the presentation was this: According to Rob's research, there were maybe two hundred "anchor donors"— wealthy individuals with names like Coors, Scaife, Mellon, Olin, and Bradley—who had created and sustained, primarily through their own philanthropic foundations, the modern Right. They were the venture capitalists of conservative America, the angel investors to a generation of ideological entrepreneurs. They had created what Rob called the "infrastructure" of Republican politics. These donors worked through a sophisticated network of Washington operatives who behaved like investment bankers, directing the money to the various right-wing groups that needed it. According to Rob, the imbalance between the two parties nationally could be directly linked to this imbalance in their underlying infrastructures. The Right spent $170 million a year on national and local think tanks; the Left spent $85 million. The Right spent $35 million on legal advocacy groups; the Left spent $5 million. The Right spent $8 million to indoctrinate young conservatives at its Leadership Institute; the Left spent approximately nothing. Those liberal think tanks and advocacy groups that did exist were desperate for funds, which meant they were always trying to outmaneuver one another for money, rather than cooperating on a common agenda.

Conservatives hadn't simply learned to win elections. They had also, over the last thirty years, changed the terms of American political debate. If you imagined the nation's politics as a gauge moving from far left to far right, then the default position of the needle, the place where most Americans lived, was no longer in the middle. Gradually, almost imperceptibly, it had tilted to the right, and this was not an accident. It was the result of a deliberate, stealthy campaign waged and funded by a relatively small number of wealthy white men whose only real political allegiance was to a radically conservative ideology. What Democrats needed, Rob was arguing, was not a better party apparatus or stronger candidates, but their own version of the message machine. They needed to build independent groups that could create and promote a progressive agenda—not for the purpose of winning the next election or the one after that, but to restore, over time, some ideological balance to the marketplace of political ideas.

None of what Rob was saying about the conservative movement was terribly new, but never had it been so carefully quantified, so tightly packaged, so nicely visualized. Moreover, Rob's argument represented a fairly radical departure from the static way in which Democratic politics had always worked. Because Democrats had been the majority party for so much of the twentieth century, their leading politicians had always run the party, and the donors existed simply to serve the interests of those politicians. Elected leaders and their consultants directed wealthy patrons to give to a series of campaigns or party committees, or to hold fund-raisers at their lavish homes for the same purpose; if the contributors didn't give money to the party or its candidates, then they weren't considered important players in the Democratic universe. What Rob was suggesting, now that Democrats had been consigned to the minority, was that the whole system should essentially work in reverse—that it was up to the donors to build their own ideological movement (indeed, that they were the only ones who could), and that the party's politicians should take direction from them, rather than the other way around.

I asked Rob what had prompted him to take all of this on. How was it that Rob Stein, a little-known political operative, had come to be sitting here in front of me, tracing the anatomy of American conservatism and plotting out the response?

Rob nodded and leaned back thoughtfully. He had been waiting for this question. "I literally woke up the day after the 2002 elections," he told me, pausing dramatically. "Picked up the paper . . ." Another pause. "Had breakfast . . ." Now he leaned in and touched my arm. "And we were living in a one-party country." He let the reality of this sink in. "And there it was. That was my wake-up call. I said, 'Okay, there's now Republican dominance down the line. It's not only that they control the House and the Senate and the presidency. But it's growing. There's no end in sight.' It wasn't only that they had reached a milestone, but they were *ascendant*."

Suddenly, Rob told me, he had felt compelled to understand what had happened, and so he had gotten his hands on reports that had been written on conservative philanthropy, along with some tax statements from various think tanks, and went to work. For months after this epiphany, he had stayed up until one in the morning, long after Ellen and their daughter, Grace, had gone to bed, scanning Web sites for clues. He went in search of what Hillary Clinton had famously called "the vast right-wing conspiracy," and he became its Vasco da Gama, memorizing its contours and meticulously mapping it for all the world to see.

A s I would learn from subsequent conversations with Rob Stein, conducted over countless cups of Starbucks coffee in the years that followed, this was how he tended to view his life—as a meandering journey connected by pivotal insights and moments of sudden illumination, unforeseen currents that guided him downstream in one direction or another. He had been a cultural outsider for as long as he could remember. The Steins were among the few Jews in Wheeling, West Virginia, where Rob worked summers in his father's chain of local lumberyards. His dad was a boastful, gregarious salesman of the 1950s variety, whose loud stories sometimes embarrassed his son, and Rob's mom was always leading some civic group or another. Rob turned in another direction: inward. He learned to hang back, to listen, to reflect. It was the easiest way to blend in on the campus of the rigid military school he attended for eight formative years, and then on the radicalized campus of Antioch College, where

Rob—something of a misfit, the only accounting major who wore a tie to class every day—once sat at a table with the young Bob Dylan, who was passing through.

Coming of age in two such radically different cultures—one based on discipline and uniformity, the other on individualism and expression—instilled in him a lifelong fascination with group dynamics and what he called, admiringly, "the wisdom of crowds." Rob's great skill was to act as a bridge between opposing points of view, insinuating himself into a discussion by listening and reacting. He revered consensus and sought it out with quiet determination. He was not, he knew, a visionary, the kind of person who walked into a room full of people with the next brilliant idea, but he was the guy who could get everyone in the room to agree on the same version of an idea, and in politics that was a marketable talent. It was the reason that Ron Brown, Clinton's secretary of commerce, had wanted Rob as his chief of staff. After Brown and thirty-four others were tragically killed in a plane crash in Croatia in 1996, a widely printed photograph showed Rob, shaken, pausing over his mentor's casket.

Rob's first great epiphany had occurred, he would later tell me, while he was sitting alone on the banks of the Colorado River in the summer of 1978. After a decade of practicing law, he had just decided to quit and do something else with his life. He was thirty-four, in a first marriage that ultimately wouldn't last, with two small children and a third on the way. Like a lot of young men who suddenly find themselves with family responsibilities, he had lost sight of what he had hoped, at a younger age, to achieve. As Rob told it, he had gone hiking with his brother-in-law and three other guys in the Grand Canyon, and one day they all split up. Rob found himself sitting by the river, tossing stones into the water and watching concentric circles radiate out, contemplating the meaning of his inconsequential life. And suddenly he thought of John Donne's famous line: "No man is an island." He couldn't get this idea out of his head.

After returning home, he continued to read widely and contemplate nature, until at last he arrived at a guiding theory of existence—a theory that revolved around the core idea that everything in nature was defined by its relationships to other things. In his mind, Rob classified these relationships into several levels: the relationships of each person to himself, to others, to his natural environment, to his possessions, and, finally, to the spiritual world. "The struggle for meaning is the struggle for embracing the quality of relationship at each of these levels," Rob told me during one of our talks. "The harmony we seek, the longing we have, is for the harmony of the universe." Guided by this new understanding, Rob went to work for a series of nonprofit groups, where he became, essentially, a professional convener, presiding over numerous forums where experts on such issues as federal food programs and Indo-Chinese immigration could get to know one another.

This kind of philosophical bent was unusual in Washington. People in the capital did not aspire to be deep thinkers; they derived their meaning from proximity to power, and rarely did they ruminate on the point of it all. You didn't interrupt a senior policy aide, during a discussion about the latest appropriations bill, to ask him to consider our larger purpose in the universe. That *was* the universe. Rob was something altogether different. He often talked like someone who had carefully read and reread every faddish self-help book to hit the shelves since the 1970s. He ruminated on "inflection points" in history and "determinative organizing principles" in everyday life. There was a searching quality to Rob Stein, a sense that he saw himself as being on a path toward belonging and purpose. The immaculately pressed clothing, the quiet tone, the thoughtful pauses—all of this conveyed an air of inner serenity when, underneath, he was rumpled and often anxious, battered by self-doubt and the perceptions of others.

I enjoyed talking with Rob. His vulnerability made him a shrewd observer of people and a fun conversationalist with an unusually keen appreciation of life's little absurdities. He was as comfortable reflecting on marriage and parenthood as he was talking about political transformation, and he approached just about any complex topic with an almost childlike fascination and good humor. To express his enthusiasm, he had an amusing habit of repeating sentences but changing the emphasis on his words. "You're going to love it," he would say, preparing to share with me some new insight. "You're . . . going . . . to . . . *love* it."

He revealed the facts of his life, though, only gradually, and with evident caution. And so it wasn't until later that I would find out, quite by accident, that the story of Rob's eureka moment after the 2002 elections was more complicated than it seemed. As it turned out, Rob had actually been studying "the conservative message machine" for more than a decade leading up to that day. It was not so much a sudden impulse as it was a long-standing obsession.

In fact, in 1995, just after Republicans had risen up to take back both chambers of Congress, Rob had pitched two Democratic senators, Tom Daschle and Jay Rockefeller, on a plan to fund and build a "communications consortium" for Democrats. The idea was to more efficiently promote Democratic ideas on cable TV and other media. Encouraged by the senators, Rob had gone to Hollywood and met with the producer and director Rob Reiner, who promptly brought Norman Lear, the sitcom impresario, and Barbra Streisand into the conversation. They had agreed to contribute seed money to the project. The idea had gained enough momentum for Rockefeller to hold a dinner at his Washington home to talk about it, with President Clinton himself as the guest of honor. In one of the seminal nights of his political career, Rob made a forceful presentation to the president, explaining how the conservative movement got its argument across using think tanks and talk radio. In typical fashion, Clinton, seemingly impressed, promised right then and there to raise the necessary cash, then promptly forgot about it. So did everyone else—except, of course, Rob.

And so the truth of his supposed epiphany on that November morning was more mundane, and more baldly opportunistic, than Rob liked to admit. It wasn't the reality of Republican dominance that Rob had suddenly glimpsed, like a vision, over breakfast. What he had seen was a fresh opening. It seemed now that Democrats might not regain control of Congress for decades to come, and the White House, too, was receding into the past, like some lakefront cottage in fond summer memories. Liberals would be desperately looking for a way back. And Rob now had a tool that hadn't existed ten years earlier: the Internet, with which he could Google all kinds of quantitative data that no one had yet bothered to aggregate. (Much of Rob's research, including the Powell memo, came from leftist Web sites that had already done a fair amount of the work for him.) Time and technology had presented Rob Stein with a chance to creatively recycle the same argument he had been making, on and off, with almost no success, for the better part of twenty years. The difference, this time, was that plenty of Democrats were ready to hear it.

O nce Rob had assembled his PowerPoint slides, the issue was what to do with them. At first, he would mention his hobby to old friends from the Clinton years when he ran into them around town. The first person to see the show was Christine Varney, who had worked as a lawyer in the Clinton White House and then as a federal trade commissioner. He also did screenings for Peter Knight, a close friend of Al Gore's who had helped run the 2000 presidential campaign, and Mickey Kantor, the Tennessean who had managed Clinton's first bid in 1992. There were lots of nods and smiles, plenty of polite encouragement. But no one could imagine much use for a bunch of slides. Rob was like some brilliant but slightly crazed inventor traipsing around town with a sleek new machine under his arm. The thing had all kinds of cool knobs and flashing lights, but what exactly was it supposed to do? Rob didn't really know. He came armed with information, but nothing like a strategy.

Then Varney introduced him to her friend Simon Rosenberg, who ran a political action committee called the New Democrat Network. Still boyish at forty, with round glasses and flushed cheeks, Simon had been blessed with many talents, two preeminent among them. The first was for pissing people off. Brilliant and fiercely ambitious, he could also be insecure and temperamental, to his own detriment. His other gift, one even his enemies grudgingly acknowledged, was a kind of political clairvoyance. Simon had a rare ability to see what was coming before it broke across the horizon—and to reinvent himself accordingly.

As the name of his group implied, Simon had aligned himself early with the centrist New Democratic movement and its rising star, Bill Clinton. He had worked at the Democratic Leadership Council before striking out on his own and setting up NDN. In 2003, however, when the DLC and other centrist Democrats began attacking Howard Dean as the latest iteration of the McGovernite Left, Simon broke with his old friends and began to align himself with the new progressives. He could feel a powerful wave of revolt coming from the Democratic base, a wave that was about to submerge the party's cautious, Clintonian establishment. Democratic activists and contributors, craving a new kind of partisanship, were begging for someone in Washington to stand up to George W. Bush. Simon saw that Dean wasn't just this year's Jerry Brown, as Washington Democrats insisted he was; he was a transformational figure from one moment in Democratic politics to the next. So rather than dismiss Dean, Simon publicly praised him, and he called on the Washington party to embrace the bloggers who were behind his campaign. The Internet, Simon preached like an apostle, would be to the new progressive movement what talk radio was to the conservatives. He was, of course, right.

The question facing Simon, by the time Rob Stein walked through his door in the spring of 2003, was how to reposition the New Democrat Network—and, by extension, himself—as the vehicle for this emerging grassroots movement, rather than as a stale remnant of the party's centrist past. Simon worried about becoming irrelevant at a moment when Washington institutions were losing their cachet. He had engaged a couple of tech-savvy marketing consultants from Silicon Valley, pro bono, to help design a strategy that could brand NDN as a leader of this new progressive uprising. Their most intriguing recommendation had been to bring together groups of potential donors in several cities to brainstorm about what kind of new organizations they could fund, outside the party apparatus. The idea was to get about twenty wealthy contributors together to serve, essentially, as the board of directors of a new progressive movement. The directors would buy their seats at the table in the same way that a company bought its seat on the New York Stock Exchange. Simon's New York–based fund-raiser, Erica Payne, had already given a name to this exclusive club, which she had taken from a Harry Potter book; she called it the Phoenix Group, as in rising from the ashes.

All of this was swirling in Simon's head when he first sat through Rob's presentation in the summer of 2003. The PowerPoint slides proved categorically what he had been saying for months now—that progressives needed their own version of the conservative infrastructure. What Rob had created was a blueprint for getting there. Eager to exploit it, Simon scheduled some confidential briefings for Rob with Democratic insiders in Washington, hoping the slide show might ignite some interest in Simon's own ideas about infrastructure. The Washington crowd, deep in the trenches of day-to-day combat against a ruthless Republican majority and already familiar with the political power of conservative institutions, mostly shrugged. One important Democrat who didn't dismiss the slide show was John Podesta, who, like Simon, had been paying careful attention to what was happening outside Washington. After seeing the presentation, Podesta remarked that he might have a master's degree in the right-wing conspiracy, but Rob had the Ph.D.

More than anyone else, it was Erica Payne, Simon's fund-raiser, who understood, instantly, the practical potential of the slide show. The problem she was having getting the Phoenix Group up and running was that it was proving impossible for a Washington outfit like Simon's to get this latest crop of wealthy contributors interested in much of anything. The donors who supported Dean over party insiders like Kerry and Gephardt thundered that Washington Democrats didn't get it, that they were feckless and timid, that "electable" was just another word for "cowardly." They were sick of giving money to Brooks Brothers–clad strategists who always claimed to have the next big idea but never managed to change the balance of power. You bought $100,000 worth of stock in a start-up, and one of two things happened: Either the stock price went up or the company went away. You gave $100,000 to Democratic Party committees or to groups like the Sierra Club and Emily's List, and the Democrats still lost—except all the same people were back six months later, asking for more checks. The donors had had enough.

Jerry Colonna, a New York venture capitalist whom *Worth* magazine had listed as one of the nation's top twenty-five young philanthropists, summed up the attitude of a lot of savvy donors when he told Erica that he was through being treated like an ATM with arms and legs. Nobody had handed Colonna his money (Colonna's dad, a journalist who covered the Nuremberg trials, had tried to drink away the memories and ended up working as a press-man instead), and he wasn't about to just hand what he had earned to anyone else. "Call me when you have something specific," he said, showing Erica and Simon the door of his Fifth Avenue office.

In the PowerPoint slides, Erica saw, at last, something specific. Some people are simply born to raise money, and Erica was one of them. A native North Carolinian who spoke quickly and bluntly, she had a Southern brunette charm that enabled her to get away with the kind of frontal assault on a person's wallet that would have seemed ill mannered coming from someone else. Like most natural fund-raisers, however, Erica aspired to more. She had a master's degree from Wharton and liked to quote liberally from *Good to Great,* the best-selling book for aspiring CEOs. She spent her spare time trying to unearth the essential philosophy of progressivism, reading and rereading everything from the works of Plato and Locke to *Harold and the Purple Crayon.* She wanted to be a player among the wealthy, not merely a conduit or a functionary. The slide show could help her get there.

She started making calls. Erica had once rented a basement apartment from Alan Patricof, a prickly venture capitalist who had been one of Bill Clinton's top fund-raisers, and she badgered him into watching Rob's presentation at his Manhattan apartment. Impressed, Patricof agreed to screen the slide show for other donors in his Midtown office. Erica had also met Jonathan Soros, the thirtysomething son of the famous billionaire, and she arranged for him to see the show as well. Soros, too, was blown away. These were people, after all, who derived their own value and power from money and its transformative qualities; unlike the Washington operatives, they had no trouble accepting the premise that a few rich ideologues had built one of the most powerful political movements in American history— and that only rich people, bonded together, could turn back the conservative tide. Twenty minutes into the presentation, Jerry Colonna, who had all but thrown Simon and Erica out of his office a few months earlier, held up his hand and cut Rob off. "I got it," he said. "You don't need to go on." The Democrats needed an investment club like the "angels" of Silicon Valley, right? Rob and Erica smiled. That was exactly what Erica had in mind.

Finally, in December of 2003, Erica decided to bring together a group of the city's top progressive donors to see the slide show and talk about the next step in building some kind of wealthy liberal alliance. Patricof agreed to host a highly confidential breakfast in his office. After George Soros said he would come, about thirty other major contributors—including Soros's fellow billionaire Peter Lewis and his son Jonathan—showed up as well, along with Rob, Erica, Simon, and Podesta. They also invited David Brock, a onetime conservative muckraker who had recently defected to the Democrats. Brock was considered a valuable asset to the party, having lived inside the very conspiracy that Rob was attempting to diagram. He was now launching Media Matters, which he intended to be the progressive counterpoint to the right's media watchdog groups. Richard Holbrooke, the Democratic diplomat who had negotiated an end to the war in Bosnia, was at the breakfast too. So was Jon Corzine, the New Jersey senator (and soon-to-be governor) who had himself amassed many millions as the chairman of Goldman Sachs.

The assemblage watched the slide show, then heard briefly from Podesta and Brock. The question was put to them: Now that they understood the underlying cause of the Democratic demise, now that they saw why their party couldn't compete in the arena of ideas or in the media, what were they going to do about it? Erica hadn't left the response up to chance. She had, in fact, carefully choreographed it. During a lull in the discussion, Jerry Colonna rose and announced to the guests, "This is exactly what the progressive movement needs." Then, as he and Erica had prearranged, Colonna pledged $25,000 on the spot for Rob to do more research on what kinds of groups the Left needed to fund. Gail Furman, a renowned child psychologist whose husband's family had made a fortune in real estate, seconded that idea and said she would commit even more. The donors asked Podesta to research the landscape for liberal think tanks, while Brock was tapped to report back on gaps in media influence.

Intrigued but cautious, George Soros said he was concerned that all of this long-term strategy would detract attention from the urgent business of unelecting Bush in 2004. After a spirited debate, the group agreed that both had to be priorities. To Erica, Simon, and Rob, what mattered was that Soros and Lewis were now part of the venture, and the Phoenix Group was, at last, a reality.

By that time, the conspiracy was already spreading across the country. Mark Buell and his wife, Susie Tompkins Buell, close friends of the Clintons, hosted a showing of Rob's slide show at their compound in Bolinas, overlooking a national park across the bay from San Francisco. In Denver, Simon introduced Rob to Rutt Bridges, a software tycoon and leader of a millionaires' cabal that was already funding more than a dozen new progressive groups in the Rocky Mountain State. Bridges happily organized a screening. Erica put together another event in Chicago, hosted by Hugh Hefner's daughter, Christy, who had seen the presentation in New York. Bren Simon, an Indiana philanthropist who often entertained Democrats at her Washington home, hosted a Phoenix Group chapter in the capital. One of Simon's longtime board members, Chris Gabrieli, brought Rob before a group of Boston Brahmans at his townhouse on Beacon Hill (directly across the street from John Kerry's).

No single person was controlling all of these meetings, and the affiliation among them was tenuous at best. The slide show was spreading virally, to the point where most donors couldn't really tell you where it had started or how they had come to see it. No one asked them for money; there was nothing to give money to. Instead, the meetings morphed into a kind of ongoing therapy session. Everyone felt frustrated and marginalized. Their country was being overrun. Here, at least, was a reason to get together over a hot buffet and bitch about it.

In Los Angeles, Rob Reiner held a showing for about a dozen Hollywood friends. Among his guests were the actor and writer Larry David and his wife, Laurie, who had become an easily caricatured promoter of various celebrity causes. Laurie David asked Rob Stein what he intended to do with this slide show, and he gave his stock answer: It was up to the people in the room. That wasn't good enough, she said. Rob couldn't just walk through the door and tell them why they were losing and not have a plan for what to do about it. Sooner or later, Laurie scolded, Rob was going to have to show some leadership. That, of course, wasn't Rob's style. The millionaires may have thought he was there to talk, but Rob had come to listen. If the Phoenix Group was team therapy, then Rob was its traveling psychotherapist. He wanted the donors to become invested in the notion of large-scale cooperation. He guided their discussions gently, expertly toward consensus. And, sure enough, as the months passed, in every city where Rob plunked down his computer and went through the slides, he left behind the nucleus of a group that hadn't existed before he got there. The slide show wasn't the plan that Laurie David wanted, but it was the gravitational force that pulled like-minded millionaires together.

In Silicon Valley, meanwhile, Andy Rappaport, a venture capitalist, had just convened his own group of high-tech honchos, the "Band of Progressives," to talk about investing in political start-ups. At Simon's request, Rappaport watched Rob's presentation in his Menlo Park office, with its rare modern art collection and lush lawns out back—as green as the felt on the full-size pool table off the conference room. When the slide show was over, Rappaport sat for a moment in silence. "Man," he said, shaking his head. "*That's* all it took to buy the country?" He invited Rob to the Band of Progressive's next dinner, and he and his wife, Deborah, flew east to attend a Phoenix Group meeting in New York.

Not long after that, Rappaport told me that the loose groups of donors around the country who were now coalescing around Rob's slide show might be able to raise, without much trouble, $100 million to help fund a small constellation of new progressive groups—groups that could, over time, act as a counterweight to conservative ideas and media. When I suggested that this seemed like an awfully ambitious goal, he tipped his head sideways and creased his brow, as if he couldn't help but feel a little sorry for me.

"A hundred million dollars," he said gently, "is nothing."

B eginning in that summer of 2004, when Rob Stein was Power-Pointing his way through the country, I began to talk with many of the liberal donors who had been dazzled by him, and who were now emerging from political obscurity. They were, by and large, more generous with their time and less guarded than most Democrats in Washington. Money, it seemed, was the very antithesis of political calculation; whereas one made you fearful of saying anything that might diverge from the party line, the other created a kind of cocoon of self-assuredness, a sense that the mere act of your saying something made it not only true, but powerfully persuasive as well.

It was the war, more than any other single issue, that had galvanized these donors. Not only was Iraq the most obvious manifestation of their own party's fecklessness, but it also reconnected them with a past for which they harbored no small amount of nostalgia. Most of the wealthy activists had been politicized at a young age by the Vietnam War, and they talked about the era in wistful tones, the same way that Americans who had grown up in the fifties talked about doo-wop and drive-ins. For middle-aged liberals, an antiwar movement was familiar space, a return to their roots. It satisfied a longing for unambiguous choices and moral clarity, for a time when they had stood firmly for what was right, even if it wasn't pragmatic.

On one of my visits to the West Coast, I made an appointment to see Rob Reiner, who was the most recognizable celebrity in the Phoenix Group. Few Americans remained as closely identified with the Vietnam era as Reiner, whose most famous television character, Michael Stivic from *All in the Family,* had served as the nation's liberal hippie archetype throughout the early 1970s. Now he had become a voluble spokesman for liberal causes and was flirting with a run for governor of California.

We sat—along with Reiner's personal political consultant, Chad Griffin—in a Beverly Hills office decorated with some of the posters from his movies: *This Is Spinal Tap, A Few Good Men, When Harry Met Sally.* Reiner, now looking all of his fifty-eight years, wore a blue oxford button-down tucked into baggy, navy blue pants and a pair of New Balance sneakers. I asked him how he had come to see Rob Stein's slide show and what he thought it might achieve. Reiner recalled for me having met Rob a decade earlier and seeing Rob's PowerPoint slides, at Simon Rosenberg's request, some months before the 2004 election. But this got him thinking about Kerry and foreign policy, and then he got onto a roll about the war, and before I could steer the conversation back to where it had started, I was leaning back on the couch, flinching a little, as Reiner let loose a tirade against Washington Democrats.

"I honestly believe that if you fight for what you think is right, people love that!" Reiner shouted. "They're not going to get mad at you." He compared the congressional vote on Iraq to the process of making pictures. "When I make a movie, there's all this stuff you have to deal with—egos, studios, *everyone.*" When a studio executive demands that something be changed, he said, "you have to ask yourself: Is this cutting into a vital organ? And if it's cutting into a vital organ, you just don't do it! You don't do it! Because you have to stand up for what you believe. People love that!"

Reiner was shouting at me now. "That's why people love Bush! I mean, he believes in creationism! He's on the wrong side of stem cell research!" He paused, looking a little helpless, as if he couldn't understand how any of this could be. Then the air went out of his cheeks and he stood abruptly.

"I've got to take a leak," he said. "Talk amongst yourselves."

When Reiner returned a few minutes later, he was carrying two sandwich bags, one full of cheese slices and the other watermelon chunks. He sat down again and, before I could ask a question about the Phoenix Group, picked up his rant where he had left off, alternately popping cheese and watermelon into his mouth.

"There is no bigger decision that a president makes than to send young men and women into harm's way," he said. "To send people off to die for a lie—I swear, I never thought I'd see that again in my lifetime! We went through it in Vietnam. To me, it's the most unconscionable thing you can do. It's beyond impeachable. If we had just one house of Congress, this man would be impeached!

"To me, the death of people at somebody's hands over the stupidity of this man is astounding! When I hear that on the weekend of the Super Bowl, an Iraqi expatriate was explaining to him the difference between Kurds and Sunnis and Shiites, it makes me want to cry! I want to cry!" He addressed me now as if I had somehow become the president himself, sitting not two feet from him on a couch. "How do you send people into a region, the most powerful superpower in the world, when you have no fucking idea what's going on there? I'm not an Arab expert. Fine. Read a book! Sit down and *learn* something." Reiner leaned forward and emphasized each word with a nod of his giant head. "Read . . . a . . . fucking . . . *book*!"

Finally, after he had spent most of his fury about the war, the president, and the Democratic Party, I asked Reiner why the Phoenix Group was important. He explained that he had given millions of dollars to Democrats over the years, and yet he had watched as the party found itself continually rolled by Republicans and beaten at the polls. "When I saw Rob's presentation about what Republicans did after 1964, I knew right away that that was what we needed to do," he told me. "They have the White House and Karl Rove and the message machine. And suddenly you say, 'OK, what do we have?' And we have nothing." He devoured the last of his watermelon and tossed the empty baggies onto the table. "*Nothing.*"

This last statement hinted at a curious irony. The liberals who were galvanized by Rob Stein's slide show couldn't conceal their awe for the conservative institutions that they saw as dominating Washington and the media. They marveled at the Heritage Foundation, with its $30 million budget, its staff of 180 and its eight-story building, complete with intern apartments and a 250-seat, state-of-the-art auditorium. They coveted the Leadership Institute run by Morton Blackwell, a Louisianan who had been inspired in his youth by Goldwater and who had, over the past two decades, graduated fifty thousand student activists and acquired his own classroom building in suburban Virginia. (In the lobby, Blackwell kept a bust of Ronald Reagan that he had specially imported from an Italian marble quarry.) Above all, they reviled the Fox News Channel, that conservative paragon with the audacity to call itself "fair and balanced," which had, in the ten years since its inception, reduced its nearest competitor, the venerable CNN, to a perennial runner-up in the ratings. All of this they envied and disdained, as surely as the Red Sox had, for so many hapless years, envied and disdained the thunder in the Yankees' dominating lineup.

The strange truth was that the zillionaires who responded to Rob's slide show had come to see themselves, however improbably, as the oppressed. They knew they were right about what was best for the country, and if the voters didn't see that as clearly as they did, then it could only be explained by some nefarious conservative plot. They imagined themselves to be victimized and powerless, kept down, somehow, by the Man. This surreal mindset was perhaps best captured by the scene at a 2004 book party for the liberal pundit Arianna Huffington, hosted by the billionaire Lynda Resnick and attended by Hollywood celebrities like Rob Reiner, Aaron Sorkin, and Larry and Laurie David. According to a few journalists who were there, Resnick, an agribusiness titan and the owner of the Franklin Mint, ascended the spiral staircase of her legendary Sunset Boulevard mansion and declared, to great applause, "We are so tired of being disenfranchised!"

It wasn't just a Republican conspiracy that was enslaving these wealthy liberals in Hollywood, Aspen, and New York. The new breed of rich and frustrated leftists also saw themselves as tyrannized by their own party and its insipid Washington establishment—and this, more than anything else, was what drew them to Rob Stein's presentation. There are, generally speaking, two kinds of political givers: access donors and ideological donors. Access donors are the people who give money to a party or campaign because they have interests to protect and expect something in return, or because they cherish a ride on Air Force One. Ideological donors, on the other hand, are those who spend on politics because they have some notion of how to save the country. Sometimes an ideological donor has a discrete agenda, like a guy I met in the Bay Area whose sole passion was a plan to turn recyclables into fuel. More often, the ideological donor has a set of broader, strongly held convictions, and what he wants, more than anything else, is for someone in power to listen.

The '90s had been the decade of the access donor. Determined to narrow the financial gap between his party and the Republicans, who had traditionally raised and spent more money than Democrats, Bill Clinton transformed the party of Jefferson and Jackson into the party of Wall Street and Silicon Valley. Aides famously rented out the Lincoln Bedroom to the highest bidder and courted wealthy Chinese nationals—schemes that resulted in two of the administration's more memorable scandals. The party became addicted to what was known as "soft money": huge checks, unregulated by the law, from individuals, corporations, and unions. It sometimes seemed as if there wasn't a high-tech CEO in America who didn't have a picture of himself, in black tie or pink golf shirt, shaking hands with the Democratic president of the United States.

For ideological donors, however, the '90s were a dismal, conflicted time. Sure, they liked the idea of a Democrat in the White House, but all they could do was stand by and quietly seethe as Clinton took the party to the center, enacting welfare reform and free trade agreements as consultants urged him to "triangulate" his positions in order to co-opt the middle of the electorate. It had been aggravating enough for these donors to have felt so marginalized during the Clinton years, to have defended the president against personal attacks even as he and his friends at the Democratic Leadership Council threw their arms around big business. It was worse yet to watch George W. Bush steal Florida and the White House in 2000 with barely a protest from Washington Democrats. And even that was only a prelude to the ultimate indignity: their own party's surrender over Bush's war in Iraq, presumably because Democrats in Congress felt the need to appear stern and patriotic. Whatever remained of the defiant Democratic Party with which the boomers had come of age—the party of civil rights and antiwar marches and forced busing—seemed finally to have been reduced to rubble, crushed under the heavy heels of craven pollsters and corporate lobbyists.

L ocal chapters of the Phoenix Group continued to proliferate throughout the spring of 2004, but nobody was in charge. Simon and Erica had called everyone to the banquet table, Rob had contributed the dazzling centerpiece, and the Soroses and Lewises had offered their blessing, but no one person could fairly be called the host. The meetings in each city were disparate and disconnected, the principals scattered across industries and interests. Inevitably, before they could go any further, Rob Stein and the donors who were coalescing around his slide show had to answer some fundamental questions: How did you build a new progressive infrastructure? Did you simply imitate the institutions that were flourishing on the right, or did you have to invent something altogether new? When you went to write the checks, whom did you write them *to*?

There emerged, over the months leading up to the election, two divergent models of what the burgeoning left-wing conspiracy might look like, and where you stood on those two models tended to depend on how you made your money—and, to some extent, whether you made it on the West Coast or the East. Venture capitalists favored the creation of what they called a "marketplace of ideas." In other words, there were progressives who had political vision, and there were progressives who had capital, and what was missing was a place where they could go to get connected. That's where the Phoenix Group came in. Under this decentralized plan, the donors themselves would create a lean, minimalist organization whose only role would be to hold meetings where entrepreneurs could pitch investors on their ideas. This model reflected the peculiarly adventurous and antiestablishment culture of Silicon Valley, which favored start-ups over established groups and high risk over steady return.

"In Silicon Valley, there is a great belief in the strength and power of individuals who are not yet a part of—and in fact, may have exclusively broken off of—the existing institutions of power," Andy Rappaport explained to me. "So there's a natural belief that David can slay Goliath, and that, in fact, Goliath inevitably will be slain. It's only a question of finding the right David. And by the way, because it's hard to find the right David, we can tolerate the fact that for every one David that slays a Goliath, there are going to be ninty-nine that won't have so much to show for their efforts. And that's OK."

A lot of the more traditional philanthropists among the group, however, who were mostly in New York and Washington, thought it made more sense for members to pool their resources, creating a central fund. They conceived of the Phoenix Group as a kind of powerful new foundation that would dole out grants to progressive groups, the way Soros's foundation gave away $450 million every year to promote "open societies" in the former Soviet bloc. Under this model, only donors who could afford to spend a threshold amount of money—in the millions of dollars, presumably—would be able to join the club, and the Phoenix Group would invest their money for them.

This west-versus-east debate was the main preoccupation of a critical meeting hosted by Simon Rosenberg and Alan Patricof in July 2004 in a conference room at the Regency Hotel in New York. About fifteen of the most active contributors ate lunch around the table, most of them from New York. Representatives of the Soros and Lewis families were there. Chris Gabrieli came down from Boston. Andy Rappaport flew in from the Bay Area. Bren Simon sent her political aide up from Washington. Rob Reiner called in from Los Angeles.

The donors mulled over a series of questions that were dependent on which organizational model you chose. How would people contribute? How many donors would join? How much money would be needed? The conversation meandered into a thicket of confusion. The Phoenix Group might have been derailed right there had it not been for Bernard Schwartz. The chairman of the aerospace giant Loral, a pioneer in the field of satellite technology, Schwartz was now nearing eighty, a native New Yorker whose legendary brashness and short temper had only sharpened over the years. He had a reputation for storming out of political meetings or exploding at others across the table, but this time he saved the conversation. Interrupting the hopeless back-and-forth, Schwartz scolded the other donors. These were not questions that they could answer by committee, he said, and he was not going to stand by and watch the Phoenix Group become another of those endless Democratic talkfests that went down in a morass of petty disagreements before it ever got started. Schwartz instructed Erica and Rob to write a three-year plan and to "think big." Come back and tell us what the plan is and how much money you need, and we'll give it to you, he said. Simple as that.

And so it was Rob, more than anyone else, who decided which fateful course the Phoenix Group should take. Typically, the donors who met at the Regency that day left without any strong notion of where Rob stood in the debate. He had seemed, outwardly at least, to agree with everyone who spoke. But Rob knew exactly where he came down on the defining question—and it was with the financiers who envisioned creating a centralized fund. Rob had intended all along for the Phoenix Group to become something larger than merely a forum for introducing people. His entire philosophy of life hinged on the harmony of personal relationships; a sterile, pragmatic marketplace of the kind the venture capitalists envisioned held no appeal for him. For Rob, a donor cooperative had to be not just about writing checks, but about bonding together all these rich liberals who barely knew each other, and who had come, over these months, to trust him. For Rob, it had to be about building a community.

CHAPTER THREE

The Thing

O f all the original leaders of the Phoenix Group, Andy Rappaport had been the one who most strongly favored a pure progressive marketplace, a sort of idea lab where donors and entrepreneurs could collide like so many atoms in a fusion reactor. When he had flown back to Silicon Valley from that last crucial meeting in New York, he still hoped that Rob Stein shared his vision. So it was disappointing when Rob called him, in the weeks after the 2004 election, ostensibly to ask his advice. Should the new group be limited to fifty members? Was a $1 million commitment from each member too high? Rappaport was alarmed; he didn't think there should be any limits on membership or any minimum ante. He didn't want any part of a secret, exclusive club of the super-rich, which he assumed would be dominated by Soros and a few other billionaires. The phone call was, effectively, Rob's way of telling him that he had decided to go in the other direction. The Phoenix Group would operate more like a large investment fund than a meeting of "angels"—the decision had been made.

Rappaport backed out. (He wasn't alone. Jerry Colonna, the New York venture capitalist who had made the first pledge at that first critical meeting in New York, and Bren Simon, the Washington socialite, also quit rather than commit $1 million to a big organization with big overhead costs.) Instead, the Rappaports went ahead and adopted their own political start-ups. For instance, Andy gave half a million bucks to Simon Rosenberg to start the New Politics Institute, which would focus on finding ways for progressives to exploit new technologies, and he quietly started putting together a private investment fund that would seek to buy up struggling media outlets and turn them into progressive platforms. His wife, Deborah, meanwhile, spearheaded the New Progressive Coalition, an online forum where interested donors could learn about fledgling progressive groups—in other words, a Phoenix Group that wasn't just for millionaires. The Rappaports called their political operation Skyline Public Works, or SPW; privately, they and the staff joked that the initials really stood for "Shadow Party West."

I visited Andy Rappaport in the Skyline office, an unadorned second-story suite in Redwood City, in April 2005, about six months after Bush's reelection. Andy was one of these storybook guys you heard so much about in the crazy '90s, an electrical engineer who showed up in Silicon Valley just in time to make hundreds of millions of dollars as a venture capitalist, gobbling up high-tech start-ups and then taking them public. He and Deborah had only recently waded into the frontier of Democratic politics, contributing about $5 million to a series of fledgling political ventures during the 2004 campaign. Rappaport was one of the smartest people I had met in politics, an amateur rock guitarist who made a fortune juggling numbers in his head but who could also riff verbally like some new age philosopher. When he thought out loud, Rappaport always began with the word "so," as if he were picking up on a thread from a few hours ago, and then proceeded to spin out complex metaphors in impossibly long sentences that somehow remained grammatically perfect.

On this day, Rappaport explained to me how to make sense of what had happened in Democratic politics since the crushing disappointment of the election. He posited that what we were seeing inside the party was the same pattern of behavior that he had seen, hundreds of times, in the large, crumbling companies he or other venture capitalists had taken over. This pattern had a predictable psychology attached to it, which unfolded in stages. He ticked them off on his fingers. First was denial: *It's not our fault. We're right, and everyone else is wrong.* Second was acknowledgment: *OK, something here's got to change.* And the third stage was a frantic search for the Thing—as in, *We have to find the thing that will save us.*

Denial had taken root almost immediately after the results of the election became clear. Over the years, Democrats had become adept at blaming other people for their losses. It was the Republicans' fault because they cheated, or the candidate's fault for sounding too cerebral, or the media's fault for not being cerebral enough. But now, in the wake of Bush's reelection, Democrats, both those inside Washington and those out in the dark blue, cosmopolitan cities of coastal America, focused their contempt on yet another conspirator, whose culpability in their undoing was a matter of record: the voters themselves.

George Soros himself had come to this view on that disastrous election night, as he glanced down from his windows onto the world's most prosperous city. He had made, he would soon tell others, a fundamental misjudgment. All along, he had been saying that Bush was to blame for America's perilous descent into darkness, but it had been naive to think that one man could be held accountable for such crimes. It was the American people, and not their figurehead, who were misguided. Starting in the Reagan era, Americans had become a people reliant on easy answers and unconvincing panaceas. This was a country that now consumed 6 percent more than it produced, that got its news from the likes of Bill O'Reilly and Jon

Stewart. Decadence—that was America's problem, and it had led to a society that seemed incapable of conjuring up any outrage at deceptive policies that made the rich richer and the world less safe.

A lot of Democrats agreed. The real problem, they concluded in those days after the election, was that all these church-going gun owners in so-called red states just weren't all that bright to begin with. One e-mail that made the rounds in Washington, chain letter–style, purported to use actual data to rank the fifty states by their average IQ scores; the top sixteen states (beginning with Connecticut, Massachusetts, and New Jersey) had voted for Kerry, while the bottom twenty-five (ending with Idaho, Utah, and Mississippi) were Bush states. Another e-mail widely circulated among Democratic activists showed the 2004 election map with the label "America" superimposed over stretches of the Democratic Northeast, the industrial Midwest, and California, while the rest of the nation—a sea of red—was labeled, in larger type, "Dumbfuckistan."

Soon enough, though, the second of Rappaport's phases—acknowledgment—had settled in. Within weeks of the election, John Podesta's Center for American Progress issued a postelection analysis for Democratic leaders that powerfully refuted the idea that Bush had been returned to office solely on the strength of mindless evangelical armies. Bush had widened his lead among all voters without college educations, not just the ones who lived in Mayberry. High school dropouts, who had voted overwhelmingly for Al Gore four years earlier, had essentially split their votes this time around. Bush had done surprisingly well among women and Latinos, and he had widened his party's lead among Catholics, one of the stalwart constituencies of the twentieth-century Democratic Party. And while exit polling showed that faith *was* a critical factor in how people voted, it turned out that religious voters were far more concerned about economic opportunity and the war in Iraq than they were about gay marriage or abortion. So much for Dumbfuckistan.

And so despondent Democrats slid seamlessly into stage three. "That's where we are now," Rappaport told me thoughtfully on that bright spring day in Redwood City. "Everybody in Democratic politics," he said, "is looking for the Thing."

Specifically, the thing Democrats were looking for was some better way to communicate to voters what they were about. This was not an unreasonable impulse. Whatever else one might have said about John Kerry, a politician of significant intellect and experience, it was hard to argue that he had been a terribly effective communicator; the man spoke like a human parchment scroll. Nor had any of the party's recent congressional leaders displayed much aptitude for the modern mechanics of messaging. After sixty years in power, during which they controlled the national microphone, Democrats in Washington had grown accustomed to expressing themselves to the voters through arcane pieces of legislation and the occasional news conference. They had continued to lecture that way long after the microphone had been killed, well after America had ceased to hear them, while their cagier Republican opponents defined them, devastatingly, as a bunch of weak, shiftless eggheads in thrall to a discredited ideology. (For every two Americans who dared now to label themselves as "liberal," more than three identified themselves as "conservative.") If Democrats thought they were being outcommunicated, it was because they were.

The party's leaders in Congress had lost faith in their standing army of famous admen and pollsters, who had, over the years, billed the party's various committees and candidates at an hourly rate that would have made any New York law firm proud, but who had, once again, failed to deliver. Instead, top Democrats began playing host to a parade of would-be saviors from the world outside the capital, marketing experts and tech entrepreneurs who claimed to have the

Thing they needed. These new gurus convened all kinds of meetings to talk about "re-branding" the party. They did things like charting the party's "hierarchy of customer needs" on a whiteboard, assigning a number to each need based on its "aspirational benefits" and relationship to "brand loyalty." They made lists of the party's "core deliverables." No one in Washington knew what they were talking about, which only served to underscore the value of their mysterious knowledge.

The party's leaders and activists veered erratically from one new theory to the next, embracing a succession of previously unknown theorists whose ideas for recalibrating the Democratic message suddenly seemed more compelling than all the accumulated wisdom in Washington. One such visionary was Thomas Frank, a progressive writer who argued in his bestselling book, *What's the Matter with Kansas,* that Democrats needed to embrace the anticorporate economic populism of an earlier day. Those dull Americans in conservative states, Frank said, had been duped into "voting against their own economic self-interest"—a phrase that became so ubiquitous, in those months after the election, that you could hardly attend a dinner party on either coast without hearing someone repeat it. Another favorite theorist of the moment was Jim Wallis, a silken-voiced, white-haired minister who surfaced, seemingly from nowhere, to insist that what Democrats really needed was to talk more about God and faith, in the way that all those ordinary folks out there seemed to appreciate. Wallis found himself invited to attend an intimate dinner party in Manhattan hosted by the former Treasury official Roger Altman, to discuss the party's strategy with, among other luminaries, Bill Clinton himself.

As it happened, seated a table away from Wallis at that dinner was the most accomplished and influential of these new self-styled strategists: George Lakoff, a Berkeley professor and one of the world's most celebrated linguists. A small, portly man with a Solomonic beard and suits that were at least a size too big, Lakoff had once been a protégé of the great Noam Chomsky's (although the two men, divided over their dueling theories of modern linguistics, hadn't spoken in forty years), and he had devoted most of his career to the study of metaphors and the human brain. In his bestselling book, *Don't Think of an Elephant!,* Lakoff theorized that Americans experienced their politics through the metaphorical "frame" of a family. Republicans had come up with phrases like "pro-life" and "tax relief," Lakoff said, which insidiously signaled to the brain that they were strict fathers who would defend the national household against outside oppressors. They used their many-tentacled message apparatus to spread this language by means of endless repetition. Democrats, the loving mothers of the political world, had unwittingly accepted these Republican phrases as legitimate terms of debate, which doomed them to failure every time.

Liberals were losing, Lakoff said, because they continued to believe that voters made their decisions rationally, based on the issues, when it fact they were responding to metaphors buried deep in their subconscious minds. In other words, voters weren't actually dumb; their brain synapses had simply been rewired, to the Republicans' advantage.

Lakoff's book was everywhere, its rise fueled by chatter on the Internet. George Miller, a liberal congressman from the Bay Area, bought copies for all his Democratic colleagues in the House. Senators carried it around in their rear pockets. Nancy Pelosi, the Democratic leader in the House, was one of Lakoff's most avid boosters. Pelosi had a self-help sensibility to go with her eerily inanimate smile; she once told me that she liked to speak to her caucus colleagues in alliterative phrases, because she'd been told they stick better in the human psyche. For instance, she liked to repeat the mantra "clarity, consensus, and credibility," to every member who walked into her Capitol suite, because, she said with that smile, "They remember!"

When I asked Pelosi about Lakoff, she told me, "He has taken people here to a place, whether you agree or disagree with his particular frame, where they know there has to *be* a frame. They all agree without any question that you don't speak on Republican terms. You don't think of an elephant!"

Improbably, Lakoff's little white book became to Democratic activists what Mao's Little Red Book had once been to Chinese Communists; just brandishing it was a statement of party loyalty. In Columbus, I saw a volunteer handing out a boxful of copies to her friends. At a base, emotional level, Lakoff's book reassured liberals that their misfortune wasn't of their own doing and that it wouldn't be so hard to reverse after all. In a more profound way, though, Lakoffmania was also about the abiding faith of Americans, and especially American liberals, in scientific discovery—the idea that every malady, including those afflicting the body politic, could be biopsied, tested, and sent into remission, if only you knew where to look. Here was a brilliant social scientist who had, at last, found the root cause of conservative dominance, deep in the neural pathways of America.

Of course, those who actually read *Don't Think of an Elephant!* should have been struck by a small aside at the bottom of page 23. "One of the major mistakes liberals make is that they think they have all the ideas they need," Lakoff wrote. "They think that all they lack is media access. Or maybe some magic bullet phrases, like partial-birth abortion. When you think you just lack words, what you really lack are ideas." Lakoff seemed to be suggesting the party needed more than a few new phrases; it needed an argument. But the Washington politicians who invariably pressed Lakoff for his version of the Democratic "bumper sticker"—the few words that would concisely explain the party's vision as effectively as "lower taxes, less government, strong defense, and family values" did for Republicans—seemed to skip right over this minor point. They were looking to rebrand the party, not reinvent it.

As many of the smartest Democratic minds did, in fact, know, the party's long-festering problems ran deeper than language. The most obvious of these were born of social turbulence. The boomers who took over the party beginning in the late 1960s—through a series of internal reforms that displaced the corrupt machines that had ruled the party during the country's industrial peak—were products of the antiwar and equal rights movements of their day. Their new party, with its emphasis on social justice, stood in contrast to the party forged by Franklin Delano Roosevelt, which had been fashioned around a coalition of economic interests and had dominated Congress largely on the strength of Southern segregationists. Upon signing the Civil Rights Act of 1964, Lyndon Johnson had predicted, famously, that he was signing away the next generation of Southern voters to the Republican Party, and he was right; for the next thirty years, as old Democrats died off and younger Republicans came of age, white voters in the South would tilt further and further away from their Democratic lineage, until, in 1994, the entire region seemed at last to have defected.

The more they retreated from the white South, the more Democrats became a party defined, culturally, by urban intellectuals and black voters, a coalition of the precious and the poor. Republicans caricatured them, ruthlessly and efficiently, as culturally smug and morally permissive. But the culture wars, at their base, weren't really all about culture; they were merely the manifestations of a larger anxiety. Something else was happening in America—something more gradual and less obvious than social divisions, and yet inextricably linked with them. Although few people in politics seemed willing to address it, the entire underpinning of the twentieth-century American economy was coming unglued, and at an astonishing rate. And nobody seemed to have any sense of what to do about it.

This kind of thing had happened before, a hundred years earlier, when agrarian America had given way, over a period of several tumultuous decades, to the automated efficiency of the industrial age. Back then, decades of bold progressive scholarship and activism had set the stage for FDR, who swept into office, following the stock market crash of 1929, with the first Democratic governing majority since the Civil War. Roosevelt and his New Dealers were flexible and creative thinkers, unafraid of change and well suited to the task of restructuring America's government and economy. Drawing on the earlier achievements of progressives like his older cousin Theodore, Roosevelt advanced a powerful argument for his time: In an age when corporations and their proliferating smokestacks were becoming a dominant force in American life, a centralized, activist government was needed to help plan and regulate economic growth and to redistribute wealth, rather than leaving workers to the mercy of the markets. From FDR's drawing board sprang the new social compact that would define American life for the rest of the century: Booming industries would create jobs for a fast-growing middle class; strong unions would secure fair wages, health care, and pensions for their workers; and ambitious government programs would assist those who didn't share in the new prosperity.

Not since ancient Rome, perhaps, had any civilization on earth experienced such heights of widespread prosperity—and all of it under the reign of the Democratic Party, whose patronage machines dominated the new industrial centers of the Northeast and Midwest. Virgin suburbs with their tract housing, broad and endless interstate highways, shining towers of public housing, unprecedented access to colleges and graduate schools, vacation homes and two-car garages, food stamps and Head Start and Medicare and Medicaid, every imaginable kind of government assistance—these were the hallmarks of a vibrant, imaginative Democratic agenda, from the New Deal through the Great Society.

But all empires fall, and by the 1970s, the industrial economy, like its highways and housing projects, was beginning to show some cracks. First came the storm of computer automation, which, unlike the advent of assembly-line machinery in the early part of the century, wiped out more jobs than it created. Who needed two guys to drop a windshield into a new Ford when a robotic arm could do it faster and just as effectively? Then came the tidal wave of the new global market, which drove down the prices of industrial goods and compelled companies to slash wages and benefits or relocate to China or Mexico in order to compete with their foreign rivals. When they did, stock prices surged, but factory towns reeled and collapsed. Unlike the slow churning of the last major economic upheaval, this one was advancing at a rate never before seen in human history. According to the economist Rob Shapiro, who served in the Clinton administration, during the thirteen years between the beginning of deindustrialization in the late 1970s and the onset of accelerated globalism in the early 1990s, America lost 2.4 million manufacturing jobs. That was bad. Then, in just the three years between 2001 and 2004, some 2.7 million more jobs fled the country, never to return. That was shocking.

These were middle-class jobs, the kind of jobs around which entire American communities had grown during the second half of the twentieth century. In a thoroughly depressing study published in 2006, three top academics—David Autor of the Massachusetts Institute of Technology, Lawrence Katz of Harvard and Melissa Kearney of the Brookings Institution—found that the American labor market had become more "polarized" than at any time in history. That is, while those at the top of the income scale were sharing in unprecedented affluence, and while lower-wage workers were watching their incomes stagnate, all the jobs in between were slowly disappearing.

Most Americans didn't care about the data, of course. What they did know was that, beginning in the 1960s, their once-thriving industrial cities and small towns, those Capraesque incubators of the American dream, were devolving into chaos. Muggings and home invasions started as urban phenomena, but soon they were suburban and rural issues, too. So were drugs and soaring rates of divorce and single parenthood, dysfunctional public schools, homeless beggars like something out of the Depression, and a media culture that reflected, if not promoted, sexual abandon and wanton violence. Americans were losing control of their communities and their kids, and as they watched abandoned factories rot and metal detectors go into their schools, they could be forgiven for wondering whether either political party had a strong notion what to do about it.

The short answer was no—there was no obvious way to reverse America's industrial decline or the social ills that stemmed from it, any more than there had been a simple solution to the passing of the agrarian age. But conservatives were in a far better position to lay blame. From the start, they had detested Roosevelt's idea of a more centrally planned government, which they regarded as a gateway to all-out socialism. And so it was easy now, as liberals from both parties sought finally to address the evils of segregation and abject poverty, for conservatives to exploit the racial and social divisions that cleaved the country, in order to appeal to a scared and angry working class. The problem, they insisted, was a government that coddled poor blacks and bused them into middle-class neighborhoods; that cared more about the criminal than the victim; that burdened the nation's employers with all manner of taxes and then gave the money to welfare moms. Liberals, they said, had throttled industry and trampled local communities, imposing their "anything goes" culture on a God-fearing country, and they had weakened the country's standing in the world by eroding its military strength and blaming America for the world's ills. If all of this could somehow be reversed, American towns and cities would thrive again.

It was a cynical argument, to be sure, but at least it was an argument. Liberals didn't really have a counterargument. Into the aging joints of the once-great and -agile Democratic Party, a stubborn inertia had settled like knobs of hardened calcium. Roosevelt and Johnson had based their innovative agendas on important moral principles: opportunity for the poor, security for the aged, equality for the excluded. Over the next several decades, however, as power had passed from the generations that crafted the new liberal ideology to those that simply inherited it, those broad principles had been whittled down to a series of programs—Medicare, Social Security, Welfare, affirmative action—so revered that they might as well have been brought down from the mountaintop on stone tablets. This new generation of Democrats had allowed the party to become almost entirely defined by a batch of statutes, each with its own powerful interest group, which they were determined to preserve, as written, in perpetuity, no matter what else in the country might have changed. So while conservatives inveighed against the set of programs that made up what the onetime presidential candidate Gary Hart, one of the latter-day Democratic Party's true visionaries, once described to me as "the Democratic cathedral," Democrats found themselves imprisoned within it, unable to articulate any argument for the country beyond a legislative agenda that predated the suburb, the personal computer, open-heart surgery and chemotherapy, the commuter aircraft, the self-employed worker, the mutual fund, and the mobile phone.

I n fact, if Democrats really wanted to understand their party's struggles, they might have employed a Lakoffian frame more useful than that of a party as a loving mother or strict father: namely, the party as an industrial behemoth. They might have studied the metaphor of General Motors, which had reigned during the postwar years as the country's largest single employer ("What's good for General Motors is good for America," went the old saw) and which had, more than any other institution, symbolized the age of American gigantism. At a time when competition was limited and consumers more credulous, GM set the standard for design and comfort, manufacturing plush, boat-sized sedans for a country that had fallen in love with the ever-broadening expanse of the open road. Each year, from its fortresslike headquarters in Detroit, the world's dominant automaker rolled out a new line of Cadillacs and Pontiacs and Buicks, and each year, millions of middle-class Americans dutifully steered them off the lots and into their brand new suburban garages.

When Japanese competitors began flooding the country in the 1970s with cheaper, more fuel-efficient imports, GM scoffed and kept right on churning out LeSabres. By the time the company realized that a new generation of Americans wasn't going to buy a car simply because GM told them to, it had fallen fatally behind on the innovation curve, and its classic brand names had taken on the stench of mothballs. By the end of 2005, as Democrats were coming to terms with their own diminished fortunes, GM's executives, after decades of denial, were preparing to issue their surrender. Having lost more than $2 billion in a single year, GM announced that its latest restructuring plan would shutter all or parts of a dozen plants and eliminate a total of thirty thousand well-paying jobs.

Why had GM so miserably failed to right itself? As with the Democrats, this question provoked many answers. It was undoubtedly true that the lifetime benefits given to its unionized employees had impeded GM's ability to compete in the new marketplace. And GM was now in an arena with foreign companies whose workers earned far less, or whose industries were heavily subsidized, making it all but impossible for GM to price its cars competitively. But the basic reality was this: GM, while still, just barely, the world's largest automaker, had stopped making enough cars that Americans wanted to buy. It had no vision for what the next great car might look like and no mechanism for listening to its customers. Instead, long after it had ceased to be the country's dominant employer, GM just kept tweaking versions of its Cadillacs and Pontiacs and Buicks and shipping them off as though nothing in America had changed, selling fewer cars to an ever-aging segment of Americans and dumping the rest onto the lots of rental car companies.

It wasn't that GM couldn't see what was happening. It was just that too much of the company's identity was bound up in its twentieth-century glory days and in the disjointed bureaucracy they had spawned. Real, fundamental change seemed too painful to consider. And so, rather than drastically overhaul its operation, GM tried, again and again, to market its way out of the problem—to find the Thing that would make Pontiacs cool among the younger set. Writing in the *Washington Post,* the consultant Maryann N. Keller, who wrote a book on the fall of GM, described how the company had reduced its corps of design engineers while relying more heavily on market researchers who used "psychographic polling," a new age mix of psychology and demographics. Keller described how GM execs hung up a picture of a rock-climbing woman in spandex who was said to be the inspiration for a sleek new SUV called the Aztek. The car, unwieldy and ugly, turned out to be a yet another disaster for GM and a joke inside the industry.

The parallels here, between the most successful company of the last century and the dominant political party of the same era, were hard to ignore. Just as GM couldn't begin to consider a world without Pontiacs, neither could Washington Democrats and their interest groups envision a world where every single liberal provision of the last seventy years didn't exist intact. This made real innovation—the kind of innovation that had launched the modern Democratic Party in the first place—all but impossible. There were all kinds of specific new policy proposals on the Democratic shelf, just as there were always new models of Buicks and Pontiacs on the drawing boards. But there was nothing approaching a plan to restructure the modern social contract for an age when Wal-Mart, and not GM, employed the most Americans, in the same imaginative way that the New Dealers had dreamed up a compact to meet the challenge of an earlier day.

Instead, like GM, the party had increasingly entrusted its fortunes to marketing gurus—in this case, the new class of celebrity admen, pollsters, and other consultants who had risen to become the most important (and wealthiest) figures in modern Democratic politics. Short of knowing exactly what to do about the slow and painful death of industrial America, Democrats came to rely on their consultants to make it sound like they did—or at least to make it sound like the whole mess was someone else's fault. Maybe it was entirely predictable that, in the days after Bush's reelection, some Washington Democrats, disillusioned with the work of their top consultants and desperate for a new answer, began to obsess over the potential of the next wave in consumer polling, which they claimed Republicans had already mastered. This hot new research method, they told me, was something known as "psychographic polling"—the very same breakthrough that had helped the marketing wizards at GM develop the Aztek.

As that spring of 2005 turned to summer in Washington, the ongoing search for the Thing seemed to lose its urgency. Democrats battling the Bush agenda in Congress suddenly found themselves in a position to which they were unaccustomed: They were actually winning, mostly because Bush and the Republicans had so brazenly overreached. Bush had responded to the narrowest of reelection victories, for instance, by announcing his intention to push through a Social Security reform plan, which, as it turned out, offered little by way of reform or an actual plan. Democrats held firm in their opposition to Bush's expensive and risky private accounts, and the entire effort collapsed. "We branded them with privatization, and they can't sell that brand anywhere," Nancy Pelosi bragged to me, using the new language of Democratic politics.

It wasn't that Pelosi and other Democratic leaders no longer believed in outsiders like Frank and Wallis and Lakoff. It was more that they believed they had learned the lesson that each one had to offer. Now they were eagerly railing against big business, talking about the budget as an issue of faith, and rolling out their own familial metaphors. And it seemed to be working.

I had asked Andy Rappaport, when we talked in Redwood City, what happened to troubled companies after the hunger for the Thing had abated. In some cases, Andy explained, the entrenched leaders of an ailing institution managed to summon the perspective and creativity to make the radical changes needed to save it. But that was rare. More often, real change didn't come from the inside, but through what Andy identified as phase number four: the shareholder revolt. Eventually, he said, shareholders came to understand that the people running the company had failed them, and that they were going to have to take control of the situation themselves.

In fact, the very same thing was just now starting to happen in the world of Democratic politics—and not just within the elite circle of Rob Stein's millionaires' club. All around the country, a far larger and broader group of ordinary shareholders, emboldened by the Internet, had begun to launch a hostile takeover of their own.

CHAPTER FOUR

The Power of the List

Six months after George W. Bush's second inauguration, on a typically sticky Saturday evening in July, I drove over to the Adams Morgan section of Washington and picked up Tom Matzzie at his apartment. Tom was the Washington director of MoveOn.org, a powerful and dynamic force in the new progressive movement, which had attracted a loyal following on much the same premise as Rob Stein's Phoenix Group—except that, where the Phoenix Group revolved around a select group of big spenders, MoveOn drew its support from millions of smaller contributors who felt a similar sense of political alienation. A Pittsburgh native who had formerly worked as a field organizer for the AFL-CIO, Tom made for a peculiar political revolutionary; he was overweight and overdressed, usually in a suit and loafers. He looked like he wouldn't be able to climb a flight of stairs without collapsing in a messy heap of Armani. He was also brilliant. He could reel off Social Security statistics one minute and run through polling in a series of congressional districts the next, all with instantaneous and nearly flawless recall. It was easy to forget that he was only twenty-nine.

It had been a big few weeks for the staff at MoveOn, who represented more than three million antiwar, anti-Bush voters—the voices of a new, unapologetic liberalism and the counterbalance to a legacy of Clintonian compromise. First, the Republicans, who loved to portray MoveOn as the modern embodiment of bong-loving, God-hating extremism, had started a campaign of intimidation designed to pressure Democratic congressional candidates into rejecting MoveOn's considerable store of campaign cash. No less a figure than Karl Rove, the president's deputy chief of staff and the most powerful political operative in the country, had accused MoveOn, because of its opposition to Bush's "war on terror," of trying to "offer therapy and understanding for our attackers." Even for Rove, this sounded more than a little overwrought.

And then Sandra Day O'Connor had resigned her seat on the Supreme Court, which meant the president would almost certainly choose a conservative ideologue to replace her, potentially endangering abortion rights and many of the other now-tenuous legacies of Democratic rule. It was time for the leaders of MoveOn—about a dozen of the kind of guys you might have expected to belong to the audiovisual club in high school, scattered in virtual offices throughout the country—to spring into action and summon the full power of their membership, like Tarzan howling out to the far reaches of the jungle. For this, they turned to the most sophisticated and effective tool yet discovered for organizing voters in this fast-moving digital age: the house party.

MoveOn members were holding more than a thousand house parties around the country that night to rally their volunteers against Bush's eventual pick for the court, even though they had no idea yet who that person would be. And so this seemed as good a time as any to find out, up close, who MoveOn's members really were. Tom and I were headed across the Potomac River to Mount Vernon, Virginia, a few miles from where George Washington's body lay in a crypt on his family farm. As I drove, Tom consulted some pages from MapQuest and explained that we were headed for the home of Chuck Fazio, who had responded to a mass e-mail sent to all of MoveOn's members asking if they would be willing to host a party in their area. Tom had never met Chuck Fazio, but every time a MoveOn member clicked a link or signed a petition, that information was logged, so that the organization knew more about each of its members than those members might have thought. Tom knew, for instance, that Chuck Fazio cared an awful lot about anything having to do with the Fox News Channel. It might fairly have been called an obsession.

Fazio's home was in a pricey suburban enclave, a two-level rambler with lots of windows, long and low in a faint imitation of Frank Lloyd Wright. In the carport were two BMWs (a convertible and a sport coupe), along with a white Ford Explorer. Chuck and his wife, Jen, were around back, near the patio and swimming pool and the stainless steel grill. The party was supposed to have started at six, but when we arrived at six thirty, Tom and I—along with Adam Green, MoveOn's press aide—were the only ones there. "We're supposed to have forty people," Chuck said nervously. He was forty-four, with slicked-back hair, a dark goatee and wraparound shades. "Where are they all?"

While we were waiting, Tom and I helped Chuck set up an eight-foot-high movie screen on the back lawn, where, he told us, he planned to show *Outfoxed,* the recent documentary about Fox News, for anyone who wanted to hang around after the party. Tom and I exchanged a quick, knowing glance. Chuck was an affable and unpretentious guy, and while we worked he told me that he owned a production company that made commercials for clients like the Independent Petroleum Association and BMW. He had purchased the house for $625,000 five years ago, but the place a few doors down had just sold for $3.9 million. There were a lot of mosquitoes buzzing around. I noticed now that Chuck's home was one of several that had been built around a picturesque canal that branched off from the Potomac.

"That guy had a mom-and-pop exterminator business and sold it," he said with a hint of disdain, pointing to one of the other houses on the canal. "That guy worked for the FAA." He moved through the rest of the houses on the inlet, pausing to describe each of the owners as he did. "Former MP in the army . . . home renovations . . . *stocks.*" This last one was a gaudy mansion that looked like it belonged on Cape Cod, with glass doors, picture windows, and monstrous dormers up top. "These people drank the Kool-Aid, man," Chuck told me. I looked at him quizzically, and he explained that they were all Republicans. "They're crazy. They don't get what's going on."

As a few guests began, at last, to arrive and saunter back to the patio, Chuck told me that he had never voted before the last election and that he wasn't a registered Democrat. He had never held an event like this before. He wasn't even sure if he was a MoveOn member or not; he couldn't remember signing up. (Of course, just by putting his name on the e-mail list he had become, officially, a member, but a lot of MoveOn subscribers didn't realize that.) His only overt political act before tonight had taken place more than a decade earlier, in 1994, when he had happened upon Oliver North, who was then running for Senate as a Republican, campaigning at the local mall. Suddenly overcome by a need to make himself heard, and realizing that he had some poster board and a Magic Marker in the backseat of his car, Chuck had quickly scrawled "LIAR" on a makeshift sign and silently held it aloft for a few minutes, until he got bored and went home. Chuck was impulsive that way.

All of this led me to ask the obvious question, which was why Chuck had decided to host a party tonight. I expected him to tell me that it was because the war had driven him over the edge, or because of a woman's right to choose, or maybe because this time he had seen Dick Cheney at the bowling alley. But his answer was more cryptic than that.

"Because I live across the street from that asshole, man."

He said this as if the asshole in question were standing next to us, but when I turned to look, no one was there. I was starting to wonder about Chuck.

"Which asshole?" I asked.

Chuck looked a little stunned. He assumed everyone knew. "Brent Bozell, man."

I had to think for a minute, rifling through my mental encyclopedia of Republican politics. Bozell was the nephew of the neoconservative icon William F. Buckley Jr. and the founder of several conservative organizations that sought to expose the media's left-wing bias and restore morality to television. He was one of those legends of the conservative movement who is known primarily to a handful of other legends of the conservative movement. That his house rested a few hundred yards from where we were standing was something Chuck seemed to find intolerable, a kind of daily torment. "At first, I didn't know who he was," he explained. "I didn't realize he was evil. But then I started Googling him and blogging." He made a face as if to suggest that what he had uncovered was too graphic to discuss here, in a neighborhood full of children. "Oh, man. I said to Jen, 'Let's go over and pee in his pool.' I just wanted to do something."

I asked if he had tried talking to Bozell, maybe striking up a conversation. I don't know where I thought I was going with this. It just seemed a shame that a man should be so uncomfortable in his own neighborhood.

"He's mean," Chuck said, shaking his head. "He scowls a lot. When I see him walking his dog, I don't even look at him. I just walk by. The rage just builds up inside me. Now that I have this . . . this . . . what would you call it?" He paused, searching for the right word. ". . . this *hatred* for the guy, I can't even go to parties around here anymore. I can't deal with it."

"And so you just decided to have a party of your own," I surmised.

"Dude, I watch Fox News every night," Chuck said. "I don't know why. I'm a masochist. It makes me so angry. My wife says to me, 'Why don't you do something, instead of just throwing Cheerios at the TV all the time?' So they sent this e-mail out. And I was at the keyboard, and I said, 'Honey, how about we have a house party for MoveOn.org?'" He did an impression of himself typing away. "She says, 'Sure, honey.' So I signed us up. A week later, I said, 'Hey, we're up to nineteen people.' And she said, 'For what?' She had no idea what I was talking about."

Chuck confided that he was frightened of the government. "When you see what's going on, and when you hear people who've been around for decades saying they've never seen anything like this before, you've got to be scared," Chuck said. "I don't want the lights coming up behind me and some cop slapping me down because he can." He said this despite the fact that he was white, drove a Beemer, and lived in a house worth more than the endowments of some charitable foundations.

"They'll do anything, these people. They invaded a sovereign country that hadn't done anything to us. They'd kill someone. I really believe they would. Dude, if you don't see what these people are doing, you have to be selfish or stupid or misinformed or . . ." He paused, counting his fingers for a moment. "What's the fourth one? Selfish . . . stupid . . . did I do 'manipulated?'"

I shook my head uncertainly, slapped at a mosquito.

"Whatever," he said. "You've got to be crazy."

By now, it was a quarter past seven, and some twenty people, almost all of them white and well dressed, had gathered on Chuck's patio. There was also a reporter from the *Washington Post,* a target of MoveOn's strategy to publicly demonstrate its organizing power. Over by the table of finger foods, I met Linda and Rick. Linda looked like the classic stereotype of a suburban, baby boomer liberal, midforties with blond hair cut tightly around her pinched, Waspy features. She declared almost immediately that she was a lifelong, card-carrying Democrat. Rick owned a wireless IT company. He said little and ate lots of chicken wings. Linda said they needed to do whatever they could politically, because Bush was trying to destroy the country, and the media just went along with whatever he said, except for the *Nation* and the *New Yorker,* for which she gave thanks every day. In fact, Linda had just read a story in the *New Yorker* about Patrick Henry College, a small Virginia school where students were taught conservative ideology. "It was so scary," she said. "Why can't *we* do that? Why aren't people on our side doing that kind of training?"

Everyone at the party was roughly Linda's age. This illustrated one of the great misconceptions about MoveOn's membership. Establishment Democrats and hostile Republicans assumed that any online forum—whether it was MoveOn or the blogs or the Howard Dean supporters who connected through Meetup.com—had to consist of tech-savvy kids who would do anything to avoid studying for exams, most of them concentrated on the coasts or in college towns with lots of storefront salons offering body art. It was a fundamental misunderstanding of the new progressive movement. In fact, about half of MoveOn's members were over fifty, and many of them lived in the most ordinary, conservative suburbs you could conjure up, just like this one. The point was that they had been so isolated for too long, entirely disconnected from one another and despondent over the rise of Republican extremism and the drift of Washington Democrats toward a kind of mushy middle. If college kids wanted to commiserate with someone over the fear and misery of life under Bush, all they had to do was walk across the hall. For affluent boomers, there was MoveOn.

What MoveOn had done, along with popular leftist blogs like Daily Kos and MyDD, was to establish a virtual clubhouse for like-minded liberals clustered in hostile places. They spent their days at corporate jobs with co-workers who probably voted Republican or who would rather talk about the upcoming football game or their kids' soccer league than about Iraq. They came home to colonial houses with neatly trimmed lawns and alarm systems and oversized refrigerators, to neighbors they barely knew except to wave to now and then. They put their kids to bed—and then, under the halogen lamp of a home office, they flipped on the computer and spent a few minutes in a welcoming place, among faraway friends who felt as culturally and politically destitute as they did. It was where they belonged.

Tom asked the little group standing around the nachos and sushi what they thought of Tim Kaine. They stared at him blankly. They had no idea who that was. Kaine was, in fact, Virginia's Democratic lieutenant governor and the party's nominee that year for governor. But no one there seemed to be politically active—in that way. They were completely detached from the Democratic Party itself and disillusioned with its candidates. Like Chuck, many of them probably hadn't voted for years before they turned out to try to overthrow Bush. They didn't really have any favored candidates of their own (besides Howard Dean); all they really wanted was to get these venal Republicans out of office.

A psychotherapist, whose name I didn't catch, said she was very hopeful about Mark Warner, the outgoing Democratic governor, who appeared to be readying himself for a presidential run in 2008. I asked her what she liked about him. Was it the comprehensive tax reform plan he had managed to push through a Republican legislature? Was it because he was bringing jobs and high-speed Internet cables to some of Virginia's forgotten rural counties?

"He's a Southern governor, and he won in a conservative state," she answered. "Remind you of anyone?"

"Bill Clinton!" Linda shouted, and the two of them shared a giddy laugh. All they knew about Warner—all they needed to know—was that he sounded like a guy who could win.

Using a wireless microphone, Chuck read from a script, downloaded from the MoveOn Web site, urging the others, once a Court nominee was finally named, to call their senators and write letters to the editor. Then he passed the microphone around so that all the guests had a chance to share their feelings about the battle to come. They didn't. Instead, much like Rob Stein's donors, they shared feelings of exclusion and anxiety. This was their moment to testify to the evil of Bush and his agenda. Twice, Chuck reminded them to focus on the Court and to keep their comments brief, but no one listened.

A gray-haired woman took the mic and said, "I was in France when 9/11 happened. I cannot believe the way America is seen around the world." Adam, the press guy, visibly winced and looked at Tom. The MoveOn crew was forever making the case that its members were everyday Americans, that the Republican caricature of them as elitist was unfair. The last thing anyone needed was for this woman to relay the view from Paris while a *Post* reporter wrote down every word. Tom shrugged. It didn't have to be perfect. The point of the house parties was that MoveOn was bringing together tens of thousands of motivated volunteers on a Saturday night to organize a grassroots campaign. No one else in Democratic politics— certainly not the party itself—could dream of doing that.

There was, in fact, something deeply impressive about MoveOn's ability to connect suburbanites civically, the way the old Democratic clubs had once pulled immigrants in off the streets of America's industrial cities to drink and play bingo. Everywhere the party had disappeared, it seemed, MoveOn clusters had sprouted, like resilient weeds from a patch of charred earth. Tom pointed out, for instance, that MoveOn had a strong presence in Oklahoma, where the Democratic Party headquarters had recently been padlocked because no one had bothered to pay the bills. MoveOn tended to be strongest in states where the party had essentially disappeared, leaving a vacuum. "People are much more interested in something like MoveOn.org than in the Democratic Party," Harold Ickes, the longtime party strategist, had told me. "It has cachet. There is no cachet in the Democratic Party."

And yet it was also true that MoveOn was intensely aware of its image problem. Tom and the others still rued the incident in 2004 when MoveOn had held an online contest for members who wanted to make their own TV ads about Bush, and one of the entries— posted briefly on the site and then removed—likened the president of the United States to Adolf Hitler. The MoveOn guys were hypersensitive to the idea that they were the official club for people who hated all Republicans. Before this party, in fact, Adam had talked to Chuck Fazio to tell him about the *Post* reporter, and Chuck, in turn, had sent a preemptive e-mail to his guests.

"We don't want to come across as leftist, liberal activists," Chuck had warned in the e-mail. "We want to come across as who we are— regular folks who are finally saying enough is enough to the extremists; that we're not falling for their extremist rhetoric anymore and we're finally going to expend the effort necessary to get our country back. Please stay on message and just know that ANYTHING you say can be taken out of context and used against the effort." Chuck added: "Oh, because a photographer will be here, might I suggest we put away our 'Bush is a Liar' t-shirts. Let's look like they do."

Chuck took the mic and tried to steer the conversation back toward the Supreme Court. "We have to send out, you know, what are they called? You know those things you sign?"

"Petitions!" someone called out.

"Yeah, go around and do the petition thing," he said.

When we left the party, Chuck invited me to come back in a few weeks. He had gotten word that Brent Bozell was planning some kind of summer party, so he intended to have a loud pool party on the same day. He was going to line the place with MoveOn signs, just to annoy that asshole. It was going to be great.

I t was easy to forget that the group that embodied the liberal back-lash against the democratic ethos of the booming '90s—the group that, more than any other, had provided an outlet for frustration not just with the excesses of conservative ideologues, but with the Clintonian strategy of meeting them in the middle—began with a defense of Clinton himself. The year was 1998, and the Republican Congress was about to successfully impeach a sitting president, for the first time since the 1860s, because he had lied about getting blow jobs, abusing a fine cigar, and generally making an ass of himself in the people's house. Like a lot of liberal Americans, Wes Boyd was incensed at the Republicans for exploiting a trivial matter at the expense of all the other things Congress was supposed to be doing. Unlike a lot of liberal Americans, Boyd was also ridiculously rich. In one of those classically weird success stories of the '90s, Boyd had invented that ubiquitous screen saver with the flying toasters, tapping into what was apparently a deep-seated American desire to see our kitchen appliances come to life and ascend toward the heavens. From their modest but elegant house nestled in the hills of Berkeley, Boyd and his wife, Joan Blades, designed a Web site and asked people to sign a petition calling on Congress to censure the president and "move on." Within weeks, they had 250,000 signatures. "You could have knocked us over," Boyd said later. "We had no idea this would happen."

Boyd bought ads in the *New York Times* and other papers, and, through his MoveOn.org Web site, he helped volunteers lobby their congressmen against impeachment. This was an extraordinary new use of Internet technology, which was just then becoming a fixture in most affluent households; no one, until then, had demonstrated a compelling use for the Web in political organizing. It was also an entirely new way for an ideological donor to spend his money. Until MoveOn, wealthy liberals had been trained to give their cash to the Democratic Party and its candidates. As Rob Stein liked to point out, this was how a majority party had sustained itself—by channeling its resources into winning elections and retaining its margins. What Wes Boyd did, without seeing Rob's presentation and without really thinking about it this way, was to entrepreneurialize Democratic politics. Someone needed to fight back against the rising forces of conservatism, and if the Democratic Party itself wasn't going to do it, then why not a rich guy in Berkeley? The days when political parties held a monopoly on organizing their constituents were over; it was just that no one seemed to know it yet. In creating MoveOn, Boyd suddenly gave thousands of liberals, people who had become estranged from politics during the Clinton era, somewhere else to go.

Even so, as the impeachment fight faded, MoveOn was considered a marginal force in Democratic politics, a small player on the party's ideological fringe. Boyd kept circulating new petitions—pushing for reform of the campaign finance system, among other things—but Washington insiders regarded him and his roughly one million members as you might the teenager with pink hair at a family Thanksgiving. They were free to express themselves, but everyone sort of assumed they'd grow out of it. And that's how it might have stayed, had it not been for the unforeseen events of September 11, 2001—and for an unusual twenty-year-old kid who watched it all unfold from the comfortable remove of his apartment in suburban Boston.

In the few days after the fall of the twin towers, Eli Pariser read the papers and watched the coverage and did what he did best: He thought. The child of public school teachers in Camden, Maine, Eli had blown off high school during his junior year and gone off, instead, to Simon's Rock, an alternative college in the Berkshires that specialized in scooping up smart, bored kids who didn't want to hang around high school to earn a diploma. (Later, when he had become, arguably, its most famous alumnus since the poet Edna St. Vincent Millay, Eli's high school in Camden would give him the degree anyway.) Like a lot of kids at the turn of the millennium, Eli had come out of Simon's Rock addicted to the Internet. Now he was doing IT for a small nonprofit, but all he could think about, as he heard the president and Congress vow to get revenge for the terrorist attacks, was how the country was about to embark on a tragic journey, and how no one seemed to be counseling restraint. Republicans wanted war, and centrist Democrats were afraid to seem unpatriotic. When it came, Eli thought, the invasion of Afghanistan or some Arab country was certain to escalate a cycle of violence, rather than abate it. He had to do something.

What Eli knew how to do was build Web sites, and so that's what he did. He created a site called 9–11peace.org, on which he urged friends and whatever other random visitors might happen by to call their congressmen. And when another friend sent Eli an antiwar petition written by a student at the University of Chicago, he posted that on his new site, too. "We, the undersigned, citizens and residents of the United States of America and of countries around the world, appeal to the President of the United States, George W. Bush; to the NATO Secretary General, Lord Robertson; to the President of the European Union, Romano Prodi; and to all leaders internationally to use moderation and restraint in responding to the recent terrorist attacks against the United States," the petition began. "We implore the powers that be to use, wherever possible, international judicial institutions and international human rights law to bring to justice those responsible for the attacks, rather than the instruments of war, violence or destruction."

Eli e-mailed the link to his site to a list of friends. He felt good about this. He had made a small gesture at a time of global crisis. He had tried, in his little way, to affect the political process of his country. And that was that.

Except it wasn't. Because when Eli rolled out of bed a few days later and, still in his pajamas, began downloading his e-mail, something bizarre happened. Two thousand messages materialized on his desktop. Then it was three thousand. They just kept coming. And then he got a call from the friend who had kindly offered to host the little Web site on his server. "Eli! Eli! The server's crashing!" he said. "What the hell are you doing? Where are all these people coming from?" Eli didn't really know the answer. This was still early in the age of broadband. Even a tech-savvy twenty-year-old college graduate didn't yet appreciate the speed at which a viral e-mail appeal could spread to in-boxes around the country and the world, forwarded by everyone he knew to everyone they knew, and so on.

Next he checked the petition on his site. More than 49,000 people had already signed it. Now the BBC was calling. "Who's the director of this Web site?" they wanted to know. "I think that must be me," Eli said. Within a few weeks, Eli's site was one of the five-hundred most visited on the Internet, and more than half a million people in 192 countries had signed the petition. A Romanian journalist told him that he had received Eli's original e-mail from five different people. There was no great marketing genius to this; it's not like Eli had linked his petition to one of those Whack-A-Mole video games with animated versions of Bush and Cheney popping out of holes. It was really pretty simple. A lot of people, however numbed by the events of that month, still believed, as a matter of conviction, in peaceful solutions, and not a single important elected Democrat was standing up for them. Five years earlier, there would have been no cheap or easy way for those five hundred thousand people to aggregate their voices. But the Internet had created a new universe of networking potential, and in that universe, with a single creative gesture, a kid like Eli Pariser could become, literally overnight, the architect of a movement.

Among those who took note of all this was Wes Boyd. The rise of the Web had also created new currencies of power. In the traditional world, people gained influence by having capital or connections. In a virtual world, however, few things were as valuable as a massive list—that is, a database of names and e-mail addresses that could be identified with a single need or interest, and thus could be mobilized with the push of a button. If you were a bank, you needed an e-mail list of consumers who were in the market for a mortgage. If you were a fledgling punk band with a new CD, few things were more valuable than a database of people who had downloaded similar music. And if you were in the business of building a political machine, no single donation could compare to the names of half a million passionate partisans, people in every part of the country who were searching for a way to wield some influence over the political process—and who probably knew, collectively, millions of other people who felt the same way. Like a kid in one of those formulaic thrillers who has accidentally come upon some incredibly valuable piece of information but doesn't know it, Eli Pariser was now sitting on a serious political asset. Boyd understood the potential of that list, especially if he could merge it with his own.

And so Eli got a call from MoveOn's executive director, and before he knew what was happening, he had quit his job at the nonprofit, moved to New York, and assumed the role of international campaigns director of MoveOn.org. Within two years, he would become MoveOn's executive director, running the day-to-day operations from New York while conferring constantly with Boyd out west. Under Eli's leadership, MoveOn played more forcefully in Washington politics, and not simply by waving petitions around. Now it raised serious money online and used it to fund candidates and buy TV ads, just like any other big-time lobby. MoveOn became the de facto voice of the new antiwar left. In 2002, as the Bush administration was laying the foundation for an invasion of Iraq, MoveOn members raised $500,000 for Paul Wellstone, the Minnesota senator who had voted against the war resolution. (Wellstone, an icon of the new progressives, was killed in a plane crash before the election.)

As MoveOn's membership list grew, so did its credibility among angry Democrats, to the point where it seemed that all Eli and his team had to do was dream up some new gimmick for collecting cash, and the money would come rolling in, most of it from people who would never have given a nickel to the Democratic Party itself. During the 2004 campaign, MoveOn held a national bake sale (like the house parties, but with brownies) and raised $750,000. When a bunch of Democratic legislators in Texas walked out of the Capitol and left the state rather than allow a skewed redistricting plan to pass, MoveOn collected $1 million in pledges to help sustain their protest. In 2005, when MoveOn asked its members to contribute to the campaign of the crusty old antiwar senator Robert Byrd—a man who, by his own admission, had once belonged to the Ku Klux Klan—Byrd collected checks totaling $800,000.

Most of MoveOn's money came in small donations; the average check was for less than $50. George Soros had given the group $2.5 million during the 2004 campaign, but when the election was over, Wes Boyd and Eli Pariser decided that, from now on, they would accept only small contributions. After all, MoveOn no longer needed any billionaire's help. Its membership list had soared to over three million, and its annual budget had surpassed $25 million a year.

Increasingly, MoveOn vowed to use its influence not only to help elect Democrats, but to help unelect some as well. It was time to let the Washington party know that centrist New Democrats and their corporate donors weren't in charge anymore. As Eli told his members in an e-mail just after the 2004 election, "In the last year, grassroots contributors like us gave more than $300 million to the Kerry campaign and the DNC, and proved that the party doesn't need corporate cash to be competitive. Now it's our party: we bought it, we own it, and we're going to take it back."

Eli, whom the political reporter Ron Brownstein, writing in the Washington magazine *National Journal,* had just called one of the fifty most powerful people in the Democratic Party, lived with his girlfriend in Brooklyn's eclectic Park Slope neighborhood, in a two-bedroom apartment across the street from a Mandee's discount clothing store and above a 99-cent shop. When I first visited him there during that summer of 2005, wet clothes were drying on a folding rack in the entryway. While Eli finished some work in his study, I sat on a futon-style couch in the living room, looking over the Vonnegut novels and academic texts piled up in pressed wood bookshelves.

Eli appeared to live like any other kid a few years removed from college. When we sat down, however, he related to me a call he had just gotten from Chuck Schumer, the New York senator who was in charge of funding the party's 2006 Senate campaigns. Schumer asked if Eli would help raise cash for Maria Cantwell's reelection bid in Washington State. Eli was noncommittal. He had already had a similar conversation with Cantwell about it, but he couldn't tell yet whether MoveOn's members would be excited about Cantwell or whether other candidates would command more of their attention. Cantwell and Schumer would just have to wait.

He wasn't boasting about any of this; he said it flatly, almost reluctantly, in response to my questioning. I had expected to find an angry young man with Birkenstocks and a Che Guevara T-shirt, but Eli was, in fact, one of the most understated and pensive political activists I had ever met. He was tall and a little awkward in his movements, with a mop of brown hair and a shy smile. Far from doctrinaire, he appeared to quietly grapple with some of the questions I asked, offering answers and then amending them as we spoke. Unlike a lot of Washington strategists, who spent most of their years in politics trying to validate whatever decades-old theory had made their work relevant in the first place, Eli seemed to enjoy thinking aloud, puzzling it all out, hypothesizing. He wasn't invested in answers he had given a thousand times before.

Eli believed the old notions of liberal, conservative, and moderate voters were hopelessly out of date. The accepted picture of the American electorate, charted along a left-right continuum, would have showed a curve of Democrats coming from the left and a similar curve of Republicans coming from the right, with the two lines intersecting in the middle, where moderate and independent voters lived. Eli saw it differently. On his graph, which he would later send to me in an e-mail, the curves representing the two parties sat on opposite sides of the political continuum, leaving a gap of nothingness in the middle. In other words, the way he saw it, no actual center remained in American politics; there were only varying degrees of liberals and conservatives, both groups battling for the soul of America. Trying to appeal to the moderate voter, as Washington Democrats were always trying to do, was a waste of time.

What's more, Eli told me, most voters were, by temperament and conviction, Democrats. They just needed a more courageous party to vote for. To Eli, who had never actually lived anywhere outside the Northeast, the Chuck Fazios of the world were, in fact, a fair representation of the average American voter, and MoveOn was simply an interest group designed to aggregate the power of average Americans in Democratic politics. Labor had its own lobby. So did blacks and Latinos and gays and seniors and environmentalists, and—most significantly of all—corporations. The individual voter had no such group. He couldn't compete with these organized lobbyists with their massive budgets and sprawling headquarters. For that voter,

MoveOn was like the chamber of commerce or the AARP—an association that used the power of conglomeration to advance the goals of its members.

Eli's grand vision was to create a government that responded to the will of these average voters by advancing bold, progressive ideas. Ever since he had hit adolescence, Eli had lived in a country that seemed to follow the dictates of an organized religious Right and the National Rifle Association. That balance could now be reversed, he thought, and technology was going to be the catalyst. Banded together online, MoveOn's members could elect their own representatives and enact their own governing agenda, just as conservatives had managed to do in the nineties.

It was important, though, that MoveOn's members, and not its leaders, determine what that progressive agenda would be. Thanks to the immediacy of the Internet, MoveOn could relentlessly poll its members, to the point where the organization had a nearly flawless understanding of their priorities. Quoting the business book *Built to Last* (by Jim Collins, the same corporate guru who had written Erica Payne's favorite book, *Good to Great*), Eli told me that every great company had to have one constant ideology that never changed. MoveOn's ideology was to serve its members above all else. When Eli thought about MoveOn, he pictured a stack of small microchip processors, wired together to form one giant supercomputer. That's why he hired people who understood technology, rather than politics. "We look for a certain geek sensibility in solving problems," he told me. "We want people who have an arcane interest in making systems run more efficiently."

In order to keep adding memory to its stack of processors, MoveOn had to keep adding more and more members. MoveOn's influence lay in the number of names on its list, and that meant that Eli and his staff had to keep finding the next issue that would motivate new people to sign up. MoveOn's staff called this issue the "message object." The war in Iraq was a powerful message object; it had already doubled MoveOn's ranks. But continuing to grow meant finding less obvious message objects. For instance, Republicans had recently tried to cut funding for public broadcasting. The engineers who ran MoveOn's supercomputer recognized that this could be a fantastic new message object, because there were lots of NPR devotees out there who hadn't yet signed up as MoveOn members— people who might care more about hearing *Prairie Home Companion* every week than they did about, say, Social Security. Sure enough, MoveOn's e-mail appeal to save NPR, widely distributed by its members and highlighted on the Web site, captured 400,000 new names in a single week. It was a huge success.

The problem with this preoccupation with growing the list was that MoveOn had become, in a sense, too efficient—a prisoner of its own single-minded responsiveness. The theme of all of MoveOn's e-mail appeals, whether they were talking about National Public Radio or Iraq, was, at bottom, the same: Republicans were evil, arrogant, and corrupt, and they had to be banished back to the wormy little holes they had crawled out of, the sooner the better. This was the only real message object its members cared about. They weren't really so concerned about reforming the Democratic Party, or about what a modern, more progressive governing agenda would actually look like. All they wanted, really, was for Bush and his war to go away, and for everything to go back to the way it had been in 1972, when they had been young, when George McGovern had headed the Democratic ticket, and when GM had still sold all the Chevy Impalas a country could possibly need.

As I sat with Eli, he admitted that he was trying to figure out what to do about this. There seemed to be a widening divide between the lofty vision of MoveOn's leadership and the more immediate goals that united its members. MoveOn's members were entirely focused on ridding the country of Republican rule. But for a complex thinker like Eli, even if Democrats could somehow win back the House or Senate in 2006 (an eventuality that seemed, when he and I spoke, about as likely as a meteorite falling on the White House), it wouldn't be enough. He wanted to change the priorities of American government. "The vision of Democrats controlling all three branches of government—that's not the vision I'm in it for," he told me. "The vision is to actually get somewhere on the issues we care about. Democrats are a vehicle. But if I'm trying to get to Boston, you know, the vision isn't Hartford." Lately, Eli had been playing with the idea of a "virtual think tank," in which progressive experts and voters from around the country could discuss and critique policy ideas online. But he wasn't sure there was enough interest to make it work.

In this way, Eli found himself in a position similar to that of Rob Stein, his friend in the new progressive movement. The emotion of the moment was an intense antipathy to Bush and his radical conservatism. It was an anger at both the president—whose approval ratings had been dropping steadily since his reelection—and the craven opposition party that seemed reluctant to confront him, and this anger made it relatively easy for both Eli and Rob to recruit and raise money among disparate groups of progressives. And yet, it also created, for both men, an unforeseen problem. They wondered, at times, how you got beyond that single, galvanizing resentment to build something positive and longer term. It was no small task to get people interested in reinventing the Democratic Party and its agenda when, as far as they were concerned, any party had to be better than the one in charge.

After we left Chuck Fazio's place, Tom Matzzie and I headed for Five Guys, a local burger joint. He told me that the week before, on the July Fourth holiday, he had been invited to view the fireworks with Harry Reid and his staff on the Senate minority leader's private balcony in the Capitol. Reid wasn't serving dinner, though, so Tom had skipped that event and went instead to a downtown party hosted by lobbyists for Citigroup, the banking conglomerate. There he had eaten miniature burgers with the likes of C. Boyden Gray, the wizened Republican insider who had been the first President Bush's White House counsel. Tom reported that Gray was a very cordial guy.

I asked him how much time he spent with congressmen and senators.

"Not much," Tom replied. He thought for a minute, adding it up in his head. "Maybe six hours a month. You know, even my colleagues at MoveOn, I think they think that I'm always, you know . . ." He paused, reaching for the right words.

"Yelling at senators?"

"No, I've done *that*," Tom said, with a little bravado. "They think I'm always sitting with politicians, and the truth is that I really don't like to spend much time that way."

Then he told me a story. Recently, Republicans and Democrats in the Senate had come to the edge of legislative Armageddon over Bush's judicial nominees. Democrats were threatening to use the filibuster—a time-honored stalling tactic that can prevent an up-or-down vote—to keep Bush's archconservative picks off the federal bench. Republicans, in turn, vowed to use what they called the "nuclear option," by which they meant that they would change the Senate rules to enable them to shut down filibusters with a simple majority. To the rest of the country, this probably sounded like a silly fracas over *Robert's Rules of Order*, but in Washington it was all people could talk about, because everyone understood that it was really about the Supreme Court. If Republicans took away the filibuster, then Democrats would be powerless to derail Bush's nominee once a seat on the high court came open.

The collision between the parties was averted only at the last minute, when a group of fourteen centrist senators from both parties forged a compromise that preserved the filibuster and seemed to hand Democrats, improbably, a tactical victory. But then rumors began to circulate that one of the centrist Democrats in the so-called Gang of 14, Colorado's Ken Salazar, was having second thoughts about the deal and was feeling inclined to cave to the Republican leadership. Liberal groups went crazy. The two big teachers' unions tried to call Salazar to see if it was true, but they couldn't get through.

Exasperated and worried, the labor guys called Tom. He put in a call to Salazar's state director and to one of his senior aides on Capitol Hill. Did he have to remind them, he asked, that MoveOn members had raised $400,000 for his campaign? They were sympathetic, but they wouldn't commit for their boss one way or the other.

So, donning his customary suit and freshly shined Bruno Maglis, Tom went down to Charlie Palmer's, a swanky new steak house on the Hill, where Simon Rosenberg was holding a reception. Tom found Salazar in the atriumlike reception area downstairs and made a direct line for him like a defensive end, thrusting out his hand before the senator could get away. "Good to see you, Senator," Tom said, looking him dead in the eye. "We appreciate your standing with Senator Reid on the filibuster."

In Tom's retelling, Salazar froze for an instant. "You've got to get the word out that I'm not bad on this," the senator told him. Just like that, Tom saw to it that the filibuster deal stayed intact.

What was telling about all this was that it showed how fast the Democratic outsiders in Washington were becoming the insiders. Not three years after most Democratic senators and congressmen had voted for the Iraq war resolution, and just eight months after Kerry and his small army of consultants had gone down in a blaze of caution, leaving a vacuum at the highest levels of the party, MoveOn was no longer an anti-establishment group fighting to seize power from the same old interest groups and deal makers. The truth was that MoveOn had become, in just the past few months, as powerful a

player as existed in Democratic politics, a constant presence in the
back rooms where the party's leaders made their most important
decisions. Far from tearing down the door of political Washington,
MoveOn's twentysomething leaders were now working it ably from
the inside.

A senior Democratic aide had told me that hardly a day went by
now when Reid's Senate staff didn't confer with Tom about strategy
or message, understanding that MoveOn was the best way for them
to get their message out and raise money among disaffected liberal
voters. Among the other senators who had openly courted Eli
and Tom in private meetings was Hillary Clinton, the presumed
front-runner for the 2008 presidential nomination, and her charm
appeared to have paid off; while MoveOn's members remained
furious at Clinton for voting with Bush on the war resolution, its
leaders refused to criticize her publicly. MoveOn was one of the most
respected voices at the table during a weekly strategy meeting among
Democratic interest groups, held at the AFL-CIO headquarters.
And MoveOn now paid hundreds of thousands of dollars to the pollster Stan Greenberg, the longtime Washington consultant who had
advised both Clinton and Al Gore.

I pointed out this irony to Tom as we munched on greasy cheese-
burgers and fries, and he shook his head in protest. "Our mission is to
connect people to politics," he said. "We have to be monastic about
that. When we start to go to Washington meetings and cocktail parties and awards ceremonies, then we won't be true to our mission." I
was dubious about this; he had already told me about the meetings
and parties he attended, and awards ceremonies couldn't be far off.
But now I had a larger question for him: Where was all of this leading? MoveOn had perfected the art of amassing power by constantly
growing its list, but how did it plan to use that power? MoveOn
could brilliantly exploit the fear and fury of liberal America, but it

had yet to offer any kind of alternative vision for the country. It was, to this point, an instrument of protest—and little else.

"OK, so there's this growing pain with MoveOn," Tom admitted. "We've built this list, and this brand, and this cachet. So what do we do with it?" He thought for a moment, then shrugged. "We're not really sure yet."

He continued to mull this over, apparently, as we drove back through the city. As I pulled up to his building in Adams Morgan, he told me about the pens at the AFL-CIO building. Every time Tom went up there for a meeting with his Democratic colleagues, he passed the wall where the unions displayed the commemorative pens that Lyndon Johnson used to sign one hundred laws of the Great Society. There was a pen for Medicare, a pen for food stamps, pens for voting rights and for civil rights. It gave you chills. That generation of Democrats had made their case with stunning clarity. Tom was trying to figure out what case his generation of progressives was going to make, now that it was their turn.

"Sometimes," Tom said as we idled, "I do think about what our pens will say, after we get power. I wonder what the MoveOn era will look like."

CHAPTER FIVE

The Road to Dysfunction

I n the fall of 2004, following Kerry's defeat, Rob Stein had set about the concrete work of building his donor collaborative. Drawing on a few hundred thousand dollars in start-up money from some of his wealthiest donors, including the Soros and Lewis families, Rob opened a checking account, rented some temporary office space in Georgetown, and set up a front company he called Copper Beech Strategies. (The copper beech tree can take as much as a century to really mature, and Rob thought it was an apt metaphor for an organization focused on changing the nature of American politics.) For a man who had searched so long and so openly for some higher purpose, this was no small opportunity. By the time he started sending out a prospectus to liberal millionaires around the country that fall, it must have seemed to Rob, a spiritual man, that all the climactic moments of his life—from sitting alone in the Grand Canyon in the 1970s to waking up, on the morning after the 2002 election, under Republican rule—had been leading him here.

If so, however, it was to be a short-lived zenith. Already, Rob was the object of jealousy among some of his peers, and these resentments would soon plunge the fledgling donor alliance into a cauldron of petty, bureaucratic infighting. Although he had now spent the better part of two years bonding with liberal millionaires and acting as their political therapist, Rob was still a peculiarly Washington figure, a mere interloper in the world of hedge funds and Learjets. And this, in the short term, would be his undoing.

Almost from the moment the previous summer when the founding members of the Phoenix Group had sent her and Rob out into the world to establish the donor alliance, Erica Payne, Rob's guide through the world of New York finance, had been openly fuming. The way she had understood it, the "partners," as they were now being called—most of whom she had personally recruited, using Rob's slide show as a tool to get them into the room—had assigned both of them, as equals, to launch the new organization. And, since Erica was the one with the business degree, the fund-raising contacts, and the entrepreneurial vision, she had assumed that she was the more obvious candidate to ultimately take charge of the venture. Rob was a brilliant presenter and a valuable resource, Erica thought, but the Phoenix Group had existed, in concept, before Rob and his slides ever came along. The way Erica saw it, his chief contribution had been to provide her with a gimmick.

Rob, of course, had made a very different assumption about who was in charge. Erica may have gotten these guys into the room, but it was Rob who captured their imaginations, who listened in that intense way he had, with his eyes narrowed and head slightly tilted, and who had drawn up the design for a new progressive movement. To most of the donors, Rob was a guru on everything connected to the conservative machine. They saw Erica as more of a fast-talking event planner. She was the kind of woman that older CEOs referred to, condescendingly, as a "fireplug" or a "pistol."

Rob knew that the partners planned eventually to hire someone to run the mundane, day-to-day operations of the new venture, which had now been renamed, confidentially, the Democracy

Alliance. (It sounded loftier and less sinister.) That wasn't the kind of thing Rob enjoyed anyway, and he told the partners that he wasn't interested in that job. It was clear to them, however, that he wanted to remain in his role as the chief architect of the movement, the guy who made the big-picture decisions. And he certainly didn't intend to share that role with Erica, whose bossy style couldn't have been more different from his plodding, consensus-building approach.

Almost immediately after the election, Erica started calling select donors to tell them that Rob wasn't up to leading the Democracy Alliance. Then she began to foment rebellion among the new staff hires, pointing out what she saw as a constant series of flaws in Rob's business plan and personal style. What had started as a productive partnership soon became a rivalry that exhausted and preoccupied both of them for many months. After yet another inconclusive meeting about the direction of the alliance in December 2004, Erica called Jonathan Soros, perhaps her most sympathetic backer, and complained that this was no way to build a business. She urged him to shove Rob aside. When Rob inevitably found out, he demanded that she quit. In January, their argument spilled out into the open at an elite dinner party in Washington, where they hissed at each other in the corner of the host's kitchen. Had Erica really thought she was going to lead the alliance? Rob wanted to know. He found that incredible.

The first full meeting of the donors—the official launch of the Democracy Alliance—was slated for April in Arizona, but the rift between its original organizers continued to preoccupy the staff and cast an air of chaos and immaturity over the entire enterprise. As the big meeting approached, Erica continued to lobby Soros and other influential partners in New York, who told her that she wasn't going to displace Rob. Just let it go, they said.

She couldn't.

They came by invitation only, stretched out in first class cabins or sipping drinks on private jets. Limousines whisked them through the red Arizona desert and deposited them at the Boulders, an exclusive, adobe resort outside Scottsdale. Most came alone or with a spouse, although the billionaires—most notably the Soroses and Lewises—came with their own entourages, small coteries of philanthropic and political advisers to whisper in their ears. The Wall Street guys wore polo shirts and slacks, the West Coast hippies wrinkled khakis and flip-flops, the Aspen crowd pastel-colored silk shirts. More than fifty of the wealthiest Democrats in America, the charter members of Rob Stein's club, arrived for their first-ever national gathering on that April weekend, just five months after the election that had left them feeling confused and deflated.

In the weeks leading up to the meeting, Rob had seemed harried and distracted as he struggled to keep up with the hundreds of e-mails that accumulated in his in-box. This first conference, he knew, had to be perfect. It had to inspire powerful people. It had to feel professional and businesslike. Erica and the staff studied each attendee's profile, memorizing spouses and business backgrounds. Rob practiced and refined his remarks. State-of-the-art computers and video screens were tested and tested again. Nothing left to chance—that was the unofficial motto of the conference.

The attendees were old money and new, financiers and high-tech impresarios, entrepreneurs and philanthropists. Susie Tompkins Buell and her husband Mark flew in from the Bay Area, as did Drummond Pike, the founder of the liberal Tides Foundation, and Rob McKay, heir to the Taco Bell fortune. Rutt Bridges came from Colorado, along with a group of progressive donors whose money had helped bring about a Democratic revival in that state, including Patricia Stryker, the heiress to a medical supply company, and Rodger

McFarlane, who ran the liberal Gill Foundation. Rob Glaser, the dot-com billionaire and chief investor behind Air America, the liberal radio network, made the trip from Seattle. Two of the nation's most successful trial lawyers—Fred Baron of Dallas and Guy Saperstein of Oakland—were there. Rob Reiner and Norman Lear made up the Hollywood contingent.

A cadre of Washington political operatives was on hand too, to lend expertise: John Podesta; David Brock, the former conservative writer now running Media Matters; Simon Rosenberg of the New Democratic Network, who had been the first to promote the slide show and who had introduced Rob to Erica; and the former White House aides Mike McCurry and Sidney Blumenthal. They were joined by the venerable journalist Bill Moyers, who had once been an aide to Lyndon Johnson. Although they were gathering, in part, to promote a more open and transparent government, the donors and their advisers met in an atmosphere of intense secrecy. Hulking security guards blocked the rooms. The staff disposed of sensitive documents with rented shredders. No proof of the meeting—not even the fancy loose-leaf binders or the tote bags they came in—was to be left behind.

Each of the donors had agreed to contribute a minimum of $200,000 a year to building the new progressive infrastructure, for a total commitment of $1 million each over five years. (This didn't include the annual dues of $30,000 for administrative costs or the one-time initiation fee of $25,000.) According to a survey taken by the donors the night they arrived, most of them were between the ages of forty-five and sixty-five, and three-quarters of them hailed from one coast or the other. Some 38 percent described themselves as "progressives," and 24 percent used the term "liberal"; only 7 percent of the contributors said they thought of themselves primarily as "Democrats." Some 84 percent said the conservative movement represented "a fundamental threat to the American way of life," and the vast majority of the donors—86 percent—said the main goal of the

Democracy Alliance should be to "support long-term objectives," rather than to show short-term results.

Rob opened the conference with a speech he had titled "Our Time to Lead." "Our children and grandchildren are watching us today," he began. "They deserve to be our beneficiaries of freedom and democracy, of prosperity and security, of a hopeful and sensible world. We have come to Arizona to invest together in their future." He challenged this inaugural class of contributors to "help create a grand vision for America, based on enduring values and grounded in meaningful, practical solutions for people at home and abroad." It was up to the people in this room, he said, to build a new generation of progressive institutions that could push back against the conservative machine. Citing this need for resistance in a dark time, Rob invoked the examples of no less a set of great leaders than Abraham Lincoln, Mahatma Gandhi, Franklin Roosevelt, Martin Luther King Jr., Nelson Mandela, and Winston Churchill.

The partners watched a perfunctory welcoming video from Howard Dean, who was as close to a political icon as many of them had, and who had just taken over as chairman of the Democratic Party. They spent most of the rest of the weekend introducing themselves to one another at open bars and buffet dinners. George Soros had been slated to address the group, but when Gail Furman, the child psychologist, saw that Bill Moyers was there, she suggested that he interview Soros onstage, instead. The donors, many of whom aspired to Soros's kind of wealth (he was among the thirty richest Americans, according to *Forbes*), reveled in the conversation between the wild-haired philosopher-billionaire and his famous interviewer.

The partners got down to deciding some critical questions. They gathered around a rectangular array of tables with their own hand-held voting devices, which registered their answers to assorted questions and instantly displayed the results, in pie charts, on a large screen at the front of the room. Three-quarters of the partners said the alliance should not "retain close ties to the Democratic Party." This led to some debate about the name of the new organization—was "Democracy" too close to "Democratic?"—but the partners voted to leave the name as it was. They decided there would be no cap on the number of partners who could join. They voted to create a "pool of funds" to be invested in progressive causes, and they decided that each partner's $200,000 commitment would be satisfied only by donating to those groups that the alliance endorsed. A strong majority of the partners—about 72 percent—said the Democracy Alliance should be based outside Washington.

The most pressing business in Scottsdale, however, concerned the election of a board of directors. One of Rob's closest friends, Anne Bartley, had decided to stand for election as chairwoman. Bartley was the stepdaughter of Winthrop Rockefeller. A smooth, blue-eyed Arkansan who had worked for both Clintons and served on the boards of several large foundations. She seemed like a lock for the job.

What Rob didn't know, however, was that Erica had chosen this moment for their inevitable showdown. Quietly, working with some of the staff and a few of the partners who were most loyal to her, she had launched a stealth campaign to undermine Bartley and elect her own chairman from among the slate of new directors. She had in mind Steven Gluckstern, a little-known venture capitalist from New York, who had been one of her last recruits to the alliance and whose confidence she still enjoyed. Erica had been arguing that it was undemocratic for Rob to simply pick his own slate of board members and his own chairman, that the partners needed to establish that it was their money and they were the ones in charge. She had managed to persuade two sympathetic board members—Davidi Gilo, an Israeli-born venture capitalist, and Rachel Pritzker Hunter, of the Hyatt Hotel Pritzkers—to lobby for Gluckstern. When it became apparent, on that first day in Scottsdale, that they had succeeded and that

Gluckstern had the votes he needed, Bartley withdrew, and the new board members promptly made the decision unanimous.

Bartley was visibly hurt, and Rob appeared to have suffered a significant defeat. The wealthy donors who had been willing to do whatever he asked before the election had now, in their first meeting together, cast aside his recommendation and chosen a leader he barely knew. He refused to so much as speak to Erica or her allies on the alliance staff, who had undermined and embarrassed him at the most critical moment of his career. He said their actions constituted a grievous breach of loyalty, and he would have been right, had they shown him the slightest loyalty to begin with.

It wasn't more than a few weeks after they all returned from Scottsdale when Steven Gluckstern—a man who hadn't even been in the room when Rob Stein first dazzled crowds around the country with his PowerPoint slides—informed Rob that he didn't have the skills necessary to lead the alliance, and that the board was embarking on an exhaustive search for a CEO who would not only administer the alliance but be its chief visionary, as well. (Gluckstern even offered himself to the rest of the board as a candidate, but he soon abandoned the idea.) Rob was given a seat on the board for five years, and, in exchange for a lucrative short-term contract, he agreed to stay on and run the alliance, guiding it through its first round of investments until a CEO could be found later in the year, after the next meeting of the partners. This put Rob in the awkward position of continuing to administer a fund for investors who clearly didn't trust him. He pointed out to anyone who asked that he had planned to step aside as CEO in any event, but he was clearly humiliated by the cold and final nature of the rejection.

At least he didn't have to worry about Erica Payne anymore. Gluckstern and the others had come around to her view of Rob Stein's fitness as a leader, but Erica's divisive campaign against him had taken its toll on her reputation, too, and by the time she finally managed to dislodge him from his vaunted position, none of the partners saw her as a credible alternative. They severed her ties to the Democracy Alliance. It was, she would say, among the biggest disappointments of her life.

With Rob demoted and Erica cast aside entirely, and with Steven Gluckstern now firmly installed as its chairman, you would have thought the Democracy Alliance could put its internecine struggles behind it and focus, at last, on its mission as an agent for political change. It wasn't to be. The tensions over who would control all this money—whether it would be hired staff or the millionaire partners themselves—would continue to absorb everyone connected with the alliance during its first two years. The mission, meanwhile, would grow ever more elusive.

Steven Gluckstern and his wife, Judy, lived in a 7,500-square-foot open loft on Spring Street in SoHo, with a spacious garden on the roof and magnificent views of the Empire State Building to the north. Two hardwood staircases, one leading up to the roof and the other down to a lower level, were suspended from steel cables, and a two-sided wall of brilliant blue Brazilian marble divided the kitchen from the living space. Everything in the place, functional or not, seemed to be a work of art, from the Danish modern furniture to the long table by the sculptor John Chamberlain and a wall-size self-portrait by the artist Julian Schnabel. A beautiful, hand-carved carousel horse sat in the dining area. Until a few years ago, Steven had owned the entire building, but he had sold the other six floors, along with the aquarium in the lobby, for about five million bucks. That was before the New York real estate boom went boom again. Now his apartment alone, he told me, was valued at around $13 million.

Steven was a genial, bearded guy in his midfifties who kept his spectacles perilously perched on the bridge of his nose. He enjoyed fielding questions about himself, and his answers often sounded like the kind of impossibly earthy quotes you would read in *Fortune* or *Forbes*. "My investment strategy is different from most people's," he told me once. "I don't really care about money. I mean, I like it. You can do fun things with it. You can give it away." In fact, Steven did seem to give a fair amount of money away—to the arts, to gay and lesbian causes, to AIDS research. The first time I met him, shortly after his surprising election as chairman of the Democracy Alliance, I couldn't help noticing that the screen saver on his computer was a photograph of a group of smiling Asian children. (By that I mean that I actually couldn't help noticing—the screen was about four feet wide.)

"Oh yeah, I own an orphanage in Nepal," Steven said offhandedly.

"I didn't know you could own an orphanage," I said.

"Well, 'own' isn't the right word," he replied, hurriedly shutting down the computer. "I fund it."

Steven had gone to business school at Stanford, but he thought of himself primarily as an educator. While still in his twenties, fresh from a graduate program in education at the University of Massachusetts, he had helped found a group of English-speaking schools in Iran, a business venture that ended abruptly when the revolution came. He then served as the superintendent of schools in Telluride, Colorado, where he and Judy still owned a second home. He made his fortune in the reinsurance industry, working first for the billionaire Warren Buffett and then with a partner, and he had recently retired from the $4 billion investment fund he had helped start. I heard grumbling from some of the other, richer partners that Steven wasn't really that good at making money, but if that was true, it was clearly relative. He was certainly better at it than anyone I knew in Washington.

Before one meeting in Steven's SoHo office, while waiting for him in a conference room, I studied what to me was an unintelligible flow chart on a wall-mounted whiteboard. The words "marine voyager" were written in big letters and circled. From that circle came a series of smaller, orbiting circles: "LPO," "DPW," "SMG," "revenue." When Steven came into the room, he explained that he had recently been on a Turkish vacation cruise when he met and befriended a man who said he was a British archaeologist. It turned out that the guy was trying to raise $4 million to build a Turkish gulet—a 150-foot boat with ancient-looking wings sweeping up from the sides, with thirteen cabins and a crew of eight. Over drinks, Steven decided to buy 48 percent of the company that would operate the boat for tours off the Dalmatian coast. The diagram on the whiteboard, he told me, represented his due diligence on the deal.

"My life is about making sure that the things I select to do are things that give me enjoyment," Steven told me. "One of my friends who's a billionaire says the thing about being rich is that you can do what you want."

It was for this reason, Steven told me, that he had decided to devote most of his time now to the Democracy Alliance. Like most of the partners I met, Steven applied the mystical language of business to his work with the alliance. He talked often about finding progressive organizations that came with maximum "ROI"—return on investment. He talked about doing "due diligence" on these groups, about "capitalizing" them so they could be "brought to scale." He talked about finding "customers" for the Democratic "product." It was clear, spending time with Gluckstern and other partners, that they felt they had identified with some precision the cause of these recurrent Democratic failures: The problem was that the party was being run by a bunch of political experts, when, in fact, it needed to be run like a business. They had grown weary of sitting despondently in their glass towers and weekend retreats, watching the Democrats flail around for a message and a market while the country slid deeper into one-party domination. It was time for the private sector to step in.

There followed from this way of thinking an important corollary, which held that the people who worked in Washington were not, by definition, the brightest flames in the human candelabra. The way the partners saw it, people who were really smart made tons of money, and if you didn't make tons of money, then you couldn't be very smart. Steven wanted the Democracy Alliance to open its headquarters in Oakland, where rents were the lowest in the Bay Area, because, as told me more than once, talented and creative people simply weren't attracted to Washington. If you were going to build a powerful new Democratic movement, you had to get some physical distance from the mediocrity of the political establishment.

From the beginning, Rob Stein had been highly attuned to this worldview. Once, when we were talking about the groups the Democracy Alliance might fund, Rob told me, "We want them to run consistent with the most cutting-edge thinking about how non-profit corporations can adopt the very best protocols to both maximize our effectiveness in the world and provide a return on investment for our contributors. There has to be a culture of excellence." And yet, much as he seemed to speak the language, he could not escape what he represented in the minds of many donors. In Steven's view, Rob had spent too much of his career in Washington. And, as if to confirm his suspicions, Rob's most recent job had been to manage a private investment fund—and still Rob hadn't gotten rich. (In fact, the fund, which invested solely in businesses owned by women, had crashed after a few years.) What did it say about a man when he started a fund and somehow didn't walk away with millions of dollars? As far as Steven was concerned, that in itself probably disqualified Rob from making the big decisions.

Of course, it was easy for these new ideological donors, the ones who hadn't played any significant role in the Clinton-era party, to dismiss Washington insiders and the Democratic apparatus, mainly because they were strikingly naive about the actual business of politics.

This became clear at various moments in my conversations with them, as when I asked Steven whether he had contributed much money to Democrats in the '90s. The question led him to recount a story.

At some point in the late '90s, after he had contributed a mere $5,000 to the Democratic Party, Steven got a call from Terry McAuliffe, who was then one of the party's top fund-raisers. "We want you to step up your giving," the Macker told him. "How about $50,000?"

Steven balked. "I'd have to talk to some people first," he said.

"Who would you have to talk to?"

"Well, the president of the United States, for one."

"Hold on," Terry said. He clicked off for a bit. Steven started to sweat. Then Terry returned to the line. "Next Tuesday at the Hay-Adams. You're having lunch with the president."

Steven showed up at the hotel the following week and found himself in a room of about fifteen contributors, all of whom sat around a table with Bill Clinton himself. Steven had given the least money of anyone there, so, of course, Terry had seated him next to the president. Steven tried to engage the president on education policy. Clinton listened closely, seemingly engrossed. He nodded a lot, trans-fixed. Finally, an aide scurried over and touched the president's arm, whispering that it was time to go.

"I'm in the middle of a conversation," Clinton snapped, and immediately he retrained his laserlike eyes on Steven. This, of course, was a classic political ploy, which Clinton—whose moves were as graceful as those of any politician who ever lived—could pull off in his sleep. Lashing out at the poor guy whose job it is to keep you moving, so that you can continue talking with this *really* interesting campaign contributor you just met, is such an old standard in Washington that a more seasoned donor would have seen it a hundred times. But, as Steven recounted this scene to me, years later, he still sounded amazed. "He was really listening," he told me. "You can't fake that." He wrote a check for fifty grand.

Steven bumped up his political giving after the 2000 election. He estimated that he had spent, in all, maybe half a million dollars on political campaigns and party contributions. It was during this time that he began to think that perhaps there was some return to be had on his investment, something he could get out of it. He already had all the money he needed. What worlds were left to conquer? When he thought about it deeply, Steven came up with an answer: He wanted to be the secretary of education. Why not? He had the master's degree and the hands-on experience as a superintendent, he'd been wildly successful, and he was bankrolling the party. That was how it worked, right? Through Terry McAuliffe and Chuck Schumer, his senator in New York, Steven was able to go down to Washington and meet with Ted Kennedy, who was said to have a lot of power in these things. He "maxed out" his donations during the 2004 cycle, meaning that he gave the legal limit—about $110,000—to the party and its campaign committees.

Steven wasn't shy about telling people that he thought he would have been in the running for the job if John Kerry had been elected—although, he was quick to add, he wouldn't have accepted the job without first having a serious discussion with Kerry. He wasn't about to waste his middle age marking time at the Education Department. He wanted to be a genuine change agent, someone who would shake up the status quo. Oddly, it never seemed to occur to Steven that the last person John Kerry could ever have afforded to make his education secretary—a cabinet post of great symbolic importance in a Democratic administration—would have been a campaign contributor, let alone a campaign contributor he didn't really know, and whose most recent experience in that area was having served on the local board of education in suburban Dobbs Ferry, New York.

The truth was that Steven Gluckstern had become just another in a large herd of classic Democratic access donors—decent, well-meaning people who assumed that their money might buy them a cabinet post or the ambassadorship they had always wanted, and who were purposely led to believe that such things were possible, because the party needed cash. Powerful politicians like Chuck Schumer and Ted Kennedy knew that it was part of their job to spend a little time indulging the fantasies of such big contributors. Those dull and unimaginative Washington insiders whom Steven held in such low regard had, essentially, fleeced him.

But now that he was chairman of the Democracy Alliance, the power dynamic seemed to be shifting. Now there was a leadership vacuum in the Democratic universe, and rich contributors had decided to take matters into their own hands. And when word got out in Washington that the chairman of this new investment fund was a guy named Steven Gluckstern, a guy almost no one in Washington power circles could remember meeting, a sense of severe anxiety began to set in among the party elite. Democrats were just now building up their financial reserves for the midterm elections of 2006, which were less than eighteen months away, and the way it sounded to party leaders, this Gluckstern guy was likely to control a whole pile of Democratic money. Of course, not even Steven yet knew exactly how the Democracy Alliance planned to spend its money, and it certainly wouldn't be entirely his decision. But nobody in Washington knew that. All they knew was that this Gluckstern was going to be a major player, and he needed to be properly schmoozed.

Suddenly, Steven Gluckstern was a popular man in Democratic politics. No meeting was beyond his reach. No call went unreturned. Everyone wanted to know him. While I was sitting in his conference room, his secretary came in and handed him a note. Steven adjusted his glasses for a moment and then broke into a grin. "Do you want to meet with Nancy Pelosi here at two thirty tomorrow?" he read aloud. He turned to his secretary. "Yes, I would be happy to meet with *Leader* Pelosi here tomorrow," he told her. Then, to me: "I've never met her."

Not five minutes later, his cell phone rang.

"What's two-one-five?" he asked me, staring down at the phone through his precarious spectacles.

"Philadelphia," I replied helpfully.

He flipped open the phone. "Hello?" He sounded annoyed. "Hi, Allyson. This is my cell phone, and I'm in a meeting. Can I give you my office line and get back to you?" He reeled off his main number. "Thank you," he snapped, and abruptly hung up.

"That was Congresswoman Allyson Schwartz," he told me, with an expression that said, you see what I go through? "She's running for reelection." He shrugged. "I've never even heard of her."

The aging white industrialists who financed the modern conservative movement harbored little ambiguity about what they believed. Their political philosophy grew directly from the writing of Friedrich A. Hayek, the Nobel Prize–winning economist whose seminal book, *The Road to Serfdom,* was among the most influential political theses of the twentieth century. An Austrian native who immigrated to England, Hayek made the case that all forms of centralized, collectivist government—whether fascist or communist—were the harbingers of tyranny. He was profoundly alarmed by the trend in the United States and Europe, beginning with the New Deal and growing more pronounced during wartime, toward centrally planned economies and the forced redistribution of wealth. These policies stemmed from all the right intentions, Hayek said, but they would lead us, inevitably, into totalitarian darkness.

Hayek's book was a libertarian manifesto, and it influenced a generation of conservative thinkers; one can draw a direct line from Hayek to the likes of Barry Goldwater and Milton Friedman. By the 1970s, wealthy conservatives like Joseph Coors, the beer magnate, and John Olin, the munitions king, had come to see themselves as

lone voices of reason, preaching individual liberty and small government against a political establishment that rushed heedlessly ahead
into an era of collectivist economics and social engineering. At the
same time, other conservative tycoons were gravitating toward social
conservatism, the idea that liberal meddling had weakened the moral
foundation and work ethic of the American family. These different
groups of donors didn't sit around a table and argue about what a
conservative movement might look like. They simply set up their
own foundations and began giving money to promising thinkers who
could make an innovative argument for a lean and restrained federal
government, one whose primary responsibility was to protect its
people from foreign aggressors.

The think tanks, policy journals, and academic programs that
these philanthropists created would eventually promote such influential—and controversial—conservative scholars as the sociologist
Charles Murray (*Losing Ground*), the economist Arthur Laffer ("the
Laffer curve"), and the foreign policy theorists Francis Fukuyama
(*The End of History and the Last Man*) and Samuel Huntington (*The
Clash of Civilizations*). Such investments would ultimately yield entire
fields of study, such as the "law and economics" movement, which
introduced free-market thinking to the nation's elite law schools,
as well as specific policy proposals like school vouchers and Social
Security privatization. This philanthropy also enabled the movement
to bridge the significant divide between its libertarians and its social
conservatives, mainly by creating an intellectual space where the two
groups could fixate on ideas that appealed to them both. Communism,
for instance, was both godless *and* an enemy of free markets—and
thus, opposing it became a focal point of both socially conservative and
libertarian scholarship.

These donors weren't trying to win elections, at least not
right away. The Republican Party interested them only as a vehicle
that might someday be commandeered; they felt almost as alienated

from liberal, mainstream Republicans as they did from the governing Democrats. Nor did they consider themselves political strategists or message crafters. They were businessmen with an ideology, and they trusted their Washington experts to handle the tactics and paperwork. The industrialists planted some seed money in journals and magazines, but the sophisticated messaging machine that Rob Stein so ably diagrammed came much later, only after the conservative argument had gained enough momentum to create a profitable market for the tirades of a raging opportunist like Rush Limbaugh.

The liberal millionaires who came to Scottsdale at one of the low moments in their party's history saw themselves, thanks to Rob's tutelage, as the modern analogs to the conservative pioneers. It soon became clear how different their situation really was. For one thing, unlike the conservative philanthropists, they didn't share any single, identifiable philosophy. They were united by their revulsion toward the Republican majority, and they shared a common nostalgia for what the Democratic Party had once achieved, but they had arrived at no consensus about the kind of government they envisioned next. They were also divided between those partners who defined success simply as electing more Democrats and those who sought, instead, to take control of the party and purge it of spineless accommodationists. And, of course, most of the partners of the Democracy Alliance had no intention of delegating the political work to so-called experts. They saw the Democracy Alliance not just as a funding mechanism, but as a vehicle for their own expertise, which they believed had been grossly undervalued in the political realm.

In an effort to define their mission, Rob Stein and a small committee of partners, led by Steven Gluckstern, began meeting in New York to hammer out some kind of broad philosophical consensus for the alliance. They were looking to distill the essential belief system at the core of Rob's vision. The end result of their work was a five-paragraph "statement of shared vision," which was submitted for review by all the partners and, after a period of comment, ultimately approved by the board. Not surprisingly, perhaps, it laid out a series of vague and unobjectionable assertions. In fact, the final document sounded less like a manifesto than like a high school project on the meaning of America.

"The Democracy Alliance is committed to the pursuit of a just and peaceful world founded on truth, transparency and trustworthiness, and on traditional American values of personal responsibility, individual rights, equal opportunity, religious liberty, and stewardship of natural resources," it began. "These principles promote human freedom and democracy, which flourish when government is devoted to the common good and respects human dignity by providing every citizen the highest quality education, affordable healthcare, retirement security, and the opportunity to earn a living wage." Elsewhere in the document, the partners embraced the "blessings of freedom" and "robust public debate" and said that "America's strength is rooted in prosperity and security."

In our conversations, Rob insisted to me that this statement, while only a beginning, had drawn some important distinctions between conservative values and progressive ones. After all, he argued, how many conservatives would include a government "devoted to the common good" and "affordable healthcare" among their most cherished beliefs? It was a valid point, and yet it was also true that you could have walked from Trenton to Tahoe without encountering a single American, from any part of the political spectrum, who really objected to anything in the alliance statement. Who in America didn't like affordable health care? Who didn't want prosperity? What made these exclusively progressive values?

As the earlier generation of conservative philanthropists might have told them, successful political movements aren't built on the common values that all Americans share, but on the arguments that lay out how, as a country, we can best live up to them. Just as a prosecutor must present to jurors his theory of the case—not simply the specific facts of the crime, but some unifying idea of why it occurred, what it means to society as a whole, and what the jury must do to ensure a just outcome—so, too, must the leaders of a political movement try to make sense of their moment, to connect the world in which people live, day to day, with the choices they're asking voters to make. It's not enough to tell people that they ought to have health care and good schools and lots of jobs; they already know this. The point of a political movement is to explain *why* these things are lacking and to advance an argument about how we should adapt to the larger forces that led us here. Ideally, a movement offers some theory that flips on the lights along the path ahead, so that the future seems a little less dark and confusing.

Arguments come and go in American politics from one campaign to the next, but some endure. The twentieth century, in fact, was dominated by the arguments of just a few popular movements and their visionary leaders. Roosevelt's New Deal, built on the progressive movement that preceded it, was based on the highly controversial argument that a more expansive and intrusive government was the only way to address the inequities inherent in capitalism—to save the unbridled market from itself. Lyndon Johnson and Robert Kennedy, affected by the equality movements of their time, picked up where that brief left off, arguing that government had not just an active role to play in the economic growth of a nation, but also a moral obligation to intervene in social injustices. The conservative movement led by Ronald Reagan advanced Hayek's argument about the inevitable evil of central planning (including taxes and forced integration) and the necessity of standing up to totalitarianism (which included "rolling back" Soviet aggression). These movements were distinguished not by their end goals—all of them sought "opportunity" and "the blessings of freedom"—but by their arguments about why those things had eluded too many Americans and what was needed to secure them.

While all of their proponents labored to make them as universal and as palatable to voters as possible, none of these arguments grew originally from a desire to win elections, nor were they designed to be immediately acceptable to the broadest swath of voters. FDR's vision inspired generations of free marketeers to detest everything he stood for, even as they reached unimagined prosperity. Johnson and Kennedy turned the entire American South away from the Democratic cause. Reagan's thesis cleaved the country, bringing on twenty years of intense polarization. Each of these arguments, in fact, infuriated large numbers of reasonable and influential Americans—but that was precisely what made them compelling and important. That was the cost of forcing people to choose between one governing path and another, and in such choices lay the fate of the republic.

Had they been able to articulate a unifying argument for governing, the Democracy Alliance partners might easily have been able to do what the conservative donors had done: aggressively search out academics and activists who shared their philosophy, build new organizations for them, and let these new thinkers figure out how to take on the establishment. The partners would have known immediately what kind of innovators they were searching for. Instead, they did what a lot of institutions do when confronted with confusion about their core philosophies: They created an unwieldy bureaucracy to fill the void.

The partners divided their potential investments into what Rob called the "four buckets": ideas, media, leadership training, and civic engagement. With this as their organizing principle, they proceeded to create all kinds of "working groups" and "project teams," along with an "investment and strategy committee" to coordinate their various recommendations. These committees were charged with finding and vetting potential "Alliance Recommended Organizations"—"AROs" for short. Soon there emerged a committee on longer-term strategy, a committee on foreign affairs, a diversity committee, and a women's caucus, whose members objected to the name "caucus," because it was actually more of a committee. The Democracy Alliance quickly became the political version of a nightmare condo association, with some partners spending twenty hours a week or more on conference calls and e-mail exchanges that frequently meandered into musings on the progressive soul but that never seemed to actually resolve anything.

Neither the partners nor the alliance staff members—all of whom, in keeping with the alliance's basic worldview, had been hired from the private sector, rather than from Washington—brought with them any experience navigating the complex topography of Democratic scholarship and activism. The partners were no better equipped to identify the best investment opportunities in Democratic politics than your average political operative would have been to identify the next big trend in the bond market. And yet, when it came to vetting potential AROs, they personally undertook the onerous due diligence process, hoping to teach these naive political guys something about the rigorous ways of big business. Think tanks that were asked to submit proposals, for instance, were given an eleven-page guide to the process, advising them to provide, among other materials, long- and short-term strategic plans, a detailed explanation of the planning process, articles of incorporation and tax documents, a brief history of the organization and a description of its operations, flow charts of the organizational structure and governance processes, biographies of board members and staff, annual reports, audits, current and future budgets, and a breakdown of funding sources, including the total cost per dollar raised. They had about a month to comply.

Next came a round of meetings with a couple of former analysts from the McKinsey & Company consulting firm, as well as with some of the partners themselves. John Podesta was probably the only potential grantee whose organization, the Center for American Progress, had enough staff and resources to comply with all of the various demands. Podesta was already getting money directly from several of the wealthiest donors in the Democracy Alliance, and yet he and his senior staff were forced to endure hours of agonizing calls and meetings with some of the partners. They grilled him on his ten-year plan, his staffing levels, his financial disclosures. After forty years in politics, Podesta could walk into any Democratic office in Washington unannounced. As White House chief of staff, he had, effectively, run the world. But here he was, defending his organization to a couple of rich guys who were brand new to politics, as if he were some failing software entrepreneur begging to be rescued by Microsoft.

As with everything about the Democracy Alliance, the strangest aspect of this entire process was the incessant secrecy. Among the alliance's stated values was a commitment to political transparency—as long as it didn't apply to the alliance. Most of the partners seemed eager to imitate the conservatives, who they believed were always hatching conspiracies in private, to great effect. Others worried, more pragmatically, about the effect on their businesses if what they were doing became public. For still other partners, however, the aversion to scrutiny came from a basic sense of wealthy entitlement. It was their money to spend however they liked, and they were accountable to no one but the IRS.

For these reasons, the process of applying for funding was anything but transparent. Groups could only apply by invitation, and they signed documents promising not to disclose anything about the alliance to the outside world. The effects of this secrecy weren't hard to anticipate. By the end of the summer, all of Democratic

Washington seemed to have heard just enough about the Democracy Alliance to feel resentful and cheated, but not enough to know why they hadn't been included in its plans.

In an effort to clarify the alliance's mission for the party's congressional leaders, Rob set up a conference call in the fall of 2005 with the party's most powerful aides on Capitol Hill—the chiefs of staff for Harry Reid, Nancy Pelosi, and Howard Dean, as well as the executive director of the Democratic Governors Association—to brief them on the alliance's funding plans. The party operatives said they wanted the alliance to direct money to an independent group that would be defending Democratic incumbents from Republican attacks in the coming campaign. "I understand the need for a long-term infrastructure," Susan McCue, Reid's chief of staff, told Rob, "but I have races I'm worried about right now, in 2006."

"I can see how that would make sense from your narrow perspective," Rob replied, a little carelessly, before trying to more thoughtfully explain the alliance's approach. Others on the call winced.

McCue seethed. "I'm not getting anything out of this call," she said, and got off the line.

Long-established liberal groups like Emily's List and the Sierra Club were furious at not having been contacted by the Democracy Alliance. Upstart groups, many of which had sprouted up in the months after the election, when it had seemed like the time was right for anyone with an answer to the party's problems to step forward, were crushed to find out that they hadn't even been invited to plead their cases to the donors. Democratic activists began to complain that the money they relied on for survival was drying up. The donors they visited told them that they were now part of the Democracy Alliance, or that they were considering joining, so they were waiting to see which organizations were recommended for funding before writing any checks. As a result, liberal groups were losing vital cash.

Among those who found himself cut off, ironically, was Simon Rosenberg, who had been Rob's earliest patron back in 2003, but who, inexplicably, hadn't even been invited to apply for funding from the alliance. Dangerously low on cash, Simon laid off most of his staff and moved, during that fall of 2005, from his longtime head-quarters near Capitol Hill to a small, dingy suite in the downtown offices that had previously housed the Kerry for President campaign. Simon and his remaining aides sat together in an open space with a single conference room. You could still see the faded patches on the walls where the Kerry posters had been. The landlord hadn't even bothered to paint.

The Democracy Alliance partners came together again at the end of October 2005, six months after their first meeting, at the Château Élan, a posh winery and resort forty minutes north of Atlanta. The event was officially dubbed the "fall 2005 investment strategy conference," and each partner received a binder with the conference logo, a gauzy yellow star set against a rippling American flag, on the cover. Inside they found information on the ten groups that had been identified by the various partner committees as the nucleus of the new progressive movement. These were the groups they were being asked to fund. It was, on the whole, an unremark-able list, focused overwhelmingly on the machinery of elections rather than the substance behind them. For all the posturing over due diligence, the plain fact was that virtually every group on the list ended up there not because it had passed a grueling test, but because it had a connection to some influential player in the alliance.

The partners promised John Podesta and David Brock, who had been in on the original Phoenix Group meetings and who were favorites of the Soroses and Lewises, a minimum of $9 million and $7 million, respectively, over two years. Progressive Majority, a candidate training outfit that had been championed by the Sandler family, got $5 million. (Herb and Marion Sandler, who weren't known for working especially well with other donors, hadn't actually joined the alliance, but their son-in-law, Steven Phillips, represented their interests at the table.) America Votes, which had been established by all three families to coordinate various get-out-the-vote drives during the 2004 election, was slated to receive at least $5.5 million for the next election cycle alone.

While neither the Soroses nor the Lewises sat on the board of the Democracy Alliance or bothered to play much of a role in all the contentious conference calls that dragged on throughout the summer, they nonetheless exercised the greatest influence on the selection process, thanks to the sheer depth of their pockets. George Soros was the single largest investor in the alliance, kicking in more than $10 million during this opening round. Peter Lewis, who had built Progressive Insurance Company and was known to be somewhat eccentric—he liked to compare himself to the Lone Ranger and had once been arrested for bringing marijuana into New Zealand—announced that he would match every dollar pledged in Georgia with twenty-five cents of his own. Those two families alone would end up contributing roughly a third of the $39 million pledged by the alliance in its first round of investments.

It was probably inevitable, at this early stage, that there would be some dissension over investment decisions. It would have been hard to get some eighty superwealthy liberals to agree on the entrée choices for lunch, much less on how to spend their money. But the opaqueness of the selection process left a lot of partners feeling especially slighted, and the mood in Georgia quickly deteriorated. It started with the three families, who had an intramural squabble over America Votes; the Lewises and Sandlers had given up on it, but George Soros insisted it be included. Then Gail Furman, the child psychologist from New York, demanded to know why the alliance wasn't creating a "nerve center" that could book progressives on TV news shows. The idea, which stemmed from a conversation with Bill Moyers, was popular with the partners, but in the rush to prepare for the Georgia conference, the alliance staff had, by Rob's own admission, "dropped the ball."

Norman Lear, the television producer, was furious that the group he had founded in the 1970s, People for the American Way, wasn't getting any money. The partners in the "ideas working group," which was responsible for identifying think tanks, complained that the staff hadn't given them enough choices. Rob Glaser, Air America's main funder, couldn't believe that the partners, for all their talk about the evils of conservative talk radio, wouldn't help the radio network, which was sinking financially. He and a group of partners had invited Danny Goldberg, Air America's CEO, to the conference, but the board wouldn't let him speak, so he just hung around all weekend, growing frustrated. This, in turn, alienated even more partners, who were appalled to see the longtime music executive and liberal activist so disrespected.

By the end of the weekend, the Democracy Alliance had passed a critical milestone, making its first round of investments in the new progressive infrastructure, but already the group seemed in danger of breaking apart. Rob could have been excused for disowning the whole mess at this point. With the first investment conference now passed, he was finally relinquishing day-to-day control over the alliance anyway. The partners had treated him shabbily, and he could have simply walked away, claiming they had undermined his vision. Instead, outwardly at least, he chose to view these early days of the alliance with unflagging optimism. Perhaps the prospect of his dream falling prey to petty rivalries kept him awake at night, but Rob wasn't about to show that to anyone else. He was an unusually patient man, and he told me that this was only the first phase of a much longer journey; after all, the conservatives, too, had overcome their share of fights and obstacles in the early days. The alliance was "an immature organism," Rob said, but it had now achieved "proof of concept."

"It's so cool," Rob told me after returning from Georgia. "It's so *cool*." He said he had made peace with having his role in the Alliance reduced. "I don't have all the skills. I know that," he told me bluntly. "But those who said, 'He *can't* do it'—I took umbrage at that. I got it this far. It's been messy, but the results are there. So I don't believe I can't do it. But I do think that running this should be done by someone who has a set of skills that I can only imagine having."

Steven Gluckstern, on the other hand, wasn't feeling nearly so upbeat. He left Georgia feeling scarred and stunned. As chairman of the board, he had overseen a bureaucratic process that had turned out to be something of a debacle. The process had divided the partners and yielded what Steven himself, in a candid moment, admitted was a less than stellar list of investments. What's more, much of the uproar in Georgia had been directed squarely at him. Other board members lit into Steven for having presided over such a confusing mess.

In all his good works, Steven had never been brutalized in quite this way. When he tried later to describe the feeling, he said he pictured himself catching spears from every direction. At the end of the conference, the partners decided that the names of five of the twelve board members should be picked from a hat, and those members would have to run for reelection at the next meeting, in April 2006. The first name Steven pulled from the hat was his own. That was just the way things seemed to be going.

Steven's best hope for righting the alliance now rested with the installation of its new CEO, the person who would finally replace Rob. After Steven had broken the news to Rob, some six months earlier, that he would not be running the alliance much longer, the board and its executive search firm had conducted a nationwide hunt for the ideal keeper of the progressive portfolio. In Steven's mind, this new chief executive would be someone with the stature and credibility to settle disputes and streamline the operation. In truth, though, the atmosphere surrounding the Democracy Alliance had already been poisoned. Because the partners lacked a clear philosophy or mission, every important strategic question was open to a hundred interpretations of what the alliance was supposed to achieve, and every decision that Steven or anyone else made was immediately met with a chorus of jeers from people who assumed that their wealth conferred on them great wisdom. It was hard to imagine that any CEO—short of Jack Welch, perhaps—was going to have much success telling them all what to do.

Less than a week before they arrived in Georgia, hoping to be able to introduce Rob's successor at the conference, the board had triumphantly offered the job to Robert Dunn, a leader in the field of corporate social responsibility and a former official in the Carter administration. Dunn seemed perfect for the $400,000-a-year job— but he shocked the board by promptly turning it down. Eager to have a name in place before the partners flew south, Steven then turned, hastily, to the runner-up in the process, a management consultant named Judy Wade, whom John Podesta had initially recommended, and who had been Steven's favorite candidate all along.

On paper, Judy Wade was exactly what the Democracy Alliance needed: liberal, tough, creative, and competent. She was a partner in the San Francisco office of McKinsey, a firm renowned for scooping up the brightest young minds on America's elite liberal campuses, and one that Democrats in particular, with their affinity for new age management techniques, seemed to idolize. Blond and hippieish, she had grown up in the Bay Area and gone to Berkeley, later earning a master's degree at Harvard's Kennedy School of Government. If the internal politics of complex bureaucracies constituted a kind of white-collar warfare, then Wade had earned a general's stars. She had recently returned from seven years in South Africa, where she had helped the postapartheid government rebuild its economy and systems. Before that, she had worked as a consultant with the New York City schools and with mining and telecommunications companies. She understood infrastructures in the literal sense; it wasn't a leap to assume she could build a political one.

Wade knew the Democracy Alliance was in turmoil, and she vowed to stabilize it fast. But South Africa, for all its tribalism, was one thing; a legion of disgruntled and entitled liberal donors was quite another. There were, from the start, partners who seemed determined not to like her, who said she didn't know enough about politics, or even that her skirts were inappropriately short. Anyone who thought Judy Wade had the political skills to overcome these suspicions and to navigate among the dueling egos and ideologies of the Democracy Alliance might have reconsidered after she showed up in Georgia and decided to introduce herself to the embattled partners with an ill-advised joke.

"You know what they say about the difference between a terrorist and a billionaire," Wade said, as the room stiffened.

"You can negotiate with a terrorist."

CHAPTER SIX

Moments of Destiny

Norman Lear lived in a banana-colored mansion in the Pacific Palisades part of Los Angeles, with a pool and tennis courts and a garden that could make you cry, all of it overlooking the quiet majesty of Will Rogers State Historic Park. In the living room, there was a bar finished in leather and a wall of cherry bookcases, in which Norman displayed hardbound editions of the scripts from his 1970s sitcom empire: *All in the Family, The Jeffersons, One Day at a Time.* You would have expected Norman himself to have become a kind of relic, too, gone the way of the laugh track and thirty-year-old coke fiends playing teenagers, but instead he remained an éminence grise of liberal Hollywood, a good-hearted mogul known as much for his political activism as for his craft. Slight and shrinking at eighty-three, Norman wore fishing hats and fishing vests and worked some derivation of "fuck" into most of his sentences. I liked Norman immensely. He was like a lovable Jewish uncle who had just been sprung from prison.

On this pleasant spring night in 2006, Norman had lent out his palatial spread, as he often did, for a book party hosted by Arianna Huffington, the relentless socialite, former gubernatorial candidate, and publisher of the Huffington Post blog. Rob Reiner was there with his wife. So was the comedian Harry Shearer and the actor Mike Farrell, who was most famous for his starring role in *M*A*S*H* and who wore a dark suit, as if he were a patent lawyer who had wandered in by accident. There were two men named Ned at the party, which I found peculiar, this being Hollywood and not Iowa. The first was an actor named Ned Bellamy, whom I recognized instantly from his hilarious guest role as a Rambo-like advertising copywriter on *Seinfeld.* The second Ned was a small, skinny guy with an earnest face who looked a little like a bobblehead doll. This was Ned Lamont, a cable company millionaire who had just decided to challenge Joe Lieberman, Connecticut's prowar senator, in a primary campaign. He had come west in search of money. Although no one in Washington thought Lamont had a chance to win, Norman introduced him to his guests as "the man who's going to take down Joe Fucking Lieberman." Lamont said a few words, none of them memorable.

At least Lamont was actually invited to this gathering of the cool clique in Democratic Hollywood. I had been forced to invite myself, which was decidedly not cool. I needed to meet up with the guests of honor: the bloggers Markos Moulitsas Zúniga and Jerome Armstrong, who had just published their indictment of the Democratic establishment, *Crashing the Gate: Netroots, Grassroots, and the Rise of People-Powered Politics.* Markos and Jerome, as they were universally known in the online world, weren't simply bloggers; they were the guys who transformed Howard Dean into the first candidate of the Internet age, and, in doing so, transformed themselves into political celebrities.

Just five years earlier, before the word "blog" had existed in American life, Markos had been designing corporate Web sites in Silicon Valley, and Jerome had been pushing his luck as a day trader in Portland, Oregon. Now Markos's site, DailyKos.com, was the single most influential political blog in the country, and he and Jerome were among the most sought-after strategists in the Democratic Party—an institution they openly disdained. The Democratic Congressional Campaign Committee had Markos and Jerome making calls to recruit House candidates in pivotal districts, the way the Yankees might have had Derek Jeter call a free agent pitcher. The party's Senate leadership had flown Markos in from his home in Berkeley to lecture senators on what they needed to do to rebuild the party. Mark Warner, the former Virginia governor, had recently hired Jerome to plot the online strategy for his much-anticipated presidential campaign.

Tonight was the opening of Markos and Jerome's West Coast book tour, and, after a few days in L.A., the three of us were supposed to drive up the coast to San Francisco, stopping at bars and book-stores along the way so they could sell some books. The tour, as it were, worked like this: The authors posted online that they would be in California for these few days, and their fans went ahead and sched-uled events for them. Everything was online, decentralized, organic. Markos and Jerome just had to check the calendar and show up. For me, this was a rare opportunity to see the blog culture—both its he-roes and its adherents—in something more than two dimensions. To make myself welcome, I'd offered to rent the car and do the driving, which also made me something less than cool, but at least then they couldn't abandon me on some roadside and then blog about it.

Arianna, whose database of phone numbers of the rich and con-nected must have occupied a small warehouse of servers somewhere in Latvia, introduced the authors. There was a small dais built into Norman's living room for just such eventualities. In her lavish Greek accent, Arianna said she had hosted Markos as a guest in her home, along with his two-year-old son, that he was a wonderful dad, and that she had "learned at his feet" while launching her own successful blog. She admitted that she didn't know Jerome very well, but she thought he was probably great too.

That introduction hinted at an unspoken arrangement between Markos and Jerome. Blond and stocky, with a soft, midwestern-sounding voice that made him seem a decade younger than his forty-one years, Jerome was most comfortable when he could hang back and observe. He had placid, blue-green eyes and a nonjudgmental expression that could be mistaken for dullness. Jerome liked to learn about other people, to figure out what they knew that he didn't, but he revealed himself only in pieces and only when asked. Markos was thirty-four and dark, half Salvadoran and half Greek, with coal-colored eyes and plump cheeks. He liked to tell people how shy he was and how isolated he had been as a kid, and yet, despite this—or perhaps because of it—he evidenced an obvious need to be noticed.

"We really are taking over the party," Markos told the dazzled crowd. "The infrastructure is getting built. The money is coming in. People are beginning to understand that it's not like there's a pendulum, and if you wait long enough, the pendulum will just swing back again. We have to change the party, because the party isn't going to change itself."

Watching Markos speak was like watching a barely controlled fire. His limbs moved in nervous, yogalike motion, elbows folding into hands, feet wrapping themselves around ankles. He had an effeminate way of talking, or maybe it was just Latin American—tilting his head every so often and thrusting his wrists out to the sides. He spoke intensely and impossibly fast. Markos smiled a lot and could be great fun, but there were moments when it was hard to miss the undercurrent of anger that animated him. What started it, who knows. Salvadoran death squads? Middle school bullies? Did it matter? Everyone is angry at something, and Markos was angrier than most.

The main problem with the party, Markos went on, was that its leaders were afraid to voice their liberal convictions, not realizing that most of the country shared them. "Washington Democrats keep searching for what I like to call the 'mythical middle,'" Markos said. "And it doesn't exist. The public already agrees with us. They're just waiting for somebody to stand up and say what we believe." He clutched his heart as he spoke.

A few minutes later, however, he came out with this: "The Democrats in Washington don't care about winning or losing. All they care about is going to cocktail parties and getting the right parking spaces and their big fat contracts. That's all they want." These two central allegations—that Washington Democrats were desperately prostrating themselves for centrist votes, while at the same time not caring a whit about whether they won or lost—completely contradicted each other, but Markos said things like this with such conviction, and at such a rapid pace, that it was hard to dwell too long on any of it.

On this night, Markos was incensed because Russ Feingold, the iconoclastic senator from Wisconsin, had just offered a motion to censure the president for authorizing illegal wiretaps, a scandal that had badly wounded the administration in recent weeks, and yet the party's leaders had distanced themselves from the proposal. "Nancy Pelosi chided Russ Feingold for his censure motion," Markos said. "She said, 'The Republicans are unraveling, so don't make news. Let's not get in the way.' They don't get that when your opponent is unraveling, that's not *getting in the way*." He made little quote marks with his fingers. "You have to exploit it. It's like James Carville used to say—back when he was relevant. If your enemy is drowning, throw him an anvil."

Inevitably, one of the guests asked the bloggers which candidates interested them among the growing field of possible 2008 presidential hopefuls. Jerome made a casual pitch for his new boss, asserting that Warner—a self-described centrist known for reaching out to conservative, rural voters—was the only guy who could win in every part of the country, including the Plains and the South. This seemed to suggest that Jerome didn't think the "mythical middle" was actually mythical after all. My head was starting to hurt from trying to keep up with all the conflicting arguments flying around the room.

For his part, Markos demurred. "They're all going to have the chance to make their cases next year," he said, "and I'm not going to make any decisions until I hear what they have to say." Two things were implicit in the way he said this. One was that his decision mattered. And the other was that when Markos heard what they had to say, it wouldn't be in a debate or a speech. It would be face to face, probably in his living room.

M arkos left the party with his wife, Elisa, who didn't love the Hollywood scene and couldn't wait to escape. Arianna graciously invited Jerome and me, however, to stay around with a small group of guests for a special screening. Between the bound scripts in Norman's bookcase there was a square of tinted glass and, behind that, a movie projector. A huge screen automatically came down in front of the French doors on the dais, turning the living room into a theater. We all sat and watched *An Inconvenient Truth,* the forthcoming documentary about Al Gore and his lonely crusade against global warming. Tom Hanks wandered in, watched for a while, and then drifted out again.

After the lights came up, a group of us, including Jerome and Rob Reiner, stood around the bar. I remarked that I had thought the film was great and very persuasive, although I wondered why Gore hadn't shown his global warming presentation during the eight years when he was the country's vice president and had the power to make policy. This seemed to infuriate Reiner, who went off on one of his tears.

"This is the only man smart enough and with enough experience to be president right now!" Reiner shouted at me. "Right now!"

"What about Mark Warner?" Jerome interjected. The son of a Forest Service officer who moved around every few years, Jerome had grown up anchored by an evangelical church, which sent him and his four siblings out on buses every summer to knock on doors and persuade people to attend traveling revivals. He seemed to be taking the same approach to his new role as Warner's Internet apostle. He had never been a senior campaign operative before, and he wasn't especially smooth at it.

Reiner, distracted for a moment by Jerome, said he wasn't sure yet if Warner was a "real Democrat." Then he turned back to me and continued his diatribe, which was aimed, I presumed, at the entire national press corps. "And you know what else? I was with Al Gore the night the Supreme Court decision came down. With him and his family! It was awful! And he took his daughter in his arms and told her it was OK. Whatever else you want to say about this man—whatever crap you want to say about him as a politician—he is a *good dad!*" Apparently, being a good dad was very important at this party.

Jerome turned to Norman, who was standing next to us, listening in. "Mark Warner is a good dad," he said.

"Huh?" Reiner, hearing this, looked completely confused.

"Mark Warner is a good dad too."

"I'm sure he is," Reiner said, in a tone that suggested this had nothing to do with anything.

It was past eleven now, and the remaining guests were meandering toward the door. One of them patted Norman's cheek as he passed. "Thank you for doing this, Norman," he said warmly.

"Get the fuck outta here," Norman growled, affectionately.

The Reiners said good-bye and left. So did Arianna. Soon Jerome and I were the only ones left. Norman and his lovely third wife, Lyn, were standing at the door, holding it open. Norman was visibly sleepy. The man was eighty-three.

"I want to set up a meeting so you can meet him," Jerome was saying, still talking about Warner. "He started out working for the DNC, you know. Then he was chairman of the Virginia Democratic Party. Then he managed Doug Wilder's successful campaign for governor. Virginia's a really red state, and he had a really progressive record there."

Norman nodded. Lyn smiled. Through the open front door, I could see the parking valet look longingly toward us from the circular driveway.

"I really think you'd like him," Jerome was saying now, even though he hadn't met Norman before tonight and really had no idea who the man was. Jerome had rarely had access to a television growing up, and he may have been the only American in a hundred-mile radius who wouldn't have known Archie Bunker from Archibald MacLeish. He once remarked to me that he liked this one show he saw as a kid, a black-and-white program about a bunch of mischievous little kids, and one of them had funny hair. He was talking about *The Little Rascals*.

"And you know," Jerome went on, "one thing a lot of people like about Warner is that he already has a lot of money and a lot of rich friends, so he doesn't need to raise money from all the same old donors. He can do what he wants. He won't be in anybody's pocket."

Norman had stopped listening. He would have agreed to put up a lawn sign right then if we would just leave already. "OK, well, I'd be glad to meet him," Norman said finally.

This was all Jerome needed to hear. He waved good night and stepped out into the pleasant California night. His work here was done.

T he rest of the schedule in L.A. featured some radio interviews, a reading, and a rally for clean elections. When we arrived early at the Santa Monica bar where the rally was being held, the middle-aged manager of the place leaped out of his chair. "Oh, you're Markos!" he cried. "You're my hero!"

"Oh, please, no," Markos said, unpersuasively. Jerome stood off to the side, unrecognized.

The first guy who walked in after us looked to be in his fifties. He stood stiffly at attention in a flannel shirt and jeans. "Markos!" he said, thrusting out his hand. "I'm Skippy the Bush Kangaroo!"

His real name, it turned out, was Gil Christner. Skippy the Bush Kangaroo was his online alias, and he had been one of the earliest bloggers—from way back in 2002. No one really knew what he had been up to recently. "He was big for a while," Markos told me after Skippy went to get a drink, "but he didn't make it." He sounded genuinely sad.

Jerome scratched his neck, deep in thought. "Wasn't he the guy who used to use all lowercase letters?"

"It was his thing," Markos replied with a shrug. Listening to these liberal bloggers reminisce was like hanging out with a group of folkies who used to play the clubs in Greenwich Village, back in the day. A few of the really lucky ones got to be Bob Dylan. Everyone else ended up the Charles River Valley Boys.

No one person invented the "blogosphere," certainly, but there was a reason they called Jerome Armstrong the Blogfather. Of all the people I had met writing about politics, no one had lived a less believable life than Jerome claimed to have led, and yet I believed every word. He had hitchhiked across the country like a nomad, working in a carnival in Nebraska and South Dakota and trailing the Grateful Dead through Minnesota and Wisconsin. He had served in the Peace Corps in Sierra Leone and Costa Rica, where he met his wife, Shashi, and had trekked through India and Nepal, where he jumped off a train and broke his ankle. He had passed a year in seclusion on Buddhist meditation retreats in western Massachusetts, Dallas,

Fresno, and up near the Cascades. He had lasted four weeks as a marketer for a potato chip company, which so traumatized him in its banality that he bought a one-way ticket to Hawaii, where he worked as a day laborer and slept on the beach until he ran out of food. (For a decade after the potato chip debacle, he refused to put on a tie.)

For a while, Jerome and a buddy ran a business importing the oils used in aromatherapy (frankincense from Somalia, sandalwood from India, oak moss from Bulgaria), but Jerome walked away when the friendship soured. He had knocked around colleges in Arkansas, Italy, and Mexico before graduating from Portland State, where he later picked up master's degrees in linguistics and conflict resolution. I tried to keep track of all these adventures on a timeline in my head, but it proved useless. To say that Jerome had done some searching was like saying that Lewis and Clark had gone on a short hike.

"I wouldn't say I've had an easy life, exactly, but a lot of doors have just opened for me," Jerome told me once. "It's like, you know when you have those moments of destiny?"

I said I thought I'd had one or two.

"Well, I have those all the fucking time," he said, prompting us both to burst out laughing.

By the late nineties, Jerome's journey had taken him to the Internet, where he started playing the market with some of his student loan money. Between trades, he visited a brand new site called Politics.com, which was the forerunner to the political blogs—a message board where interested Web pioneers could talk to one another. For Jerome, political sites were extensions of his trading obsession; he and the other early adapters would predict the outcomes of races for fun, in the same way that he tried to guess the trajectories of the markets. That was his only real stake in the process. Jerome had rarely voted, and he didn't identify with either political party. The closest he had come to caring about a presidential candidate was Gary Hart, and after Hart's career was derailed by scandal, Jerome was so despondent that he voted for Ron Paul, the Libertarian.

What brought Jerome back to politics after all those years—and this was true for many of the online activists whom Markos and Jerome had dubbed "the netroots"—was, first, the impeachment of Bill Clinton, and then the disputed election of 2000. He thought that the election had been stolen and that Bush was a menace. The president and his conservative following reminded him too much of the zealots he had known at church as a kid; it wasn't the religion he had turned against, but the inflexibility of the doctrine, the extremity of the black-and-white moral contrasts. After Florida, Jerome declared himself a Democrat. In addition to commenting on the message boards, he had established his own Web site, which he called MyDD.com. (The "DD" stood for "due diligence," the initial idea being to offer stock tips for traders; later it was changed to "direct democracy.") MyDD became Jerome's personal blog, and in 2002, following the lead of a few other early blogs, he began letting other people comment on his posts. Soon MyDD was a central meeting point for a growing number of liberals who were seeking one another out online.

This nascent blog movement grew out of a particular moment, not just in American politics, but in American life. It stood at the intersection of three interrelated trends that had little to do with ideology. The first was, of course, technological. The advent of the Internet made it possible for thousands of liberals, scattered around the country, to convene without leaving their bedrooms. The second was a yearning for connection. Americans at the end of the century had largely given up on the civic and political organizations that had sustained their parents and grandparents, and that isolation had left them searching for some sense of community, which the Web made possible in new ways.

And, third, American society was experiencing a general devaluing of expertise. At exactly the moment when old, authoritative institutions—from television networks to Major League Baseball and the Catholic Church—found themselves mired in scandals and lawsuits, the Web was tearing down the walls that had separated those who possessed knowledge from those who wanted it. Now, if you were looking to invest your money, you didn't trust a broker; you went to E*Trade and did your own research. If you had a rash, you went first to WebMD, and then you shared your own diagnosis with your family doctor. No one trusted the professionals anymore; why should politics have been any different? The proliferation of twenty-four-hour cable news had brought forth a legion of barely informed pontificators, armed with glib witticisms and baseless predictions, whose job it was to comment all day long on the latest political story. It was inevitable that a lot of avid news consumers would watch this cavalcade of arrogance and think to themselves, "Why shouldn't I be a pundit, too?" Online, they were.

Among the people who posted regularly on MyDD was a brash, combative writer who went by the alias "Kos." It was the nickname Markos's army buddies had given him while he was an artillery scout stationed in Germany. His decision to join the military, Markos would later say, had been tied to the helplessness he felt as a boy in his native El Salvador. It was Uncle Sam's army, he would often say, that had made him believe in centralized government programs. What other institution was as socialist in its philosophy as the military, with its subsidized health care, meals, and housing? His liberal audience loved this riff. Of course, a skeptic could have pointed out that, in exchange for these socialist programs, the military also demanded uniformity of thought and appearance and unconditional obedience from its subjects. But Markos's gift was that he didn't traffic in such tortured intellectual complexities. He could make political arguments sound so simple, so binary. Like the president he so despised, he had a genius for self-certainty.

After his discharge, Markos got a law degree from Boston University, although the idea of being a lawyer interested him about as much as baling hay. Then, like a lot of ambitious young men of the time, he struck out for Silicon Valley, hoping to get in on the ground floor of something, or take it public, or spin it off—whichever tired phrase of the tech boom might lead to some kind of quick and spectacular wealth. The thing was, he got there too late. The bubble started letting out air, and Markos wound up building Web sites. He was bored. He hated the clients. Most days, he couldn't wait to get home and sink into his second life as a blogger on MyDD. In 2002, he struck out on his own and created DailyKos.com, bringing a lot of MyDD readers with him.

When, on the eve of the midterm elections that November, Jerome became the first blogger ever to be interviewed live on CNN, an excited Markos called to offer his congratulations. "Don't forget us little people when you're famous," Markos said.

B y then, Jerome had already found the man who would become the online movement's galvanizing force. For months after the attacks of September 11, most Washington Democrats were cowed by the president's 75 percent approval rating and wary of confronting him directly. Howard Dean wasn't—and the bloggers took notice. Almost no one outside Vermont had even heard of Dean, but Jerome had a vision for how to change that. "Here's what Dean could do to transform his weakness into his strength," he wrote in a prescient 2002 blog post. "Exploit the Internet. His current Web site is sparse, not updated, and not very interesting. What he needs to develop is a Web site that gravitates the online discussion of 2004 toward him."

Jerome created his own, unofficial Web page for the Dean campaign. Then he drove up to Seattle, where Dean was set to address the King County Democrats, and handed it to the candidate himself. Before long, Joe Trippi, Dean's new campaign manager and an early blog devotee, was holding conference calls with Jerome and Markos on Web strategy. It was Jerome who first mentioned to Trippi a new online phenomenon called the "meet up," which brought thousands of Dean supporters together for parties in scores of cities. Jerome soon took a hiatus from blogging to move Shashi and the kids to Burlington so he could work full time on the campaign.

Ultimately, of course, for all the Internet passion he inspired, Dean won only a single primary state—his own. But he emerged from the 2004 campaign as a transformational figure, bridging the distance between the broadcast era that had dominated politics for the last forty years and the digital moment that had now arrived. By 2005, *Advertising Age* would report that thirty-five million American workers were spending a chunk of their workweek on blogs of one kind or another. According to a report financed by Simon Rosenberg's New Politics Institute, the ninety-eight most-read liberal blogs now logged a total of more than fifteen million page views per week.

The bloggers, it was fair to say, were the most obsessive of the new progressives; without them, there would have been no movement at all. MoveOn's members logged on to the site, on average, a few times a week; the bloggers seemed to live on their sites twenty-four hours a day, as if it were their only vocation, which, in some cases, it was. If the donors of the Democracy Alliance were roughly analogous to the conservative philanthropists, and if MoveOn operated much like the National Rifle Association or some other membership-based group on the Right, then the bloggers were the progressive movement's equivalent of the evangelical ministers who had hijacked Republican politics. They preached the word with unbridled zeal, and their diatribes were a more trusted source of news for a lot of progressive voters than the *New York Times* or CNN. The most active donors read them, and so did a growing number of elected politicians.

To the extent that a single philosophy united all of the people doing this incessant clicking, it wasn't any kind of governing agenda for the country. Rather, the netroots stood chiefly for the principle of unyielding partisanship. Like the members of MoveOn.org, the bloggers detested a Democratic establishment populated by adherents of Clintonian triangulation, which sought the safety of middle ground on every issue. According to the blogger ethos, Republicans, whether staunchly conservative or not, were to be stomped, beaten, and generally humiliated. And any Democrat who didn't pursue that goal— who saw value, say, in cooperating with Republicans on a deal to reduce farm subsidies or to extend a package of tax credits—needed to be taught a lesson. It was a common theme among the bloggers that Bush was tilting toward dictatorship, and that those who didn't condemn everything he did were appeasers whom history would harshly judge. Some bloggers started referring to collaborators within their own party as "Vichy Democrats."

It wasn't just that the bloggers wanted to stiffen the resolve of the party's Washington apparatus, however. They argued that the apparatus itself was no longer relevant. The party and its leaders derived their power from a single source: money. Only the party could raise the cash needed to run campaigns, and, for that reason, the party got to decide who the favored candidates were, what they should say, and which of the cautious Washington consultants would help them say it. But the Internet was sapping that power. Just as MoveOn could raise millions of dollars for its own ad campaigns, and just as the Democracy Alliance could divert millions more into its own progressive infrastructure, so too could the blogs recruit their own candidates and raise their own funds. Dean had raised an estimated $25 million over the Internet alone—an amount that would have been unimaginable just four years earlier. To the bloggers, this signaled a revolution: Now the activists would control the party, and not the other way around.

Every era has its icons, and the first genuine celebrity of this new digital world turned out to be Markos Moulitsas Zúniga, whose blog had become, in a sense, the official headquarters for America's liberal resistance. More glib and more audacious than Jerome, with a defiant voice more ideally calibrated to the resentment of liberal baby boomers, Markos emerged from the 2004 election as the most outspoken and influential blogger in America, and one of the first to actually make a living at it. By the time we ran into Skippy the Bush Kangaroo in Santa Monica, Daily Kos was drawing some 600,000 readers every day—more than all but a few daily newspapers in the country, and more than all the old progressive magazines and journals in America combined.

"Hey, I know what my next book is going to be," Markos told us. "'The Libertarian Democrat.'" He went on a short riff about how the party needed to reposition itself as the defender of individuals against an intrusive conservative government. Markos said he considered himself more a true libertarian than a traditional liberal. I asked him if he had ever read F. A. Hayek.

"No," he said.

One of the hallmarks of netroots culture was a complete disconnect from history—meaning, basically, anything that had happened before 1998. The political consciousness of most of the bloggers seemed to begin sometime around impeachment, when they had first tuned in. Whatever had gone on before then, the fight between Clinton and the liberal establishment, the very real debates inside the party over trade and taxes and defense—all of these things felt as ancient to the bloggers as the underlying causes of the Peloponnesian

War, and about as useful. It wasn't just that the bloggers didn't know much about the political world before impeachment; it was that they didn't want to know, either. So burning was their contempt for "Washington insiders" and the "mainstream media" that they were moved to dismiss not just the individuals who fell into these categories, but all the knowledge such people had accumulated. In a sense, the way the netroots saw it, the more you knew about Democratic politics before 1998, the less relevant you actually were.

Jerome Armstrong, I found, was a rare exception. This was partly because he had an unusually curious mind. (What kind of guy took it upon himself to visit all nine remaining Native American tribes in Oregon?) But it was also because Jerome had decided that his newest destiny was to help Warner get elected president, and in this pursuit, he was determined to find out everything he could about what worked and what didn't. One day near the end of our road trip, Jerome and I spent two hours in the bookstore on the Stanford campus, while he rifled through every book in the politics section, as if the answer he was seeking might be scribbled in a margin somewhere. In presidential politics, Jerome told me, it was the things you didn't know that would kill you, and he wanted to make sure he knew as much as possible.

"Hey Matt, do you know Pat Caddell?" Jerome asked me as the three of us drove down La Cienega in my rented Taurus.

"Who's that?" Markos asked skeptically.

I said I did, in fact, know Pat Caddell.

"You think you could introduce me while we're out here?" Jerome asked.

I said I probably could, although as soon as the words left my mouth, I wondered what I had done. Caddell was one of the great political minds of his generation, a boy genius who had started polling for politicians in high school and had made a business of it while he was still an undergraduate at Harvard. He had been a mercurial and much-feared strategist for Jimmy Carter and Gary Hart, among others. Then Pat declared himself sick of politics and disillusioned with this new breed of centrist Democrat, and he moved out to the other coast, where his projects included a consulting gig on the drama *The West Wing,* and where eventually he grew as broodily contemptuous of Hollywood as he was of Washington. Pat lived in a house no one ever saw in the hills above the Sunset Strip—one of those houses, fittingly enough, that always seemed on the verge of sliding into oblivion—amid what sounded, from his descriptions, like towering stacks of arcane papers and articles that he was always running off to consult. Friends knew he was capable of disappearing for weeks at a time, only to resurface as a guest on the Fox News Channel, with his eyes bulging and his face slack, as if he hadn't slept in days.

I consulted Pat about politics every so often, the way one might consult the Delphic oracle. Now I left a message for him, and, surprisingly, he called back a few hours later, having just flown in on a red-eye. He had read about Daily Kos and the blogs, and he was intrigued. A populist at heart, Pat always argued that Democrats had prostituted themselves to Wall Street during the '90s (he once described the party as being controlled by "a confederacy of gangsters"), and he was forever waiting for the party to regain the moral bearings he remembered from his early days in politics. He hoped that these bloggers could return the party to its roots.

We met Pat for a late breakfast at our hotel on Sunset Boulevard, in a lounge off the lobby that was, like most everything in L.A., a little overdone, with dim lamps and red velvet upholstery. Markos sat with his arms crossed and feet up on another chair, looking bored. Jerome and I stared at Pat, who looked like he had slept in his denim shirt and jeans, his mop of gray hair tossed about on his head. Conversations with Pat were never really two-way affairs. It seemed that every few weeks he woke up, discovered some new object of outrage, and immediately launched into a soliloquy that lasted for days. A few times he had called me late at night, only to vent, almost without interruption, until the battery in his phone died midsentence. It was worth every minute; Pat shared at least one brilliant insight for every half hour he spoke.

Today, Pat was incensed at the Democrats in Congress over the issue of immigration. In December, the Republican House had decided to designate illegal immigrants as criminals, but they had debated whether the crime should be a felony or a mere misdemeanor. The issue had come to a vote, and House Democrats, by a margin of 191 to 3, had voted down the more lenient amendment, allowing the brutal felony provision to pass. The reason for this had been entirely tactical: While they generally supported a gentler bill, Democrats wanted to force the Republican majority to pass the more draconian measure so that Democratic candidates could use it as an issue in the November elections. The bill wasn't likely to become law anyway. It was just good opposition politics.

This sequence of events had been eating at Pat like bacteria. It was a disgrace, he said. What kind of party torpedoed a more humane law, a law that nonetheless took action against the serious problem of illegal immigration, just so it could make its opponents look mean? Why couldn't these Democrats just do the right thing now and then? This was why people rejected the Democrats, Pat thundered as he devoured a plate of steak and eggs. They had no convictions—only tactical maneuvers—and they were willing to endanger helpless immigrants to score a few points.

In making this argument, however, he was running smack up against the guiding ethos of the blogs, which held precisely the opposite. As far as Markos and Jerome were concerned, tactics were all that mattered. And voting for a Republican amendment—even a good Republican amendment—would have been an act of treachery. Before long, the table erupted in argument. Wearing a crooked smirk, Markos waved Pat's ranting away. Why, he asked, should

Democrats have voted to make illegal immigration a crime, period? It was a Republican idea, and now it was going to hurt Republicans in the elections.

Jerome agreed. "This issue isn't going to divide the Democratic Party," he said. "It's going to divide the Republicans." That Pat wasn't talking about which party risked fracture over the vote—that he was actually talking about the merits of the immigration policy itself—seemed lost on them. Caddell and the bloggers might have been speaking the same language, but they were communicating in vastly different dialects.

"Let me tell you something," Pat said. He laid down his fork noisily and pointed a long finger at Jerome. "That's what destroyed the Democratic Party and American liberalism. That attitude right there. All you want to do is exploit an issue for political gain. You don't give a shit about the issue."

"We're taking back the party," Jerome said. "We're bringing people into the party."

"Yeah," Pat shouted, "but you can't *keep* people in a party if it doesn't stand for anything!"

Markos seemed amused by this outburst. Pat shoveled the last bit of his steak and runny eggs into his mouth and shook his head bitterly. These new-model Democrats were no better than the ones he'd left behind.

One of the reasons Markos had amassed such power within Democratic politics was that he kept telling people how much power he had. "I told Reid's chief of staff that if Joe Lieberman leaves the party, we're going to demand that he be stripped of his committee assignments," Markos told me. It had been rumored for weeks that Lieberman might run for reelection as an independent. "We want Democrats in those seats," Markos said.

At another point he told me, "I don't own anything, and no one owns me. I say what I want. I already told one reporter that I want to find someone to run against Pelosi for Congress. I don't care. She should know what we think."

No doubt Pelosi did know what the bloggers thought. The more elusive question, though, and the subject of a robust debate in Washington, was whether she or anyone else really should have cared. High-profile Democrats such as Harry Reid now held regular conference calls with bloggers around the country. But a lot of old Democratic hands—the powerful consultants and senior aides who really were the Washington establishment—privately dismissed the blogs as just a lot of noise. After all, the bloggers still reached a relatively small number of people, all of whom, presumably, were already ardent Democrats. Mostly, they were talking to themselves. And while no one liked reading nasty things about himself on a blog that some junior staffer had read and sent around the office, it hardly had more impact than some guy in a bar trashing you to his friends. To let a few kids who spent all day at their computers start running the party, these Democrats argued, was a kind of insanity.

As I drove the Taurus north on the Pacific Coast Highway, headed for Santa Barbara, I put the question directly to Markos, who liked to sprawl out in the back seat while Jerome sat up front. Why did the blogs even matter?

He answered by talking not about politics, but about his and Jerome's newest business venture: SportsBlogs, Inc. They had been going around gobbling up small, low-budget blogs dedicated to various professional teams—a Yankees blog called Pinstripe Alley, an Eagles blog called Bleeding Green Nation—by offering to host the Web sites on their technological platform and to sell the ads in exchange for the rights to the blog itself. The brilliant idea was to amass a small empire of sports blogs that could then be sold, as a package, to a large investment group.

"Why does Billy Beane talk to Tyler, our sports blogger in Oakland?" Markos asked me, referring to the general manager of the Oakland Athletics. "Because that's where the influentials are. Last year, when Billy Beane traded his two aces, Tim Hudson and Mark Mulder, in a single week, opinion on the blog was running against him, 90 to 10. Fans were really angry. The next week, he called Tyler, and he explained what he had done and why he had done it. He went through his whole plan for the team, his whole rebuilding process, and Tyler posted the entire transcript on the blog. After that, they supported him 90 percent to 10. The blog is where the influentials are."

Markos was probably right. It hardly mattered whether the progressive blogs were reaching 500,000 readers or 5 million. However many people came to blogs like Daily Kos, they were the people who cared the most about politics, and, thus, they were the most likely to evangelize everyone they knew. The advent of the broadband Internet had made viral marketing the single most efficient means of getting an idea across to select consumers, and the political blogs were about as viral as bird flu.

I asked Markos if he had read *The Influentials,* the business book he had just been citing. I wasn't surprised when he said no and changed the subject.

A t the moment, the influentials were gathering at Elsie's, an unmarked bar near the center of tony Santa Barbara with purple and green walls and Tiffany lamps. Standing by the front door, I met a guy named Doug Ingoldsby, who was holding what looked like a framed print under his arm. It turned out to be the original artwork for the liberty banner that was Daily Kos's recognizable logo. Doug explained that he spent about four hours a day on Daily Kos, blogging under the pseudonym "Kdud." A few months ago, he had purchased the banner for $2,500 in an auction on the site; the proceeds were going to the first-ever physical gathering of the Daily Kos community, an event that had been dubbed "YearlyKos" by its organizers and that was scheduled to take place in Las Vegas in just a few months. Doug showed me the back of the canvas, where Markos had scribbled, "You are now the owner of what used to be one of my prized possessions. Enjoy it." Doug said he considered it an investment. It was like buying the NBC peacock in 1960.

At every stop along the book tour, I found myself amazed at the community that Markos and Jerome and others had created, almost from nothing. The history of American media was the story of new technologies connecting big personalities to an ever-growing number of people—families who gathered around the radio to hear FDR's fireside chats or around the TV to watch Ed Sullivan. But it was hard to think of any big personality, before the bloggers, who had enabled so many people to connect to one another. The bloggers themselves often talked about this phenomenon as the birth of a kind of classless utopia, a place without arbitrary barriers and rules, where any voice could be heard. From the outside, this was true. And yet it was clear that the blogs comprised their own social strata, just like everyplace else.

At the top rung of netroots society were the bloggers themselves—a handful of people, like Markos and Jerome, who attracted their own followings. This group numbered maybe a hundred in all, and they spoke to one another—arguing over ethics and terminology or suggesting strategies for some upcoming political fight—on a secret e-mail list known as "Townhouse," named for the Washington bar where a group of them drank on Sunday afternoons. Below the bloggers, you had the main outside contributors to each blog. These were people, known by aliases like DavidNYC and Georgia10, who had posted so often, and with such obvious skill, that they had become mini celebrities to the other blog devotees. Daily Kos, for instance, always had four front-page writers, some of whom Markos paid more than $50,000 annually as "fellows." Their "diaries" were featured atop the Web site, and thus they were considered part of an elite circle, close to the founder himself. Their entries on a given day could be at least as incisive as, and a lot funnier than, what any newspaper columnist had to say.

And then you had the whole rest of the lot: techie nerds and housewives banging away in their kitchens, lawyers and midlevel managers on their lunch breaks, acid critics spewing rage at the morons of the "mainstream media," sycophants hoping for a word of praise, old-school lefties complaining about the lack of diversity or inciting the world's workers to unite. These lesser-known characters fell under the general rubric of "bloggers," but really they made up the unruly proletariat of the netroots. And while you might have thought that such loyal followers—"Kossacks," as they were known on Daily Kos—would evoke some stirring of paternal pride in their online icons, that turned out not to be the case. Markos and Jerome talked about some of the people who posted on their blogs as if they were shut-ins who had forgotten to take their medication. Markos rolled his eyes at all the wannabe bloggers who tried to impress him with praise or argument, and he couldn't stand all the single-issue liberals who were always rambling on about abortion or global warming.

This dismissiveness sometimes showed in their presence. Markos snapped his head around when he overheard one guy at Elsie's mistakenly refer to Jerome as "Jerry." "It's *Jerome*," Markos barked, as the poor Kossack withered.

We spent that night at Susan Gardner's house, way up in the mountains above Santa Barbara, where you wouldn't be surprised to find a bear in your backyard. Susan—or SusanG, as she was known online—was one of Daily Kos's vaunted front-page writers and paid fellows. She was an example of all that was inspiring about the blogs. Susan was forty-eight and had once been a reporter for the local paper, but she had long since quit to raise her four children, the youngest of whom was now sixteen. Just five years ago, the closest she had gotten to national politics was a subscription to the *New York Review of Books,* and even that arrived late. There still wasn't any cable TV or satellite in the hills where she and her husband, Michael, a private investigator and a Republican, had settled. They had only been able to get a high-speed connection through their telephone line since 2004, about the time Susan discovered Daily Kos. She started sharing her thoughts online, and she posted for about two years before others in the Daily Kos community nominated her for a front-page slot. Markos had chosen from a dozen candidates, and now she was a major figure in the netroots, cited frequently on dozens of other blogs.

Susan spent about forty hours a week trolling for information on the Web and writing dispatches for Daily Kos. She had been the first to expose Jeff Gannon, a credentialed White House correspondent, as a conservative plant with a false name; the national press had followed her posts for days. In this way, the blog world was a true meritocracy—the rare sphere where the quality of your insight and your ability to express it mattered more than who you were or where you worked. Georgia10, one of Susan's fellow front-page writers, was really Georgia Logothetis, a twenty-three-year-old law student who lived with her parents in Chicago. The *Chicago Reader,* a weekly paper that profiled Georgia10 in 2006, called her the most widely read political writer in the city.

Susan's son, Jackson, made us sandwiches while we all banged away on our laptops. Markos was reminding his readers at Daily Kos that they really needed to buy the book, which had been well reviewed in the *New York Times,* among other venues, but which wasn't selling as spectacularly as he had hoped. After dinner, Markos and Susan stayed up talking in the kitchen. They gossiped about some of the other main writers, like Em dash and Armando. They laughed about some of the Kos community romances that had

developed and about how someone had sent naked pictures to someone else. Markos evidenced a lot more interest in the lives of Susan
and the other front-page writers than he had in the socially awkward
admirers who had come out just to shake his hand at Elsie's. I
thought back to what he had told me about being a painfully bashful
kid, afraid to stand out in a room. I wondered if perhaps those grateful Kossacks, who loved him for having given them a place where
they felt they belonged, reminded him a little too much of himself.

I n the morning, we headed up the coast to a town called Pacific
Grove, just a few minutes inland from John Steinbeck's Cannery
Row, where Markos and Jerome addressed a crowd of white-haired
partisans in a tiny second-story art museum. As at every other stop on
the tour, no one asked a substantive question about the party's agenda
or the new challenges the country faced. All of the discussion centered on tactics and the ubiquitous subject of "message," and on how
they could fight the corporate-owned media, which was conspiring to
deceive the public.

The next event, in Santa Cruz, fell through for lack of organization, so Markos rented a car and drove the two hours back to Berkeley, where he spent the night with his wife and son. Jerome and I
headed on to the hippie haven of Santa Cruz, where he had booked
us some rooms on Priceline.com. We wandered aimlessly through
the town, ordered up some Jamba Juices, and took in a movie starring
Denzel Washington. We also talked a lot about Jerome's future. By
now I had realized that Markos and Jerome were pondering, each in
his own way, a question that no one before them had ever had to
answer. (And how many of us can say that in our lifetimes?) They
were the first of the celebrity bloggers, and they were trying to figure
out what a celebrity blogger does next, after he finally grows weary
and impatient with the tedium of online idolatry.

Jerome had decided that after years of living as an insurgent in the political bush, he was ready to clean up, put on a tie, and give life on the inside a try. He was graying around the temples now and raising two children in the northern Virginia suburbs, and twenty years of blurred scenery, changing phone numbers, and parting paychecks was enough. And anyway, Jerome had a theory about Democratic politics that he needed to test. He believed that the Web wasn't going to change just the nature of the party, putting power into the hands of anyone who had a hard drive and some passion. It was also going to fundamentally change the balance of the country's blue and red electoral map. Like MoveOn, the blogs could inspire and organize not only those progressives who lived in the old industrial states, which tended to vote Democratic already, but also the pockets of disaffected liberals who lived in the South and on the Plains, people who had long been ignored by the party's Washington establishment and who had all but given up on the prospect of a Democratic resurgence. The right candidate, someone who could harness that energy deep in the heart of conservative country, could blow up the two-party balance of power and redraw the map for decades to come.

This is what Jerome saw in Warner: not the committed centrist who had long been linked to the Democratic Leadership Council, or the governor who had eagerly collaborated with his Republican legislature, but, quite simply, a guy who really got it. Warner was a tech entrepreneur who had made hundreds of millions of dollars off mobile phone licenses. He seemed to understand intuitively how technology could move the tectonic plates of politics; this was why he wanted Jerome in his inner circle. Jerome had no ideology. He didn't care about the governing part—that was someone else's problem. He just wanted to vanquish these venomous Republicans, and for this he needed a candidate who was willing to try it his way.

There are people in politics who just grasp the coming moment more clearly than others, who, for whatever flaws they possess, always seem to see the bend in the arc when everyone else sees an endless straight line. Pat Caddell had been like this, and so had Joe Trippi. And it seemed to me that if anyone in the netroots was poised to succeed them, it was probably Jerome.

Markos had other ideas about a second act. He was already making six figures, but whenever Markos talked about his future, it seemed to involve more serious wealth. He wanted to buy a condo in Chicago, where his brother lived, along with season tickets to the Cubs. He had just purchased a turbo-boosted Subaru sports car, along with the first house he and Elisa had ever owned, and he talked about installing a room-to-room stereo system with iPod docks throughout the house. He envisioned becoming a Democratic venture capitalist, like the partners in the Democracy Alliance. "Hopefully, in five years, I'll be writing checks for a living," Markos said.

Markos talked about leaving politics altogether. He was a classically trained pianist, and his dream was to score movies. He had thoughts of a career in interior design. Of course, just about everyone in politics will tell you that they intend to get out after one more campaign, but with Markos, it sounded believable. Politics for him was a means to an end, and the end seemed to be about money and freedom. The most likely vehicle for achieving this end was the sports blog business. From California, Markos was going to Madison, Wisconsin, to meet with some interested buyers.

Whatever Markos lacked in humility he more than made up for in ingenuity and bluster, and it wasn't hard to see him as a successful CEO, reclining in his box at Wrigley Field. In hindsight, it was tempting to think that anyone with an ego and an opinion could have made it big in the early years of the blog revolution, but the fact was that Markos had made it bigger than anyone else, and there was a reason: He was simply a master of niche marketing and self-promotion. He didn't give a second's thought to the perils of economic transformation or the new threat posed by nonstate actors with advanced weaponry—

identifying the progressive argument was someone else's job. He was, however, the single most successful entrepreneur of the progressive movement. Had I been one of these rich venture capitalists in the Democracy Alliance, I would have written Markos a check for $5 million and told him to go build his next Internet business. He probably would have doubled my investment.

As Markos and Jerome gave their last talk of the tour to a packed crowd at Kepler's, the venerable Menlo Park bookstore, I gathered up my bags and prepared to catch the red-eye from SFO back to Washington. By now, we had grown so accustomed to traveling together that Markos and Jerome had even prevailed on me to introduce them at one of their readings. Seeing me head for the door, Markos interrupted himself to introduce me to the audience, saying that he wanted to thank me for driving them all that way.

When most of the hundred heads in the audience swiveled around to look at me, however, they weren't smiling. They looked confused, even a little disturbed. What were the famous bloggers doing with the evil mainstream media? A writer for the *New York Times,* no less—that voice of the timid establishment. I could see them wondering, just for that moment, whether Markos and Jerome had left behind the little people after all.

CHAPTER SEVEN

The Argument

While the bloggers were busy storming the party's Washington establishment from outside its towering walls, the man who was their political icon had somehow slipped inside, taking the fight to the innermost sanctum of the Democratic machine. Howard Dean had swept into Democratic headquarters promising to rebuild a moribund Democratic Party— his way. Like Rob Stein and the Democracy Alliance partners, Dean, too, talked about building a permanent "infrastructure," but when Dean said it, he didn't mean think tanks and media watchdogs. He meant organizers on the ground in every state, a volunteer chairman in every county, and a volunteer captain in every voting precinct in America. He called this the "unsexy" stuff of politics, the inner pipes and cables that made the party run and that its leaders had allowed to rust and fray over the years. As chairman, Dean instituted what he called his "fifty-state strategy," under which the national party would spend an unprecedented amount of money—as much as $8 million in 2006 alone—to hire new organizers in states where the party had all but disappeared.

"We're going to be in places where the Democratic Party hasn't been in twenty-five years," Dean liked to say. "If you don't show up in sixty percent of the country, you don't win, and that's not going to happen anymore." Which is why, at the end of May 2006, Dean decided to show up in Alaska, a state so remote that if you accidentally pass it, you end up in Russia. Dean was the first national Democrat in several years to set foot in the state, which hadn't sent a Democrat to the House or Senate in more than thirty years.

When I heard about the trip, I invited myself along. I had learned a few things about traveling with Dean, which I had done many times since we first met in 2003. The first was that you never brought a bag that had to be checked at the airport, because Dean didn't wait for baggage; he brought only the suit he was wearing and a few L.L.Bean wash-and-wear shirts, since he thought $1.25 was way too much to pay for dry cleaning. Second, it was best to show up with something chocolate—cookies or brownies, maybe—because this tended to lighten Dean's mood and help him forget that he was enduring your presence. "Don't mind if I *do*," he would say when offered sweets, wiggling his fingers in the air.

It was pouring when we landed in Anchorage. The wide-chested cinder block of a guy who picked us up from the airport introduced himself as Jonathan Teeters. He was twenty-five and a former offensive lineman at the University of Idaho. Teeters was among the first class of organizers hired under Dean's fifty-state strategy. Before, the withered Alaska Democratic Party had consisted of two staff members for the entire state: an executive director and a part-time fund-raiser. The party hadn't even kept a list of volunteers. Now the DNC was paying Teeters to set up local committees spanning every acre on the vast Alaskan frontier.

As we drove through the rain, wipers swishing furiously, Dean asked Teeters how many organizers the state party now had on the ground. "It's just me," Teeters said, almost apologetically. The DNC, he said, had also hired a press aide for the state party. Dean grunted and stared out the window at the soggy landscape. Then he suddenly decided that one organizer simply wasn't enough. "In most states, we have three or four," he said, thinking out loud. "Seems like you should really have more. We should be able to find that money in the budget."

Teeters nodded. I could imagine what he was thinking. After five minutes in a car with Howard Dean, during which he had probably been instructed not to say very much, he had somehow talked the chairman into spending even more money in Alaska. He probably would have been rewarded with a promotion, if there had been some job to get promoted to. Maybe if he hung around Dean for another half hour, there would be.

That night, after meeting with Dean at the sad little storefront office that housed the state party, Alaska's party chairman announced to four hundred Democrats assembled at a fund-raiser that Dean had just decided to spring for another organizer in Alaska. The crowd erupted in applause. I could see Dean's personal aide, Chris Canning, standing to the side of the room, gently roll his eyes and begin typing a text message into his mobile phone. He was telling some poor staffer back in Washington that they were going to have to find another thirty-five grand for Alaska, of all places. Dean sat there beaming, basking in the adulation.

There had been a time, when Dean had first taken over the party, when other Democrats in Washington had found this kind of impulsive behavior mildly amusing. Endearing, even. In those bleak months after the election, Democrats had been willing to try pretty much anything—even if it meant dumping the party's precious resources into a vast wasteland like Alaska. After all, at that point, a lot of analysts had posited that Democrats had slid into an irreversible and permanent minority status. Mark Gersh, a nerdy statistical expert who was the party's most trusted source of demographic projections, told me then that it was hard to envision a scenario—given the huge advantage for Republicans in the new exurban communities that were the fastest growing in America—where Democrats would regain control of Congress over the next decade or two. It was theoretically possible, Gersh allowed, that the war or some scandal could create a "throw the bums out" kind of year that would hand Democrats the majority in one or both houses. But the demographic data told him that if this kind of once-in-a-generation political cyclone didn't sweep through Republican Washington very soon—before 2012, in his estimation—then Republicans would solidify their hold on Washington for decades to come.

By the spring of 2006, however, it appeared that just such a storm might be swirling on the capital's darkening horizon. A top Republican lobbyist with ties to the White House, Jack Abramoff, was headed to jail. Tom DeLay, the majority leader known as "the hammer," had been forced to resign. And then there was the unraveling of the president himself. More than any one failing, it was the cumulative impact of so many governing debacles—the aggregation of the arrogance that prevented the president or his advisers from ever admitting a mistake—that had eroded Bush's standing and left his party perilously exposed: the botched attempt to privatize Social Security, the languid response to Hurricane Katrina, spiking gas prices, and rising economic inequity. The ongoing and intractable war in Iraq was a real calamity with real costs, but it was also a powerful symbol of an administration that seemed to have lost control of its own ill-fated agenda. In the nineteen months between election day 2004 and the end of June 2006, the United States lost almost 1,400 soldiers in Iraq, an average of more than two a day. Bush's approval ratings, which had reached as high as 55 percent after his reelection, tumbled to 31 percent. And if Americans couldn't vote against Bush himself in November, they seemed increasingly warm to the idea of punishing his party.

Now, suddenly, even pessimistic Washington Democrats saw a very real chance to take back one or both houses of Congress, ending the long era of Republican rule, and they were determined not to let it slip away. The party's House and Senate leadership zeroed in on about a dozen Senate races and some forty House districts in perennially competitive states such as Connecticut, Pennsylvania, Rhode Island, Florida, and Ohio. These were the states they had to win, and they asked Dean—begged him, really—to help them do it. They needed the national party to pay for TV ads and field programs in the places where every dime mattered, and where Republicans would enjoy a financial advantage of tens of millions of dollars.

Dean's response was a polite but firm no. This was the problem with the Democratic Party, he argued: It was always lurching drunkenly from one campaign season to the next, wantonly throwing every dollar it had into trying to win the next election, while local Democratic parties got smaller and weaker. Dean wanted to spend his money reaching out to all those voters whom the party had effectively written off over the years: white, rural men and their families in the South and on the Plains, the kind of people who didn't think "Bible study" referred to a college humanities course. He was investing the party's cash in a way that would yield returns further down the road, and no one was going to talk him into pulling off now and blowing it all at the nearest all-night casino, no matter how tantalizing the odds.

So there was Dean, soaking up the ovations on the edge of the Arctic tundra, while virtually everyone else in the party could think of nothing but battleground states and the coming election. The Democratic establishment was stunned. Washington insiders had never liked Dean or what he stood for, and the feeling was plenty mutual, but they had granted him an uneasy truce since his election as chairman. Now, over expense account lunches at Charlie

Palmer or the Capital Grille, party lobbyists and consultants asked each other the same questions over and over. What in creation was going on in Dean's addled brain? Just what was that little fucker trying to prove?

I f there was an analog to Howard Dean in modern politics, it was probably not a leftist like George McGovern or Jerry Brown, but Ronald Reagan. Like Dean, Reagan ran for president and lost, first in 1968 and then more seriously in 1976. Reagan's followers were disgusted with an equivocating Republican establishment that was willing to embrace activist government and break bread with Communist regimes. His 1976 campaign inspired thousands of movement conservatives to plunge into politics, take over their local parties, and attempt to dethrone the reigning Republican hierarchy, which they managed to do just four years later. Dean wasn't the communicator Reagan was, nor did he have the same kind of commanding presence, and he had not come nearly as close to the nomination. But his symbolic importance, in defeat, was just as imposing. Even if Dean hadn't actually become the Democratic chairman after 2004, the turbulent party that emerged from that campaign, at least at the activist level, wasn't John Kerry's or John Edwards's or Hillary Clinton's. It was his.

To party insiders, Dean had always been a confounding and irritating figure. He had his admirers on Capitol Hill, but most Washington Democrats saw him as the worst kind of spokesman for the party, a polarizing liberal afflicted with the political equivalent of Tourette syndrome. It was an unfair caricature. If you really wanted to understand what Dean was about, it helped to study some of the seemingly trivial clues from his past. For instance, Dean, the son of a New York stockbroker, had grown up a Yankees fan, but after moving to Vermont to get married and practice medicine, he had declared himself a steadfast member of Red Sox Nation. In the Northeast, this was roughly equivalent to switching religions—and, as it turned out, Dean had done that, too. He had walked out of the Episcopal Church in the early 1980s, becoming a Congregationalist instead, all because of a dispute with the church over where to build a bike path. Dean simply wasn't the kind of guy who invested much of himself in inflexible worldviews or unshakable faiths. He mostly adapted to circumstances. Once he decided he really believed something, however, Dean expressed that belief with unwavering moral firmness, as if he had believed it all along, and as if it were the only thing that any sensible person could really believe.

To the extent that Dean had any consistent ideology, it was more medical than political. He was the classic doctor: smart, gruff, and clinical. Dean's philosophy of life was essentially diagnostic. He looked at the problem, processed the complaint, and, more often than not, quickly and decisively arrived at an inviolable course of action. This quality had made him a pretty good governor in a small, independent-minded state, where people expected their chief executive to act more like a technician than an ideologue. In an odd way, it also made him ideally situated for the emotional climate he encountered when he set out to run for president in 2002.

The other Democratic candidates, mindful of Bush's popularity and immersed in all the moral complexities of governing in a time of war, tried to calibrate their words carefully, so as to preserve their options for a general election. That just wasn't Dean's way, and, in any event, he had little to lose by speaking candidly. Bush was a cancer on the country, and he was going to excise it, and that was that. After Congress authorized the invasion of Iraq, Dean dithered briefly—some advisors told him it was suicide to oppose the war—but ultimately offered what he considered to be the obvious diagnosis. The invasion of Iraq would be a crime, and Democrats were complicit.

As a governor in the nineties and a disciple of the Democratic Leadership Council, Dean had been a devout centrist, infuriating liberal groups and proudly receiving the endorsement of the National Rifle Association. ("I was a triangulator before Clinton was a triangulator," Dean told me once, riding through Iowa.) Had he been the kind of person to stay consistent with some guiding ideology, Dean would have missed his opening. But when antiwar crowds suddenly began responding to his plainspoken opposition to Bush as if he were the reincarnation of Bobby Kennedy, Dean simply shrugged and embraced the role. Just as he had with the Yankees and the Episcopalians, Dean easily shed his third-way philosophy when the moment called for it. He put away what had been his standard pitch about health care and balanced budgets and started railing, instead, against all those jelly-spined compromisers back in Washington. Grassroots Democrats were craving a resonant voice of protest, and, as it happened, Dean had a rock-hard baritone that rattled your chest.

It wasn't just Bush he was indicting with his rhetoric. It wasn't just Washington. What he had tapped into was a current of resentment that went to the heart of the modern Democratic Party, the same current that ran through MoveOn and the Democracy Alliance and the blogs. Dean would never actually say so, but he was running against Clintonism and everything that it stood for. He was dismantling the political legacy of the party's most dominant living figure—and middle-aged liberal voters, the people who had felt so marginalized during the nineties, were screaming in the aisles.

Campaigning for president, Dean became aware, for the first time, of the true state of the industrial-age Democratic Party. During a stopover in West County, Missouri, he met a woman who said there was no longer even a Democratic Party to join in her county. Inspired by Dean, she and twenty other supporters had started one, and soon two hundred fifty more people had joined. The situation was even worse in rural states that had become reliably Republican, places where no Democratic nominee since Carter had even bothered to stop for refueling. Through the years, as the party's presidential prospects had grown ever dimmer throughout the South, the Heartland, and the frontier West, the national party had become obsessed with the notion of "targeting"—that is, focusing its money and energy on an ever-narrowing number of swing states that the party thought it had a reasonable chance of winning. So if you lived in a targeted state like Ohio or Pennsylvania, you could hardly avoid seeing the Democratic nominee on TV—if not in person—every four years. If, on the other hand, you lived in Nebraska or Wyoming or virtually anywhere below the Mason-Dixon Line, you might not know there *was* a Democratic Party. Targeting meant that Democrats no longer even tried to be a truly national party.

Rattled by this realization, Dean found himself urging people to start their own local parties, or, better yet, to start their own organizations, completely outside the stodgy, bureaucratic party structure. Throw out your copy of *Robert's Rules of Order,* he would scold—just hold some parties and start keeping lists of the people who show up. He was outraged. No wonder Democrats kept losing. Over the past twenty years, Republicans had professionalized their state parties, pouring in money and expanding their competitive reach into every region of the country—while, at the very same moment, Democrats had sounded the retreat in every county that didn't have a Starbucks or a skyscraper. How, he wondered, could we have let this happen? When exactly had the mighty Democratic Party decided to close up shop in half the country and call it a day?

The problem for Dean, of course, was that, at some point in all this, his campaign became more about changing the party than it was about fixing the country. When it all came crashing down—after the Iowa caucuses, when he gave his famous and strangely captivating "scream speech" through clamped teeth, like a man trying his damnedest to give an upbeat toast at his ex-wife's wedding—Dean blamed everyone else for the collapse. He blamed Joe Trippi. He blamed the media. He blamed his opponents. Later, though, in moments of clarity, he would say that he had simply let the anger hijack his campaign. The voters had needed to see him pivot away from fiery rhetoric and toward some kind of governing vision, and he had failed to make the leap.

Still, he had helped to create a state-by-state uprising inside the party, and the question now was what to do with it. Immediately after he dropped out, Dean formed a political action committee called Democracy for America, whose mission was to raise money for progressive candidates, from mayoral and congressional seats down to the local water board. This was revolt on a small scale, however, and Dean continued to seek some grander strategy. He considered forming a third party, but that felt quixotic; not since the Civil War had any third party done much more than pester the other two.

A few months before the general election, Jerome Armstrong walked into the Democracy for America offices, in an industrial park in Burlington, and sat down with Tom McMahon, Dean's trusted aide-de-camp. Jerome and Markos expected Kerry to lose in November (Bush had just gotten his postconvention bounce in the polls), and that meant control of the party would be up for grabs after the election. The bloggers had an idea: How about Dean for party chairman? There was no way he could lose; all he had to do was win a majority of the 447 members of the Democratic National Committee, and most of them were state activists, not Washington types.

As it happened, McMahon had been talking to Dean about the very same thing. At first, Dean had dismissed the idea. Why would he want to spend his time in Washington, of all places, or out raising money? But McMahon and his allies had been slowly changing Dean's mind. For months, he had been telling Democrats around the country that it was time to take the party back. Here was his chance to do exactly that.

From the way the party's congressional leaders reacted to news of Dean's campaign for chairman, you would have thought a mob of Visigoths was preparing to descend on the capital and ransack its marble monuments. Harry Reid and Nancy Pelosi tried, with almost comic ineptness, to find a candidate who could stop him. First they got behind Tim Roemer, a former Indiana congressman and respected centrist, which seemed like a fine idea for a while, until it surfaced that Roemer was against the right to an abortion. In the rush to derail Dean, no one had bothered to ask. Then they tried to recruit Jim Blanchard, a former Michigan governor who hadn't held elective office in fourteen years, though not for lack of trying. That juggernaut went nowhere. Finally, the insiders threw their support to Martin Frost, a Texan who had, until recently, served with quiet distinction in the House, and who now, washed out by Dean's celebrity mojo at candidate forums, appeared barely to exist. The outcome was never much in question.

This unlikely turn seemed to both excite and confuse Dean's diaspora, now scattered throughout the country and among the various portals of cyberspace. On one hand, they marveled at what they had achieved. Here was this guy whom everyone in Washington had dismissed as nothing but a marginal protest candidate, a nobody from Vermont, and he had taken over the party. *They* had taken over the party, just as Eli Pariser had proclaimed in his e-mail message after the election. But now that Dean controlled the apparatus, did that make him an outsider or an insider? Were they supposed to work with the Washington party, or against it?

Dean wasn't exactly clear on that question either. His triumphant arrival in Washington—not the inaugural parade he would have chosen, certainly, but triumphant nonetheless—was conspicuous for its awkwardness. He had, after all, spent the last two years running around the country portraying the party establishment as one step up from La Cosa Nostra. On his first official visit to the newly renovated DNC building a few blocks from the Capitol, Dean was greeted in the lobby by his predecessor, Terry McAuliffe, who was, to Dean and his supporters, the very symbol of a party run by cash-obsessed hacks. The Macker, in his usual winning mood, pointed to the new wall-size glass building dedication in the lobby, which featured his name at the very top, followed by a list of contributors. "Now, Howard," he said, brandishing a finger, "don't you go chiseling that down."

The Howard Dean who showed up in Washington, however, was not the Dean that a lot of insiders had expected. Dean could be the red-faced, confrontational orator that Washington Democrats had seen on TV, but, like most politicians, he could also be surprisingly insecure and solicitous. For all his experience in state government and as a presidential candidate, neither Dean nor the small cadre of outsiders he brought with him from the campaign knew much about the inner workings of the party they had castigated. Dean had vowed during his campaign for chairman to work cooperatively with the Washington crowd, and now he tried to make good on that promise. His transition team consisted of seasoned Washington operatives, and he invited the party's leading strategists into his office for informal group sessions so he could get their counsel. John Podesta, who had never met Dean before he attended one of these early meetings, would later recall being taken aback by Dean's demeanor. Podesta had expected to encounter the gruff, defiant candidate who thought he knew better than all these cynical centrists. Instead, he found a vacillating chairman who seemed in over his head, unable to choose among the varying streams of advice that were flowing his way.

Dean was, in fact, a little lost, and nowhere was it more apparent than in the one area that was most central to the mission of the modern party: money. The DNC during the Clinton years, had catered almost exclusively to a few hundred top donors and fund-raisers—

people like Bernard Schwartz and Alan Patricof—who treated it like their private club. Prompted by changes in the laws governing campaign finance, McAuliffe had begun the process of attracting more small-dollar contributors through direct mail—something the Republicans had been doing, with huge success, for many years. Dean's team, however, came in with a plan to transform the DNC in the same way that they had revolutionized presidential politics. Dean was going to take the DNC fund-raising campaign online, where, the theory went, the same grassroots donors who had made his campaign viable would pour millions of dollars into the national party, effectively replacing the oligarchy that owned it.

For the first six months that Dean was in office, he didn't bother reaching out to many of the party's top contributors, most of whom he'd never met. There was, between Dean and the donors, a presumption of mutual contempt. A lot of wealthy donors complained to friends in Washington that Dean would visit L.A. or New York without even calling. They heard about his travels after the fact, and it was insulting.

The problem with Dean's plan was that getting small-dollar donors excited about an established party organization proved a far more arduous task than getting them excited about an insurgent campaign. Party donations only came through carefully calibrated appeals and sophisticated modeling; you couldn't just put a button on the Web site, like you did at the height of a campaign, and expect the money to fly in while you were sleeping, as if deposited there by little elves. The situation grew perilous, and Washington Democrats started to panic. By the end of 2005, the Republican National Committee had raised twice as much as the DNC and enjoyed its largest advantage in "cash on hand"—the amount you kept in the bank for the purposes of bludgeoning the other side—in more than a decade. By that time, Dean had relented, firing his finance director and bringing aboard one of McAuliffe's old acolytes, a lawyer named Jody Trapasso, to fix the debacle. Trapasso called the big donors and smoothed things over, then guided Dean through a few hours' worth of fund-raising calls every day, until at last the checks started rolling in.

The other main part of the chairman's job description, aside from fund-raising, was getting the party's message out. Here, too, Dean did little to reassure his critics in Washington or in more conservative states, where leading Democrats sometimes declined to share a stage with him. In June 2005, Dean made headlines when he charged that Republicans had "never made an honest living in their lives," then outdid himself a few days later when he said, "They all behave the same. They all look the same. It's pretty much a white, Christian party." During a subsequent appearance on MSNBC, Dean accused Republicans of playing "hide the salami, or whatever it's called," with nominations to the Supreme Court. He was stunned to learn from aides, on his way out of the studio, that he had just suggested that Republican leaders were copulating in the cloakroom. Dean had had no idea what the term meant. It had just kind of popped into his head.

Fortunately for Dean, he had made a few unlikely and influential friends in Washington, and if they couldn't keep him from playing word association on national TV, at least they could help him overhaul the party apparatus. During his presidential campaign, Dean had gone out of his way to strike up a friendship with Tina Flournoy, a savvy and well-connected operative who had worked with Al Gore and Joe Lieberman during the 2000 race. Flournoy was also a charter member of an informal and little-known dinner clique whose members referred to themselves, cheekily, as the "Colored Girls." The core group included several African American women who had reached the highest echelons of Democratic politics. Donna Brazile, the veteran organizer who had managed Gore's presidential campaign, was a regular. So were Minyon Moore, a consultant who worked in the Clinton White House; Yolanda Caraway, a public relations specialist; and Leah Daughtry, who had been McAuliffe's chief of staff (and whom Dean retained). Guest speakers at their dinners frequently included probable presidential candidates and top members of Congress.

During the chairman's race, Flournoy had brought Dean in as well, and he quickly clicked with the group. The Colored Girls became his informal cabinet. Senior aides inside the DNC learned that if they wanted to get Dean to sign on to some idea, or if they wanted to avoid having their decisions reversed, their best bet was to take it to Flournoy first.

It was an odd alliance—this pairing of a blue-blooded Vermonter with a group of black women—but, in addition to sharing some genuine affection, both sides were getting something important out of the deal. As those close to him knew, Dean had always been self-conscious about race. He had, after all, been the governor of a state whose population was only half a percent African American (only three other states in the country were less racially diverse), vying for the leadership of a party that was deeply dependent on black voters. And he had been personally stung by Al Sharpton's observation during the campaign that he lacked any African American advisers. Dean often defended himself by telling the cringe-inducing story of how he had requested an African American roommate at Yale, which generally led him to discourse on just how darn comfortable he felt around African Americans. Linking himself to the Colored Girls gave him political cover, but, more to the point, it also made him feel good about himself. It was an added bonus that Flournoy and the others happened to be exceptionally well schooled in the art of Washington combat, and that they now had Dean's back.

They also had their own agenda. Like Dean, they harbored a resentment of the elite Washington Democrats who had always run the national party. They had attained star status in the party, and they were considered powerful insiders, but they never actually thought of themselves that way. This was partly because they were black women in a party dominated by white men—men who often seemed to prize them more as symbols of diversity than for their expertise. But it was also because all of these women had come up in Democratic politics as local field operatives—that is, as young organizers who knocked on doors, principally for Jesse Jackson—in an era when all the power in the party was concentrated in the hands of the Washington consultants who made TV ads and polled the electorate. They had never enjoyed the kind of easy access to McAuliffe and other DNC chairs that the pollsters and fund-raisers had. Dean came to Washington vowing to take power from the insiders and give it, instead, to the ground-level activists who had long been ignored. For the Colored Girls, this was a chance, finally, to get their hands on the party machinery.

More than anything else, Flournoy and the others helped Dean transform the culture of the party headquarters from a centralized, top-down organization to one that was more diffuse and bottom-up—turning the party, in effect, upside down. No longer was the DNC a clubhouse for the money guys and the Washington elite, a place where state parties and their volunteers were considered a general nuisance. Under Dean, top Washington reporters and senior aides on Capitol Hill found, for the first time, that they couldn't get their calls returned, while state activists rarely had to hold the line for more than a minute. Dean, with Flournoy's hands-on guidance, hired his political team from the states, rather than from the same old pool of Washington retreads. The Colored Girls introduced Dean to a relatively obscure African American pollster, Cornell Belcher, who became a fixture at meetings with Dean. (At one early briefing on the Hill, Harry Reid, who knew every major pollster in the party, actually asked Belcher to recite his qualifications.) Like past DNC chairmen, Dean traveled constantly to headline fund-raisers in the states—but, unlike his predecessors, he was in the habit of letting the state parties keep all the money. In a telling demonstration of how he felt about Washington, Dean himself never even moved to the city. He stayed at the Capitol Hill Suites a few days a week, then headed back home to Burlington.

Quietly, and beneath the notice of most Democrats and journalists, the party was increasingly riven by the uprising that Dean had incited. In the states, political newcomers who considered themselves part of a new progressive movement—much like Reagan's conservative followers after the 1976 election—were seizing control of beleaguered party organizations, casting out the rusted patronage machines that had controlled Democratic politics for much of the previous century. In states such as Maryland, North Carolina, Colorado, and Arkansas, outsider candidates, many of them inspired by Dean, swept into office as state chairmen, defying the will of powerful elected leaders. In Texas, Fred Baron, the trial lawyer who was a partner in the Democracy Alliance (and who had supported John Edwards over Dean in 2004), led a privately financed effort to rebuild the Texas state party from the ground up—initially, at least, without the consent of party leaders.

Meanwhile, the netroots, loyal to Dean, were fomenting sporadic local rebellions. Bloggers at Daily Kos and MyDD began writing about obscure local party elections with the obsessiveness of rotisserie baseball fans, tallying the score as they went. Democracy for America, the political action committee founded by Dean, held training sessions around the country for online activists who wanted to run local campaigns against party insiders. Chris Bowers, an influential blogger on MyDD, called for readers to go take over their local parties. Setting his own example, Bowers, a lanky, long-haired doctoral student in American poetry, got himself elected captain of his local precinct in Philadelphia's Twenty-seventh Ward and then won a seat on the party's state committee.

What these new progressives wanted, chiefly, was a national party that would try to win everywhere, rather than trying to target "winnable" states and districts. The tension between the activists and the Washington party blossomed into a public and heated argument in the summer of 2005, after a special election in Ohio's Second Congressional District, one of the most solidly Republican areas in the country. The bloggers embraced the Democratic candidate, Paul Hackett, a swaggering Iraq veteran and political neophyte who referred to Bush as a "son of a bitch" and a "chicken hawk." (When *Mother Jones* asked him if he regretted that last one, Hackett replied, "Bush *is* a chicken hawk. Tough shit.") A group of bloggers traveling full time with the campaign helped raise half a million dollars online, almost two-thirds of Hackett's campaign stash. Meanwhile, in Washington, the Democratic Congressional Campaign Committee, the arm of the party that raises and spends money on House races, kept its distance, airing ads only in the campaign's final days, when it was apparent that Hackett actually had a chance to win. He didn't win, but he came within four percentage points—closer than anyone in Washington had thought remotely possible.

It was a remarkable coming-of-age moment for the bloggers. They had, for the first time, financed their own candidate, and he had nearly pulled off a remarkable upset. It proved, they argued, that the party's strategy of targeting races was a relic left over from the machine age. Hackett's district was the kind of place where the Washington party generally didn't even bother to recruit a candidate; the insiders saw it as a lost cause. What the bloggers were saying, though, was that now, with the advent of the Internet as an organizing and fund-raising tool, Democrats could field a credible candidate in every district in the country, and local activists could make a lot of those races competitive. This not only meant that Democrats had a chance at winning more Republican seats, but it would force Republicans to spend money to defend their candidates in rural areas, rather than letting them save all their resources for the most contested states, which was what usually happened.

Back in Washington, however, Rahm Emanuel and Chuck Schumer, the congressman and senator who were leading the campaigns to take back the House and Senate, respectively, thought this argument absurdly naive. And all but a few of the party's elected leaders agreed with them. Had these people screaming on the blogs ever actually worked on a political campaign, they wondered? (The answer, in most cases, was no.) What could they possibly know? Politics, after all, was the art of resource allocation; you had a certain amount of money to spend and a certain number of races you had to win, and the strategy lay in making difficult choices. Of course, everyone liked to *say* the party would compete for every seat—it was one of those grand abstractions, like saying you were going to provide a good job for every American—but no one in the world of professional politics actually believed it.

It was pretty clear where Dean stood in this debate—and it wasn't with his fellow party leaders. "This is like deciding to go to a psychiatrist," Dean explained during one of our conversations. "The risk of staying the same has to be greater than the risk of changing. And right now, in the history of the party, that's exactly where we are. The risk of doing nothing, the same old thing, is enormous. The risk of trying something new is much smaller. The risk of the fifty-state strategy is much smaller than if we continue to do what we've been doing."

Under Dean's plan, Mississippi, which had no targeted races in 2006, was getting four organizers from the DNC, while Pennsylvania, which had a pivotal governor's race, a Senate campaign, and four competitive House races, got only three. Dean was vowing to spend some $12 million on the party's 2006 races, but that included his funding for the fifty-state strategy, which meant a lot of that money was going to states where Democrats didn't stand a chance.

When Emanuel, a trained ballet dancer, heard that Dean was actually sending the party's money not only to Alaska and Hawaii, but also to local Democrats in the U.S. Virgin Islands, it made him want to dig a steel toe into Dean's skull. A onetime Israeli army volunteer and then an enforcer for Bill Clinton, Emanuel spoke in violent bursts of shrapnel, profanities flying in all directions. The way he saw it, the real lesson of the Hackett race was clear: Americans were souring on Bush and his war, and if Democrats could make 2006 an up-or-down vote on the president, they might have a chance at a historic comeback. All he was asking was for the party's chairman to provide a fraction of the help that his Republican adversaries surely would.

The tension finally exploded during a meeting that May among Dean, Emanuel, and Schumer in Dean's executive office. Emanuel told Dean that the fifty-state strategy was a waste of money. Dean shot back that winning elections wasn't only about buying TV ads. Emanuel wanted to know what Dean was doing to help in California's Fiftieth District, where voters were about to hold another special election. When Dean said he had organizers on the ground, Emanuel erupted. "Who?" he demanded. "Tell me their names!" Dean couldn't, and Emanuel stormed out of the meeting to go to a vote on the House floor, cursing as he marched down the hallway.

What was remarkable about this test of wills, as it dragged on throughout that summer of 2006, was just how public it became and the extent to which it seemed to be pulling influential Democrats into its vortex. It pitted donors against politicians and consultants against activists, as if all the latent intraparty tensions of the past several years were now spilling out into the open. It wasn't just an argument over whether the DNC should be paying for barbecues in Anchorage or ads in Columbus; it was about where the power in Democratic politics was ultimately going to reside. For decades, the party's

Washington establishment had controlled its agenda and strategy, mainly because it controlled the money. What Dean wanted to do was redistribute power back to the local level. At bottom, his plan was to "devolve" the centralized Democratic Party in the very same way that Reagan and the movement conservatives had tried to devolve the federal government—by choking off its funding and returning control to the states.

And so the feud touched an emotional nerve. Bren Simon, the wealthy Democratic patron from Indiana, warned Emanuel and Schumer that she wouldn't write them any more checks if they didn't stop harassing Dean. Donna Brazile ran into Emanuel on the steps of the DNC building and started loudly lecturing him about his attacks on the chairman, in full view of party employees. Paul Begala, one of the main strategists behind Bill Clinton's White House campaigns, went on CNN and railed against Dean and his wacky fifty-state plan. "He says it's a long-term strategy," Begala said. "What he has spent it on, apparently, is just hiring a bunch of staff people to wander around Utah and Mississippi and pick their nose."

That comment lit up the blogs. "These inside-the-beltway assholes really hate the thought of Howard Dean building a 50-state party," Markos wrote on Daily Kos. "Begala—one of the Clintons' favorite consultants—thinks spending time building a national party is a waste of time. And he insults Utah and Mississippi in the process. Won't these Clinton-era jokers please go away? We tried their way and look where we are. Time for new blood."

Shuttling that summer between Dean's office on the third floor of the DNC building and Emanuel's digs on the floor below, I found myself sympathizing, to some extent, with both sides. The party's congressional leaders were surely right that winning back control of Congress would have far-reaching effects—not the least of which would be shutting down a Republican agenda that seemed increasingly and brazenly tilted toward the wealthy. Still, Dean had a point. Every Democrat in Washington, after all, professed a desire to expand the party's reach beyond its coastal enclaves, but only Dean, among his party's leaders, had been willing to argue that there was a choice involved, that you couldn't actually invest for the long term unless you were willing to forgo at least some short-term priorities. That took some courage.

No matter who was right, though, the whole debate was premised on a fundamental assumption about politics that no one on either side seemed to question—that money and tactics alone could revive the party. Emanuel and Schumer were arguing that ads and field programs would enable you to win the 2006 elections, and that once the party controlled Congress, it could hold lots of hearings to investigate the president, and that this would, in turn, enable Democrats to reclaim the White House in 2008. Dean was arguing that local organizations were critical, because, over time, if you had lots of county chairmen and precinct captains pestering their neighbors, you would turn out more voters in more states. The whole discussion closely mirrored the tactical conversations going on outside the party among the new progressives. The Democracy Alliance was debating the value of market segmentation versus a media-booking center. The bloggers were arguing over message and party discipline. There was very little real discussion about what anyone was actually going to do for a country in the throes of a historic and painful transformation, beyond the usual abstractions and thirty-year-old proposals.

Almost as an afterthought, when they weren't scuffling over which tactical maneuvers might deliver them from the political wilderness, leading Democrats tried to settle on some kind of slogan, something that would at least give the impression of a modern and meaningful worldview. As far back as the summer of 2005, Dean had put together a "messaging project," in which the party's top elected officials huddled around one of those ubiquitous whiteboards and tried to figure out how to nicely encapsulate their public philosophy. Cornell Belcher, who acted as a facilitator for the summit, prepared a ten-page discussion guide, which began by asking a series of questions of the nation's most senior elected Democrats:

- What have our message problems been?
- How do you think most Americans view Democrats?
- What are some of your ideas and thoughts about what the Democratic message should be?
- How do you think we turn this around?

Belcher asked the Democratic leaders to discuss a series of possible strategies for the party, such as "identify Democrats as the party of change, optimism and hope" and "use Democratic Party history and founding values to strengthen the brand." Then all the elected Democrats took turns trying to come up with a "bumper sticker" for the party. The entire discussion revolved around the question of what language might "move" voters to the Democratic side; no one seemed even to consider the possibility that the difficulty in settling on a slogan might have something to do with a general lack of clarity about the party's philosophy. At one point in the meeting, when the participants agreed that it was important to go into the midterm elections with some kind of positive message, rather than just attacking Bush and the Republican Congress, Rahm Emanuel, who hated circular discussions like this in the first place, shook his head in disgust. "I have my knee on their vertebrae," Emanuel snapped, "and I'm not going to let up on the pressure until I hear the vertebrae snap." There followed a brief moment of frightened silence.

Emanuel, in fact, had his own idea for the message: In a memo to House leaders, he proposed that the party issue a "Declaration of Independence from Special Interests and Lobbyists." This would be accompanied by news conferences and ads in which Democrats would wave this declaration around and declare themselves to be the champions of cheap prescription drugs, lower gas prices, and an end to corporate tax breaks. The leadership dismissed this idea, however, as "too risky." Instead, at Dean's branding session, Pelosi suggested that Democrats call themselves "the people's party." This slogan was quickly and wisely rejected, as it sounded like a communiqué from the party headquarters in Pyongyang.

Ultimately, after much polling and all of this endless brainstorming, as if the most powerful Democrats in the land were running an ad agency rather than a great political party, it was decided that what Democrats really needed to say was that they weren't the Republicans. And so the party's leaders ended up choosing a new slogan: "Together, America Can Do Better." Even this pallid marshmallow of a slogan briefly plunged the caucus into chaos, as lawmakers who might have been scrutinizing the war or reinventing American health care spent forty minutes arguing over the precise language. "We were divided on using the word 'together,'" Evan Bayh, the Indiana senator, quipped.

The plan had been to follow up the unveiling of the new slogan with a policy agenda for the midterm elections. But by the fall of 2005, Bush's approval ratings had slipped below 40 percent, so party leaders decided that it was better to let the Republicans collapse of their own weight than to offer an actual agenda and risk the possibility that some voters might not like it. Instead, to make their case for governing the country, they rolled out a pamphlet they called "Six for '06," in keeping with Pelosi's view that people always responded to catchy phrases. The six Democratic principles included such vague and obvious selling points as better jobs, lower gas prices, and affordable health care.

The problem with all of this, of course, was that the party's top insiders had fallen into the same trap that had ensnared the outsiders of the Democracy Alliance. They could throw a bunch of issues together well enough, but they seemed at a loss to articulate any larger, more meaningful argument for the times, something that might replace the boundless and dated activism of the New Deal. Instead, they kept harking back to the way things used to be, before the evil Republicans got there—as if George W. Bush had created Islamic fundamentalism, invented the robotic arm in GM's factories, and drawn up the plans for an integrated world, rather than simply having failed to deal with any of it. They fell back on vapid slogans, as if the American voter were a housewife wandering around the aisles of the political supermarket, eager to have her most obvious desires parroted back to her in cheery logos and money-back guarantees. Better jobs? Check. Cheaper gas? Check. Together, America can do better.

"Tell us what you want to hear," the party seemed to say, "and we'll be sure to put it in our pamphlet."

There had been, since John Kerry's defeat, a growing tension in the party between those few who still believed that Democrats needed a new argument, some big idea for governing the country, and a much larger contingent in Washington who said it was only the machinery of politics that held the party back. According to this latter, more vocal group of Democrats, big ideas in general were overvalued, and the popular notion of a Democratic Party adrift was really just a myth perpetrated by conservatives. They argued vociferously, in magazines like the *New Republic,* that Democrats had all the policy ideas a party could ever need; it was just that nobody ever wrote about them in the newspapers because they were too cerebral and complex. After all, hadn't every Democratic contender during the last election proposed some version of a health care solution, usually by expanding the web of existing programs? Hadn't Democratic policy experts written entire books full of provisions that would increase college grants and preserve Social Security? This stuff was sitting around on the cobwebbed shelves of every think tank in America, and yet somehow critics still persisted in saying what Gary Hart had said way back in the early 1970s—that Democrats were somehow out of ideas.

Besides, this theory held, the modern campaign obviously wasn't about ideas anyway. Hadn't Al Gore and John Kerry had more to say about policy than George W. Bush? Had voters or the media actually given a rat's ass about any of it? No, if a man as intellectually and grammatically challenged as Bush could win, they reasoned, and not once but twice, then clearly elections at the turn of the century were vapid affairs, detached from any meaningful content. To have thought otherwise was what Democrats now considered their crucial mistake. The Republicans had proven that campaigns were won and lost on charisma and the common touch, on turnout models and media manipulation and dirty tricks on election day. You needed the right kind of candidate, someone who could down a beer and belch with the best of them, and you needed to be tactically ruthless. But you certainly didn't need a lot of bright, new ideas.

From the day I first met him in 2003, walking down a street on Capitol Hill where not a soul yet recognized him, Howard Dean seemed profoundly conflicted about where he stood on this question. In moments of unguarded candor, he would betray a palpable frustration with his party's inability to modernize its agenda in the face of such dizzying change. He had told me, more than once, that Democrats needed to start an open debate about trade and the sagging social safety net. "I need your help, because we need *idears*," I heard Dean, after his election as chairman, tell a group of Asian American lawyers in Los Angeles, pronouncing the word, as he always did, with an *r* at the end. "We have to have something other than the New Deal. We can't fall back on the same thing we've had for seventy years. We have to have some new idears."

At other times, though, Dean would say that the party's agenda wasn't the problem and that there really was no confusion about how Democrats would govern the country, beyond whatever confusion Republicans had been sowing to their own nefarious ends. As party chairman, Dean was consumed with the mechanics of branding and party building, so that he sometimes came to sound exactly like those squishy and manipulative Washington consultants he had so maligned as a presidential candidate. During that same trip to L.A., Dean sat down with John Emerson, a former Clinton White House aide who was now a prominent West Coast fund-raiser. When Emerson asked about the party's message for the midterm elections, Dean, a little apologetically, recited the new Democratic slogan: "Together, America Can Do Better." "The pundits and the intellectuals hate it," Dean explained, "but it polls off the charts." Emerson just sat there looking at him blankly for a moment, as if to say, you've got to be kidding me.

As the head of a movement, Dean fell victim to the same political shortcoming that had cost him his party's nomination for president. He was a truly inspiring figure for liberals all over the country. He was a political risk taker who recognized a need to make the party more inclusive, more responsive, and more democratized. With his argumentative style, Dean imbued ordinary Democrats with a sense that they were, at long last, drawing a line and standing firm against the inexorable creep of mean-spirited conservatism. But what, exactly, was he arguing *for*? What was the most pressing challenge of the new century? What was the post–New Deal iteration of American government supposed to look like? How were progressives going to redefine a social contract that dated back to a world before telecommuting or flextime or contract workers? By what doctrine were they going to stamp out the new generation of anti-American forces across the globe, now that the strategies of "containment" and "mutually assured destruction," which had worked so well for forty years against the Soviets, no longer applied?

Of course, Dean, like the bloggers, would have said that this wasn't really his problem to solve, and he had a point. He had chosen a different career path now, and the role of a party chairman was to raise money and tinker with the party apparatus. Dean woke up every day thinking about how he might make it possible for progressives to take back American government. It wasn't his job, or even his place, he figured, to tell them what, exactly, they were supposed to do with it.

But whose job was it, then? Rob Stein had premised his slide show on the notion that transformative ideas didn't begin inside political parties, but with the outsider movements that shaped them. Rob had argued that the party's elected leaders were too narrowly focused on the battles of the day, and properly so, to indulge in philosophical debate; that kind of thinking had to be done elsewhere. That was what the founders of the conservative movement had managed to do. And now other influential progressives were coming around to the same point of view. They had their own passionate followings, and they had the Internet, which gave Americans of diverse backgrounds, and with all kinds of expertise, a powerful new way to convene and share their own ideas, rather than having to wait for someone else to show them the way. Maybe, they reasoned, this business of articulating the progressive argument wasn't up to party politicians and their experts, after all. Maybe it was up to them.

CHAPTER EIGHT

Beyond the Message Object

The MoveOn colossus had been built on the idea that ordinary people could rise up to rebuild their party. And now, with Democrats poised to take back control of Congress, Eli Pariser thought those same people should be the ones to dictate the long-term agenda. And so, not quite a year after I had eaten nachos on the patio at Chuck Fazio's house in Alexandria, I found myself headed for another MoveOn house party. This one was only a few miles from Chuck's regal, bayside neighborhood, but it might as well have been another part of the country. Staring alternately at the address in my hand and the street atlas in my passenger seat, I navigated through a mostly black, mixed-income neighborhood on the south side of Arlington. This wasn't typical of the MoveOn constituency as I had come to understand it, but it was, perhaps, far more typical of Democratic America.

The party, it turned out, was in a tiny, first-floor apartment overlooking a parking lot and tucked into the rear of a brooding brick complex—the kind of all-too-common 1950s adventure in mass housing that seemed to have been inspired by the architecture of Soviet-era Warsaw. The place belonged to Gayle Fleming, an animated woman who looked to be in her forties, although she was actually a decade older than that. She had short, spiky hair and a broad, engaging smile. Gayle had arranged all the couches and chairs she could find in a circle in her living room, which was about the size of a large SUV. Her kitchen table was piled with snacks that her guests—about fifteen in all—had brought with them. There were tortilla chips, lemon cake, strawberries, and pepperoni slices, which Gayle told me were the first meat she could ever remember having in the apartment. A bumper sticker on the refrigerator said, "Global warming is so uncool."

I sneaked a glance at the pictures on the wall, featuring Gayle's strikingly beautiful daughter and her daughter's husband. He looked startlingly like the comedian Chris Rock. I looked again. He *was* Chris Rock. What were the odds of that? I tried to imagine Gayle's famous son-in-law sleeping on the old couch during Christmas in Arlington, then found myself wondering why he hadn't taken the time, between lucrative and mostly terrible movies, to buy her one of the plush new condos that were popping up like mushrooms a few miles up the road. It seemed impolite to ask.

Gayle's guests were a diverse lot that included five senior citizens, several middle-aged African Americans, and a few young women who looked to be college students, probably from nearby George Mason University. One guy, baby-faced in a blue blazer and tan slacks, like something out of the J.Crew catalog, stood around looking out of place. He introduced himself to the others as Paul Ferguson, the vice chairman of the Arlington County board. He had that scrubbed and self-important look of a bush-league politician, and, sure enough, before the party officially began, he felt the need to stand up and introduce himself to all the guests. "The MoveOn, the blogging—I'm still new to it," he said. "It's just so exciting to me." Then he left.

Ben Brandzel, who worked for MoveOn, was there, too. Stubbly and bushy-haired, Ben was in his early twenties and hailed from

Berkeley. He was overseeing all six hundred MoveOn house parties taking place tonight, and he had chosen to address them, via cell phone, from Gayle's apartment. This was to be a seminal moment for MoveOn. At tonight's parties, for the first time ever, its members would be proposing and voting on "positive goals" for the country. Each party was going to select the three agenda items its attendees thought were most important, and then MoveOn's members would have a few weeks online to winnow this list to three initiatives. No longer would MoveOn exist solely to find the next message object; now it would also become a lobbying force for its own, demo-cratically selected, long-term agenda. The "MoveOn era," as Tom Matzzie had put it, was about to begin.

There was a handwritten sign tacked to a bookshelf in the living room, and on it were the main rules for the evening, which MoveOn had issued to all of its hosts. At the top it said, "Guidelines for Goals." It continued:

1. Specific enough to know when you've done it.
2. Focus on goals, not details.
3. Focus on positive.
4. Keep it to 5 words.

As we waited to get started, Gayle handed out notepads she said were for brainstorming. This was the first MoveOn party she had ever hosted. "When I got the e-mail that said 'positive,'" she said, "just that word—positive—got me so excited. We can get so nega-tive. We've been so negative for so long. So that we can do something positive is just so exciting to me." It occurred to me that Gayle herself had the skills to run for office. She probably would have that joker from the county board begging for mercy.

Ben dialed a number into his cell phone, to which he was tethered by a wired earpiece, and suddenly he was speaking to more than a hundred thousand MoveOn members at parties like this one all over the country. After introducing himself, he asked everyone at Gayle's party to scream enthusiastically into the phone, like he was one of those morning deejays broadcasting live from Hooters. Then Ben explained some of the rules for the evening. This was MoveOn's opportunity to forge a "bold and positive agenda," rather than just to criticize Bush and the Republicans. *Positive*—he couldn't stress that word enough. To illustrate this point, Ben gave an example. "Keeping Diebold from stealing elections," he said, referring to the voting machine manufacturer that was at the center of various liberal conspiracy theories, was a negative idea. On the other hand, "having elections that every American can trust" was a positive way to express the same thing. (It also consisted of seven words, not five.)

"Good luck, everyone," Ben said, a little nervously, reading from a script that he had just printed out on Gayle's home computer. "I can't *wait* to see what we all come up with!"

Everyone at the party broke into groups of three and wandered outside to deliberate. Each group would nominate three big ideas, and then all the party guests would reconvene to pick the three best. Watching the groups fan out, I was reminded of what Harold Ickes had told me, that MoveOn had a cachet among ordinary liberals that no party could match. Right now, in cities and towns all over the country, tens of thousands of these little clusters of people were seated around garden tables or on front porches or on the rooftops of apartment buildings, debating and discussing the political issues that mattered most in American life. It was hard to imagine the Democratic Party pulling off anything like this, with or without Howard Dean as its chairman.

I strolled out onto the little front patio, where an elderly man was lecturing the two college students on why it was critical for immigrants to learn English. The students were nodding awkwardly and looking anxious. They had fifteen minutes to solve the nation's problems, and this was not how they had planned to start. The old guy just kept going. This collision was too painful to watch, so I made my way through the front garden and down some steps to an alley that ran the length of the apartment building and was bordered on the other side by a chain-link fence. Here I was relieved to find Gayle, our host, who was sitting on a wood retaining wall with two other women.

Gayle's group had very quickly come up with three very general agenda items: health care, global warming, and energy. Now they were trying to figure out how to turn those generalities into something more specific. Gayle wasn't entirely satisfied with the selections, however, and she continued to raise other options. This seemed to annoy one of her colleagues on the wall, an older woman whose name tag said "Barbara." She wore a sour expression and was staring off beyond the fence.

"I think we have three good ideas," Barbara said impatiently. "I propose we use the rest of our time to concentrate on language."

Gayle seemed not to hear this. She was deep in thought. "Immigration," she said. "How do we frame that progressively?" I was less surprised than I should have been to hear her use George Lakoff's buzzword; by now, every Democratic voter with cable TV seemed to talk like a pollster. Immigration led Gayle to consider the issue of wages. "You know, raising the minimum wage is a really good issue," she said. "How about 'fair wages for all workers'?"

Barbara closed her eyes and dug her nails into her temples.

"'Fair wages for all workers—including immigrants,'" Gayle said, trying again.

"You can write it down, then," Barbara sighed, rolling her eyes. "I'm just trying to think of a way to say these things that isn't this tired old language that doesn't *mean* anything."

Now the third woman piped up. She looked to be about Gayle's age and wasn't wearing a name tag, which led me to think she might be a tad rebellious. She said she couldn't believe people were now talking about trying nuclear energy again. That was terrible.

"What's another word for 'plan?'" Barbara asked, ignoring this digression. It wasn't clear to me which of their three ideas she was talking about, but all of them required some kind of plan.

"I don't think we need to parse these words," the no-nukes woman said.

"Yeah, I don't think so," Gayle agreed.

Barbara plowed on, undeterred. "But if it's not a plan, what is it?" she demanded.

"It *is* a plan!" Gayle replied testily.

"The thing about five-word sound bites is that things really are more complicated than that," the no-nukes woman said. The other two women nodded and sulked for a moment. They hadn't realized how hard this would be.

"Let's go back in," Gayle said finally, "and maybe somebody can actually help us with the words."

We made our way back up the steps to the apartment. Discussion time was almost over. I heard an elderly woman suggesting that it was time to bring back Roosevelt's WPA. "Oh, like a Marshall Plan!" a guy on her team said, and everyone nodded.

Meanwhile, the old man on the patio had moved on to gay adoption. "Now, is that child better off in an orphanage, or with two parents who love him?" he was saying, while the students, dejected, looked around for help.

Everyone gathered again in the living room. Gayle had a whiteboard, and it was her job to write down the suggested ideas from each group, so that everyone could vote on them. I could gauge the potential of each suggestion from the reaction it got from the crowd. "A foreign policy that wins friends" got lots of "ahs" and nods. "Enough in the budget so that no child is left behind" drew an immediate rebuke from Gayle. "We can't use that!" she said, explaining that "no child left behind" was the president's phrase. One clever group came up with "affordable housing, education, and health care." This was roundly rejected on the grounds that it encompassed too many ideas to be a single agenda item.

"Reversing the tide of corruption!" one group leader called out. Gayle looked puzzled. Now, she asked, was this corporate corruption or government corruption? She was told it referred to both.

"Oh, wait, remember?" Gayle said suddenly, looking alarmed. "This has to stay pos-i-tive!" There were noises of assent. The idea was reworked to become "rebuilding public trust."

"This keeps it on a positive note," Gayle said. "Thank you for that."

"Full benefits for veterans!" another group leader called out.

"Ooh," Gayle said excitedly, hovering over the whiteboard. "Good."

"What does that mean—health benefits?" someone else asked.

"We don't know," came the reply.

"Well, you have the right idea to target veterans, anyway," said the guy who had wanted a Marshall Plan of some kind.

One of the last groups to report back suggested "fully funded educational opportunities." Barbara, who still seemed to be fighting a migraine, shook her head quietly. She leaned in toward the man next to her, whose name was Arnold.

"You know," she whispered in his ear, "there's more money for education today, per student, than ever before." He nodded. She leaned back in her chair sullenly, realizing that raising this point would do no one any good.

W hen the votes were tallied, Gayle's guests had voted for "affordable health care for all," "a foreign policy that wins friends," and "create a comprehensive energy plan." They turned out to be pretty much in agreement with MoveOn's membership as a whole. A few weeks later, after online debate and voting, MoveOn would unveil its agenda:

- Health care for all
- Energy independence through clean, renewable sources
- Democracy restored

"Most groups would say this is a far too risky way to make such a big decision," Ben Brandzel would tell members in a triumphant e-mail. "But it's the grassroots consensus that makes this agenda different—and powerful." MoveOn's new agenda would "push Democrats to think big and fight hard," he said.

These weren't entirely novel ideas, of course, nor were they all that specific. (Where was democracy supposed to be restored? Ohio? Congress? Afghanistan?) But then, never before in the history of the country had ordinary voters been expected to navigate their own course through economic and foreign threats with so little guidance from their elected leaders, and, when you looked at it that way, the experiment had been a qualified success. MoveOn's agenda was more specific than a vapid slogan like "Together, America Can Do Better" and more compelling than the cynically crafted "Six in '06," which didn't even bother to set real priorities. One could see, in the final product, the faintest outlines of a progressive argument for the country—the idea that government at the dawn of the global economy suffered from a kind of cautious incrementalism, when what it really needed to do was adopt the more radical, spend-whatever-it-takes kind of approach that had once propelled America, like a rocket, into the age of industry.

And, if nothing else, at least MoveOn's members—thousands of them—had been willing to sit down and think hard, not about what message might "frame" Bush's failures or "move" voters in the Sun Belt, but about what they actually thought a progressive government could achieve in a new century. There weren't a lot of Democrats in Washington doing that.

Gayle's guests—all except poor Barbara, at least—clearly felt invigorated and proud as they rose to leave that night. They felt as if they had exercised an affirmative voice in the affairs of the country— and, in fact, they had. Where else in modern American politics, besides maybe on the blogs, could a voter actually do that anymore? You called your congressman and got some generic voice mail. You sent him a letter, and by the time they finished checking it for anthrax powder, you were lucky if an intern ever opened it. MoveOn actually listened and took action. The members who turned out to wrestle with their own agenda were doing, in effect, what an earlier generation of progressives—those who espoused good government and conservation and women's suffrage—had done a century before, in private homes and social clubs. They had taken the business of public policy upon themselves, and it was ennobling.

As the giddy partiers snacked on the last of the lemon cake and filed out into the night, Gayle suddenly leaped up, as if she had just remembered something. "Before you go!" she shouted, reaching for a stack of paper that she had printed from the MoveOn Web site. Quickly, she handed out flyers for MoveOn's newest initiative, Operation Democracy, a plan to help members conduct "rapid response" campaigns against the Republican talking points in their communities. Positive hour had come to an end.

CHAPTER NINE

Backward Compatible

J udy Wade, the former McKinsey consultant who had taken over from Rob Stein as the managing director of the Democracy Alliance at the end of 2005, had her own vision for what the alliance should become. She had left McKinsey for the alliance partly because she had been bored at the firm since returning from her long South Africa stint, and she was looking for something new, but also because she was the kind of person who actually liked to debate public policy. She wasn't a political person by temperament—she had never run a campaign or worked for a senator—but, given the chance, she thought she could help define the progressive argument for the twenty-first century, in the same way that she had helped businesses and foreign governments adapt their missions to the global economy. Wade loved highbrow political forums. She had first met John Podesta, her connection to the Democracy Alliance, at a conference sponsored by the hyperintellectual Aspen Institute, and she served on the board of the Kennedy School of Government, the official academy of liberal intellectuals.

And so this was how Judy Wade saw the potential of the Democracy Alliance, or the "D.A.," as she liked to call it—not simply as a funding mechanism for liberal groups, but as the chief convener of the progressive conversation. Democratic factions were always too jealous and competitive to talk much to one another; the alliance, through the power of money, could spread its wide, paternal arms and draw them all into one peaceable dialogue. She pictured the Democracy Alliance conference as becoming a "mini Davos," referring to the global economic summit that, once a year, brought together all the biggest brains in government and industry. "Only the D.A. can do that," was Wade's catchphrase, by which she meant that only people with all that money could realistically hope to fill the intellectual void in the new progressive movement.

She clearly meant to showcase this mission at the alliance conference in May 2006. About eighty partners descended on another absurdly posh getaway: the Barton Creek Resort, perched on a hillside outside Austin and flanked by gated communities of Spanish-style McMansions. Wade had titled the conference "Transformation in Action." The conference had its own soundtrack piped in over speakers (music by the anti-Bush Dixie Chicks) and its own logo (a pale blue fast-forward button like you might find on a TiVo remote), which graced a series of backlit fiberglass displays scattered throughout the resort's dining and meeting areas. The partners wandered around this sleek-looking set in resort shirts, with name tags and sunglasses hanging from their necks, like tourists in Tomorrowland.

I was there, too—the first outsider allowed into one of these conferences, although a lot of the partners were less than pleased about it. Since I had been following the alliance from its earliest days as the Phoenix Group, Wade, Steven Gluckstern, and Rob Stein had all endorsed my being allowed into the Austin conference. But a few of the board members had vetoed the suggestion, saying they preferred to keep their involvement confidential. I had then informed the partners that I planned to show up in Austin anyway; nothing personal, but it seemed to me that a group plotting to dump $100 million of unregulated money into American politics didn't have much of an expectation of privacy. This standoff led, remarkably, to hours of emergency meetings and conference calls among the partners, until at last it was decided that I could attend only the first twenty-four hours of the conference, and only under the most restrictive of guidelines.

In the conference materials for the partners, Wade included a letter explaining that they were under no obligation to acknowledge me, and that they could, in fact, turn their ID tags around if they wished, so that I wouldn't know who they were. I was issued a big black credential—the color of death—so that everyone could easily identify me in a crowd. As a final precaution, the alliance retained the services of Paul Clark, the head of crisis management in the Washington office of the public relations giant Hill & Knowlton, whose job it was to monitor my every movement in Austin. I felt bad for Clark, a Republican aide from the Reagan era who seemed unable to marshal much enthusiasm for the assignment. I told him that the whole thing reminded me of my last such experience with a full-time minder, while traveling in Saddam Hussein's Iraq.

The centerpiece of the Austin conference, as Wade had designed it, was to be an opening night panel discussion on a twenty-first-century economic agenda, featuring an appearance by Andy Stern, the president of the service employees' union. Stern was one of the most powerful Democrats in Washington—which was, in itself, a meaningful statement about the direction of the American economy. The 1.8 million Americans who carried the union's purple-emblazoned card toiled at the low-wage, low-respect jobs of the new American workplace: They were the home nurses who changed bedpans, the security guards who fought to stay awake all night, the janitors who scrubbed their hands raw cleaning office-park toilets. While most of the rest of American labor was falling toward irrelevance (the number of American workers who belonged to unions had dropped from a third in 1955 to barely one in ten now), the service employees were the fastest-growing union in North America and, as such, a major source of cash and manpower for Democratic campaigns. When Andy Stern called a Democratic Senate office, he was never on hold for long.

It was what Stern had chosen to do with that power, however, that made him a hero to the new progressives. A small, wiry man who had studied social work at the University of Pennsylvania and who easily could have passed for a professor or a psychologist in his trademark purple shirts, Stern had gone through a private and public transformation. In 2002, his fourteen-year-old daughter, Cassie, died suddenly from a freak infection after collapsing in her father's arms. His marriage of twenty-three years broke up soon afterward. And then, strangely liberated by misfortune, Andy Stern began to act like a man who had nothing left to lose. He began to say, publicly, that the labor movement had become the chief enabler of a bankrupt Democratic establishment. He and his fellow union bosses, Stern argued, had been giving all their members' hard-earned dues to politicians who either voted with big business every time or who continued to defend a series of outdated, industrial-age programs that weren't remotely adequate to the challenges faced by the itinerant, unskilled workers of the new economy. And why did labor leaders do this? Because they got to ride on Air Force One or have their picture taken with a bunch of smiling senators. Venting decades of frustration, Stern said he didn't want to be part of the club anymore. He wanted to blow it up.

And so he had. In 2005, on the fiftieth anniversary of the AFL-CIO, the federation of unions known familiarly as Big Labor, Stern led three other unions in walking out of the annual convention. Those renegade unions and three others broke away and formed their own federation, taking 40 percent of Big Labor's membership and money with them. They vowed to increase their political muscle by expanding the ranks of their workers—and to use that muscle to pressure entrenched politicians who didn't vote in the interests of their members, no matter which party they belonged to. This was something completely new in modern American politics: a labor movement that meant not simply to elect Democrats, but to actually hold them accountable as well.

Having essentially offered his middle finger to the rest of the labor movement and his party's elite, Stern became the most influential interest-group leader to cast his lot with the progressive outsiders. He forged new friendships with progressives such as George Soros, Markos Moulitsas Zúniga, and Eli Pariser. He watched Rob Stein's slide show, and he decided that the service employees should invest in the Democracy Alliance—making the union the only institution to sit alongside dozens of millionaires. (Later, the AFL-CIO, not to be outdone, had purchased its own seat in the alliance.) In fact, Stern's union had done more than simply join the alliance: By the time the Austin conference was over, the service employees' union would have committed more than $5 million to alliance-sanctioned groups, making it one of the most generous partners in the alliance, up there with the Soroses and Lewises.

Stern was also housing the alliance's offices in the union's new, high-tech headquarters on Washington's Dupont Circle. The environment-friendly building featured glass walls accented with stainless steel and teak paneling, along with purple leather couches, matching ottomans, and high-tech video phones in the waiting areas. It was unlike anything the labor movement had ever seen.

Like anyone who had spent his life on picket lines, Stern maintained a natural suspicion of his wealthy alliance partners, but he also reasoned that if he wanted to modernize the Democratic agenda for a new economic age, his best bet was to try to work with them. The party's economic policy, Stern had told me, "is basically being opposed to Republicans and protecting the New Deal. It makes me realize how vibrant the Republicans are in creating twenty-first-century ideas, and how sad it is that we're defending sixty-year-old ideas." If the Democracy Alliance really did intend to be the funding source for innovative ideas that would change the party, then Stern was determined to help shape its priorities.

So far, however, he had been disappointed. He had expected the progressive donors to stand up against the party establishment, to embrace ideas and strategies that were as heretical inside the party as Stern's ideas were inside the labor movement. Instead, they mostly seemed timid. Stern had personally asked many of his new alliance partners to contribute money to labor's public relations campaign against Wal-Mart. His strategy was to simultaneously pressure and open a discussion with Wal-Mart, to explore feasible ways for the company to do right by its workers while also punishing it for every day that it didn't. The partners resisted. He had the impression that they found it distasteful to take on the nation's largest employer, with whom some of them had business dealings. Stern was coming around to the belief that the donors were just like his colleagues at the AFL-CIO; their idea of a bold vision for the new economy was to help Democrats win elections, as if that alone were going to magically solve the problem.

In the months since he had brought about the breakup of Big Labor, Stern had become, in certain business quarters, a celebrated apostle of change. He spoke to gatherings of CEOs and corporate conferences. Recently, he had been the guest speaker at a private retreat for McKinsey consultants. His shtick was that the twentieth-century economy was gone and that the great programs that industrial-age Democrats had built around it were insufficient to protect the new working class. His audiences cheered loudly. Sometimes they told him he should run for president. But Stern knew what was really going on. The truth, he told me, was that he confounded their notions of what a union boss was supposed to look like. Here was a labor leader in a lilac shirt who had gone to an Ivy League school, who wouldn't attack you just for making money, whom you could actually imagine having in your home. Audiences loved Stern because he didn't seem like a *worker*. He admitted to feeling patronized, even a little disgusted. But he needed these people. If you were going to build a movement among Democrats around the idea of creating a new social contract, then you had to enlist the guys who signed the checks.

"Let me try to frame the discussion this way," Stern told the partners on that first night in Austin. "Tomorrow morning, when you all come down to breakfast, someone is going to clean your room. Let's call her Maria. She's probably making seven dollars and ten cents an hour. She has no benefits. So if all the things you're doing don't help Maria, then it isn't worth anything." There were nods and murmurs of assent from all sides of the room.

People like Maria weren't going to get health care from their employers anymore, Stern said—those days were over. They weren't going to get lavish pensions or help with child care, either. Businesses in the ruthless, global marketplace had neither the resources nor the inclination to do what GM had done for its workers in an earlier era. Stern's essential point was that a progressive government would have to be more expansive—but also less wedded to the liberalism of that past. Yes, he was advocating a government that invested huge sums of money in national health care and child care and better public schools. But he was also saying that maybe that meant dismantling some entitlement programs, or experimenting with school choice, or overhauling the tax code. Simply blaming Republicans and big business for Maria's problems wasn't enough, and neither was a dogmatic adherence to old programs. You had to ask yourself what kind of liberal government you would create today, as if you were looking at an entirely different kind of society — which you were.

No single generation in American history had ever witnessed such immense societal and technological change, Stern said, speaking quickly and passionately, his shirtsleeves rolled up, hands slicing the air for emphasis. "You can't *stop* globalization," he said. "You can't stop trade. That debate is over. I like to say to people who want to return to the New Deal that we are now as far from the New Deal as the New Deal was from the Civil War. I don't think Franklin Roosevelt looked back to Lincoln to decide what to do. And I don't think we can look back to FDR."

He ended his talk by again raising the specter of Maria, who deserved a government that made sure she was paid a living wage, that her doctor's bills were covered, and that her kids could get a decent education. "That's the America she needs, and we have the ability to give it to her," Stern said with finality, and the ballroom erupted in shouts and cheers, the partners rising to their feet.

Next the program took a twenty-minute break so that each table could hold its own discussion on the twenty-first-century economy. I was at a table in the back, between my minder and a guy named Rob Johnson. Long-haired and long-faced, possessed of a healthy sense of wonder, Johnson had, at one point before the collapse of the Democratic era, served as chief economist to the Senate Banking Committee. He'd made his millions years ago working for George Soros, and now he lived in a stately Victorian along the shoreline in Greenwich, Connecticut. Although he dabbled in music management and had even run his own blues record label (one project with Ike Turner had been nominated for a Grammy), Johnson seemed to devote most of his time to chairing the alliance's powerful "strategy and investment committee," and he and I had exchanged long and thoughtful e-mails over some of the pieces I'd written on Democratic policy. He was the only donor I knew of who had joined the bloggers' "Townhouse" e-mail list. He was also vehemently anticorporate and as close to a practicing socialist as I had ever met.

Anne Bartley, the Rockefeller heiress, was our designated "table captain," so she led Johnson and several other donors sitting with us in a conversation about the panel we'd just heard. All anyone wanted to talk about was Maria. How could we help her? What were we going to do about Maria? I almost started humming strains from *West Side Story*. I wondered if they actually understood that Maria was a composite, or whether this whole discussion was going to end with their marching upstairs to find her, so they could hand her a couple of hundred-dollar bills.

Quickly, however, the conversation veered, almost imperceptibly, from how they could improve Maria's life to how they could secure Maria's vote. What message should the party have for Maria? How should its issues be framed? One partner suggested that Democrats needed to talk in "aspirational" language. Another said the party had to convince Maria that it cared about her standard of living. Finally, Rob Johnson interrupted. "We're not the smart people," he said. "We're just the people with money. We're the guys who write the checks. So the question is, how do we get rich people energized to have the camaraderie and the compassion to help Maria?" In other words, the best thing the wealthy partners could do for Maria was to find more wealthy partners. There was a certain logic to this, and the other partners nodded.

Our attention was then brought back to the stage, where Stern and his fellow panelists were now joined by representatives from three alliance-funded think tanks: the Center for American Progress, the Economic Policy Institute, and the Center on Budget and Policy Priorities. Their role was to talk about the agendas they were busy crafting that would catapult Democratic politics into the economic future that Stern had so chillingly described. Only they didn't. They spent the next forty minutes or so, one at a time, pillorying the

Republicans in Washington—how they had inflated the deficit and cut taxes for the rich and created more inequality. On and on they went in a bleak and endless recitation of conservative crimes against Maria. All of these allegations were true enough, and yet they were all well known and had nothing to do with the need for an alternative argument. Instead, the deep thinkers onstage made only vague and passing allusions to some better tax plan, to preserving Social Security and doing something about this darn health care problem.

From the back of the room, I could see Stern's chin slowly sink toward his chest. He folded his arms and stared straight ahead. He seemed to be suppressing the strong impulse to send his chair hurtling toward the banquet tables. "Look, we are all mispositioned in the twentieth century," he complained, waving an arm in exasperation toward the others onstage. He said he didn't think the inflexible government programs of the last era were the answer to the current crisis. "How we got to be the party of government, and not of small business, I just don't get," Stern said finally, almost as a non sequitur.

Oddly, the other panelists and the audience seemed not to notice that he was criticizing them. Instead, they went right on cheering him as if they couldn't have agreed more, as if he spoke for them. "You want a center-left agenda?" one of the panelists concluded triumphantly. "In my view, you've heard it here tonight." The donors clapped approvingly, as if glad to have finally cleared up that whole new-economy mess. I kept my eyes trained on Stern, who was staring at his shoes with his arms folded, as if wishing he were somewhere else.

Later, Stern would reflect on his frustration in Austin. The Democracy Alliance was supposed to have been about taking risks and debating the next generation of progressive ideas. "What we admired about the conservative movement wasn't just that they built a political machine—it was an ideas machine," Stern told me. "Where are all the ideas? For all the people like George Lakoff we heard about after the election, what has it gotten us? People just don't realize that we are living through the most fundamental economic change in our history. They don't want to think about it. I've lost faith that traditional politics will provide anything but incremental answers to problems, rather than fundamental answers."

Stern's own effort to forge a new economic agenda, similar in its approach to MoveOn's search for the "bold and positive agenda," had been an online contest called "Since Sliced Bread." The idea, molded by Stern's communications team and some tech guys from the Dean world, was to do something modeled after the reality show *American Idol*. Real, live Americans would submit their ideas, and the winner would get $100,000. A panel of distinguished thinkers—people like Bill Bradley, the onetime presidential candidate, and Carol Browner, the former head of the Environmental Protection Agency—would act as the Simon Cowells and Paula Abduls of economic policy, judging the entries and presenting the finalists for an online vote.

On some level, like the MoveOn experiment, it was pretty inspiring stuff. More than a hundred thousand people visited the Web site, which had its own blog, and more than about twelve thousand submitted ideas. From the perspective of the organizers, who mostly wanted to use the Web to engage voters in policy, the contest had been a huge success. They had turned the movement's future over to ordinary voters, and the voters had responded with admirable thoughtfulness, coming up with a few worthy, if general, proposals. (The winning idea, submitted by a forty-one-year-old environmental project manager in Seattle, proposed taxing polluters to pay for new sources of sustainable energy.)

Mostly, though, the entrants proffered the same kinds of ephereal notions that liberals had been talking about for twenty years at least: reforming public education, investing in public works

projects, and so on. Other, less lofty submissions ranged from building a new industry in "scratch-n-sniff clothing" to hundreds of vari-
ations on a simpler idea: "Fire George W. Bush." In the end, Stern
himself had to log on and try (unsuccessfully) to quell a small revolt
on the site after some devotees complained loudly that the finalists
chosen by the judges hadn't submitted anything that hadn't been
suggested by other Democrats and their candidates a thousand times
before.

The truth was that if the new progressives had anything in common with the party's Washington insiders, it was this: Both suffered
from a kind of bunker mentality when it came to thinking big or
differently about government. This was, in a way, the great tactical
victory of American conservatives. They had spent so much time
attacking the policy achievements of the New Deal and the Great
Society, and had done so with such devastating effectiveness, that
Democrats and their interest groups now thought themselves justi-
fied in devoting all their energy to trying to preserve the party's
legislative legacy, rather than to update or build on it. And those
Democrats who did aspire to something bolder were immediately
assaulted by a conservative response that tainted them as profligate,
McGovern-era liberals. How would you pay for it? Were you going
to *raise our taxes*? "We're so weak," Andy Stern told me, "that we
think that if we have a big idea, we're going to lose."

The result was that Democrats and their leading think tanks
practiced an entirely defensive kind of politics. When they talked
about new ideas, they were almost always talking about ways to
protect or modestly enlarge existing programs—extending Medicare
to cover more Americans, enlarging the Head Start rolls. Any
Democrat who dared to wonder if these programs were still optimal
under an entirely new set of economic conditions was immediately
accused of siding with conservatives and trying to destroy the social
safety net. You couldn't have a real debate about building a modern

retirement program that wasn't financed by a payroll tax that hurt wage earners and the self-employed but left big-time investors untouched; or about a portable, comprehensive health care plan that might replace Medicare and Medicaid; or about updating affirmative action to address economic disadvantage, rather than skin color. The working, if unspoken, assumption was that Democrats would never again be able to enact the kind of transformative solutions that had defined the twentieth century, and, therefore, even talking about the need to reimagine any of those programs was the same thing, effectively, as aiding those Republicans who wanted to dismantle them.

The only way to protect activist government from conservative marauders, Democrats believed, was to remain unified and obstinate in defense of an old agenda, whether or not it was the best possible agenda for the times. This was the theme that dominated discussions on the blogs and at MoveOn house parties, and inside the Democracy Alliance, too—how to present a united front, how to ensure that no one in the party strayed from decades-old orthodoxies, how to stave off cynical attempts at "reform." There may have been some political realism to this, but it came at a cost, which was that it deadened the party's intellectual impulses and it added to the perception that Democrats had nothing to say beyond opposing Republican reforms. The new Democratic mission was essentially to protect the old one.

A friend who does corporate consulting explained to me once that software designers often have to contend with something called "backward compatibility." Simply put, it means that each new software release has to incorporate the programming code from previous versions in order to be viable. In other words, Microsoft unveils a new operating system called Vista, which it hails as the great new innovation of the computer age, the successor to its ubiquitous Windows program. But in order for Vista to succeed, it has to be compatible with every program that already uses Windows. And, for that reason, Vista isn't really a fundamental innovation after all; it turns out to be

really just a fancier, more refined version of Windows. In order for
Microsoft to actually build an entirely new operating system, the
company would have to break with its Windows platform and start
all over again—something it simply can't afford to do.

Democrats in Washington were running up against the same
problem. They, too, felt bound to entertain only those ideas that were
backward compatible—that is, ideas that fit the same basic approach
to government that they and their interest groups had been perfect-
ing since the dawn of the industrial economy. Anything else was
bound to cause a revolt among their consumers, and it would have
led to the reasonable question of why they had clung so mightily to
that approach in the first place. There was also the issue of habit and
experience: Democrats of a certain generation simply couldn't envision anything other than the centralized, inflexible programs of the
assembly-line government. And so they proposed no end of modest
adjustments to old programs, a library full of complex plans that
were meant to sound like innovation but that, more often than not,
started with decades-old answers to distinctly modern questions. In
the face of this transformation Andy Stern kept talking about, the
argument at the core of the party—a relic of the New Deal—
remained largely untouched.

Ideally, the partners of the Democracy Alliance would have used
their vast fortunes to mitigate this problem. This was precisely
what the conservative donors they so admired had done. Joe Coors
and his fellow investors had recognized that there was no space in the
political dialogue of the 1970s for academics who wanted to challenge
the liberal status quo of either party, because anyone who advanced
controversial views couldn't get funding for their work. There was
certainly no constituency in either party for libertarian, antigovern-
ment ideas. So what these donors did was to find unconventional

policy thinkers and offer them a source of sustained funding. Those theorists who received grants didn't have to worry so much about whether their work offended the powers in the Republican Party, or even whether it contradicted what other conservative thinkers believed, because they had funders who relished the fight. In this way, the conservatives had insulated their brightest and least conventional thinkers from the vagaries of the political marketplace, and they had reaped a significant return.

Money from the Democracy Alliance, however, came with a very different message. Perhaps things would have been different had progressives just experienced an election like 1964, had they seen their nominee demolished at the polls the way Goldwater had been. But the way the Democratic donors looked at it, they had come torturously close to winning back everything, not once but twice, so they were in no frame of mind to push short-term, electoral considerations into the background. Their main goal was to rid the country of conservative majorities, preferably in the next election, and they were determined to unify the progressive opposition, not tear it apart with academic debates.

This probably explained why a major think tank like John Podesta's Center for American Progress styled itself primarily as a bridge between the party's factions, rather than as an ideological provocateur. In just a few years, Podesta had done a brilliant job of building a nerve center connecting Democratic Washington to the new progressive movement, with a staff of more than a hundred and one of the most widely trafficked blogs in America. In any given week, the think tank hosted a number of lunchtime discussions on critical subjects like military preparedness or outsourcing. And CAP had offered a few genuinely bold ideas, such as replacing the employee's part of the payroll tax with a progressive version of the flat tax, and compensating teachers for classroom successes—an approach that the powerful teachers' unions generally opposed.

For the most part, however, CAP had been careful to steer clear of challenging Democratic orthodoxy on the most important issues of the day. After all, the vast majority of CAP's funding came from the same three families—the Soroses, Lewises, and Sandlers—who provided some 40 percent of the alliance's funding. What would have happened had CAP floated a proposal to replace, say, Social Security or racial quotas with a more modern, progressive solution? Podesta's funders would have revolted. Little wonder, then, that CAP became more effective, at least in this early incarnation, as a daily war room than as an incubator for risky ideas.

A few months before the Austin conference, Andrei Cherny and Kenneth Baer, both former White House speechwriters, decided to launch a new publication, in print and online, called *Democracy: A Journal of Ideas.* Their vision was to create a serious forum where Democratic thinkers could propose new ways of looking at foreign and domestic policy without having to fit into one ideological camp or another. Early pieces included Karen Kornbluh, Barack Obama's policy chief, on a way to fundamentally rethink entitlement programs by focusing on the concept of "family insurance"; Jeff Faux, a left-wing economist, on the need to speed the process of globalization, rather than slow it down; and two Berkeley Ph.D. candidates, Naazneen Barma and Ely Ratner, on the counterintuitive idea that China's main threat to the United States was not economic or military but, in fact, moral and ideological.

Democracy was an endeavor that fit perfectly into Rob Stein's initial vision for the alliance. Among the most influential vehicles in the conservative movement had been small-circulation journals like *Public Interest* and *Commentary,* which operated outside the Republican mainstream and showcased some of the theories that would in time become the guiding intellectual tenets on the Right. This was, so to speak, a no-brainer for the fledgling progressive movement.

Cherny and Baer figured they needed about $500,000 to start—a fraction of what the partners had committed to David Brock's media-monitoring operation, and well less than they were about to give to a handful of groups, such as Sojourners and the Gamaliel Foundation, that were supposed to help progressives appeal to religious voters. The service employees contributed some seed money to the journal, and Andy Stern himself took a seat on *Democracy*'s advisory board. Gara LaMarche, who ran George Soros's Open Society Institute and represented him to the Democracy Alliance, came up with $50,000. But when Cherny and Baer traveled the country to meet with other alliance partners, they found only a few who were willing to write even a small check.

One of the founding partners of the alliance bristled when Cherny suggested that they hadn't really invested in intellectual innovation. "No, that's not true," he said triumphantly. "We've put money into Air America!" (Not only was this an odd way to define big ideas, but it was also untrue. A group of alliance partners promised to invest in Air America, but the deal repeatedly fell through. Eventually the network was forced to declare bankruptcy.) In the end, the Democracy Alliance sent Cherny and Baer a check for $25,000—less than what the alliance probably spent on all the limousines and logos in Austin.

McKinsey & Company is known in the business world for its unique and brainy culture. The firm, which says its clients include two-thirds of the Fortune 1,000, prides itself on recruiting the brightest and most eager young thinkers in the country; in any given year, it might hire more Harvard Law School graduates than most elite law firms. Its consultants traffic in numbingly esoteric and abstract techniques, the effectiveness of which is debatable. Writing in *The New Yorker* in 2002, Malcolm Gladwell noted that McKinsey had exalted one of its most prized clients as a prime example of its talent-driven philosophy: Enron, which later became synonymous with fraud and corporate malfeasance.

Judy Wade spent sixteen years immersed in this world, and, almost immediately, she set out to McKinsey-ize the Democracy Alliance. She sensed, accurately, that the partners had no cohesive notion of what they actually believed or what they were trying to accomplish, aside from beating back Republicans. And so she provided to the partners a thick set of charts and diagrams titled "Framework for Developing Our Strategy," which laid out the three essential theories that the alliance needed to quickly develop: a theory of victory (what the alliance was trying to achieve), a theory of change (the critical elements in achieving the theory of victory), and a theory of action (what the alliance could do to cause the theory of change to occur). These diagrams included lots of circles and squares and squiggly shapes that resembled porcupines, arrows going this way and that, input boxes and output boxes, and a picture that was supposed to represent "transformation," which looked a lot like a ray of light going through a hubcap. Wade established yet another new committee to tackle these questions and report back.

The partners on the committee tried gamely to wrestle with these abstractions, as some of them had with the original vision statement for the Democracy Alliance, but their deliberations again illuminated the philosophical confusion at the core of what they were doing. "I believe voters are looking for deep convictions," wrote Jonathan Heller, one of the partners on the committee, in one e-mail exchange. "What are ours? Once we know them, we can frame them for voters." In the same chain of e-mails, Charles Rodgers, who ran a family foundation in Boston, added earnestly: "What are our values and beliefs?. . . Do we have a progressive counterpart to the conservatives' *The Road to Serfdom* by Hayek? What is the responsibility of government versus the individual in assuring economic prosperity?

What do market forces regulate well and where is government intervention needed? Who are the thinkers that best articulate a vision of a progressive country, who have a point of view on the role of the individual versus the community? The list goes on. . . ."

Most of the partners, however, considered it a waste of time to delve into such deep questions. What seemed destined to be another close election was now fast approaching, and all they could think about was funding any group that seemed to have a strategy to deliver the House and Senate. When he had first established the alliance, Rob Stein had made the case for large, multi-year grants to political entrepreneurs who were trying to work outside the party establishment. Now that vision crumbled, replaced by an explosion of smaller, single-year grants to many of the same well-funded groups that had been part of the party's election machine for decades. In Austin, the Alliance partners doled out grants to eighteen more groups, including several that had complained about being ignored during the first round of funding: Emily's List, the Sierra Club, People for the American Way, and ACORN. (Simon Rosenberg's advocates managed to finally get NDN back on the list as well.)

Gone were all those onerous, time-consuming requirements for due diligence that the partners had preached before. About the only groups that didn't get money in Austin were those few that dared to buck liberal orthodoxy or which didn't follow the prescribed talking points in Democratic Washington. Several partners, for instance, tried to get funding for Third Way, a new centrist group that was working closely with congressional Democrats. Third Way had challenged the party to reevaluate its stances on social issues and to embrace free trade, and it had stood with Hillary Clinton, among others, to call for an increase of a hundred thousand American troops to fight terrorism. Third Way's funding request was torpedoed by another contingent of alliance partners, led by Guy Saperstein. The alliance, these partners said, didn't have room for self-described centrists whose main goal was to appease Republicans.

Wade tried to impose some order on this chaotic process. Just before the Austin conference, she decided to delay the next round of funding until the alliance could sort out its larger mission, but the partners overruled her and tossed aside her flow charts. They didn't like her personal style, which could be needlessly undiplomatic. They also didn't like the way she harped obsessively on her time in South Africa; some partners in Austin actually turned it into a drinking game, sipping their wine whenever she mentioned the country. The crux of the conflict, though, was really control. To the partners, Wade was hired staff, like a financial adviser or a political aide, and they didn't take orders from staff. The alliance was their vehicle to personally change Democratic politics, and no one was going to tell them how to spend their millions—not even a brilliant McKinsey consultant.

By the time the partners met in Austin, it seemed clear that one side or the other—either Wade or the partners who opposed her— would ultimately have to prevail before the alliance could shake free of its bureaucratic paralysis. The constant infighting had already disillusioned most of the founding partners from New York, who skipped the Austin meeting and seemed on the verge of quitting altogether. The embattled Steven Gluckstern, who had tried in the months leading up to the Austin meeting to act as a bridge between Wade and the board, had essentially given up and detached himself from the day-to-day drama. He announced in a letter to the partners in Austin that he had decided not to seek another term on the board, ending his stormy chairmanship.

Rob Stein, meanwhile, in his now-diminished role, pleaded with the board members to adopt a plan that would temporarily freeze the number of groups in the portfolio so they could take some time to figure out their longer-term strategy. Rob urgently warned them, coming out of Austin, that if they didn't stop fighting over who was going to control the Democracy Alliance, there soon wouldn't be anything left to fight over.

O n Friday night, the second night of the conference in Austin, the alliance partners boarded two coach buses and headed to the nearby state history museum for a party hosted by Fred Baron, the Texas trial lawyer. On the ride over, the staff handed out margaritas as both buses buzzed with an intriguing rumor, which was soon confirmed. Wade had been saying that a "mystery guest" would be appearing at the conference Saturday morning, and now the partners heard that the mystery guest was none other than Bill Clinton himself, who was in town to address the University of Texas's graduating seniors. When the Democracy Alliance had first invited him, Clinton had responded by asking for a sizable contribution, in the hundreds of thousands of dollars, to his global initiative to fight AIDS. In his postpresidential life, Clinton rarely spoke to such a large audience for free. The Democracy Alliance, a collaborative of some of the wealthiest progressives on the planet, had declined to give. Even so, at the last minute, the former president had decided to drop by, probably out of loyalty to old friends like the Buells and Bartley. It was a decision he would soon have reason to regret.

Most of the partners seemed to greet the news of Clinton's appearance as validation of their place in the political universe, even if their views of Clinton himself were somewhat varied. Some partners counted Clinton as a personal friend. Others had never met the man, and while they admired his celebrity, they disdained his third-way, middle-of-the-road politics, which they blamed for two presidential defeats and, most tragically, for the decision Democrats had made to support the war. The way the ideological donors saw it, senators who voted for the Iraq war resolution—including, significantly, Hillary Clinton herself—had done so not for principled reasons, but because they felt compelled to demonstrate their strength and patriotism and because they were more in thrall to centrist voters and corporate donors than they were to their own ideals. They were, as Howard Dean had put it, afraid to act like Democrats—and this fear was the heavy, lingering cost of the Clintonian argument.

And yet I had been amazed to find, during my hundreds of conversations with the new progressive donors, that almost all of them had somehow managed to draw a distinction between what they saw as the evils of Clintonism and the man himself. Maybe this was because he was the most glamorous figure in Democratic politics since Robert Kennedy. Maybe it was because he had been so thoroughly and viciously pilloried by the conservative machine, which made him, in a strange way, a victim. Whatever the reason, for all their contempt for what the politics of the '90s had wrought, the progressive outsiders never directly challenged the man who had invented it. The former president had remained, at least until now, a figure beyond public reproach. And Clinton, in turn, had never betrayed any sense that he felt personally assailed by the movement.

Clinton got an enthusiastic ovation when he entered the ballroom. He arrived ten minutes late, in a suit and tie, looking rested and exuding that Hollywood aura. He delivered a standard, twenty-minute stump speech on globalization and technology, an easy lob for a notorious night owl asked to speak on a Saturday morning. He mentioned, as he always did now, his anger at the Republican tax cuts, which, if repealed, would yield $700 billion back to the treasury. "That's a lot of money, even to a roomful of people like you," Clinton added, eliciting laughs. Somewhere in there, he mentioned the Iraq war. The question now, Clinton said, wasn't whether individual Democrats had been right or wrong to vote for the war resolution, but what they were going to do about it going forward, now that the occupation of Iraq seemed headed toward unmitigated disaster. This was the issue that mattered.

When he finished, Clinton sat down in a leather wingback chair onstage and fielded questions from the audience. He talked about the youth vote. He answered a softball about global warming, which he said was the single greatest issue of our time. He waxed eloquent on the importance of faith in politics. As he spoke, a few of the partners furtively exchanged skeptical glances or even whispered remarks, but they remained typically respectful.

Guy Saperstein was seated at one of the front tables, stewing. Before his retirement twelve years earlier, Saperstein had been a legendary civil rights lawyer, building the largest and most lucrative civil law practice in history. He was also a classic antiwar liberal of his era, a veteran of the unrest at Berkeley, who retained an intense interest in foreign policy and was an ardent critic of the Iraq war. (He had even commissioned his own private poll on homeland security, which he then disseminated, with a strategy memo, to the party's congressional leaders.) Saperstein headed the alliance's foreign policy committee, and he was incensed by Clinton's comments about Iraq. Like a lot of the progressive donors, he believed that the outcome in Iraq had been, in fact, entirely foreseeable, and that the Democratic acquiescence in it had been a classically Clintonian act of craven moderation. How could Clinton say that how you voted on the war didn't matter? Did he really believe he could excuse his wife's vote so blithely? Did he suppose no one would notice?

The same issue had arisen the day before, during a roundtable of foreign policy experts, when a group of partners had lectured the panelists on the ways in which Washington Democrats should have apologized for leading the nation into war. Now Saperstein rose and challenged Clinton directly. He pointed out that John Edwards, Kerry's running mate and a certain candidate for president in 2008, had already apologized for his vote on Iraq. Why shouldn't every Democrat who had voted for the war—including, presumably, Hillary Clinton—do the same thing? How were Democrats supposed to have any credibility if they wouldn't admit when they had been so calamitously wrong?

Clinton's face reddened. He leaned forward belligerently and pointed a finger at Saperstein. "You're just wrong," he said. "Everything you just said is totally wrong. Wrong, wrong, wrong." While the donors sat, stunned by his tone, Clinton then went on to explain why the vote on Iraq had not, in fact, been a vote for war. It had been a vote to authorize the president to use the threat of force—as a means, in fact, of avoiding war. Bush had said that such a vote was the only way to get the weapons inspectors back into Iraq, thus defusing the confrontation. This was a fair point—Hillary Clinton had, in fact, said this very thing when she cast her vote back in 2002—but her husband wasn't finished. Just as he appeared to be winding down his argument, Clinton's voice started to rise again, and he turned remarkably personal.

"Look, if that vote was a mistake, then it's a mistake I would have made," he said. "But you're just wrong." He stared directly at Saperstein and lost any semblance of restraint. "This is not productive! You're asking people to flagellate themselves! What you do tomorrow is all that matters. Only in this party do we eat our own. You can go on misrepresenting and bashing our own people, but I am sick and tired of it. Stop looking back and finger pointing, and ask what we should do now.

"Let's get real here," Clinton went on. "Go ahead and give Edwards a gold star because his mea culpa is better than Hillary's. Do it," he said, "and lose."

The ballroom was dead silent. No one said a word. Spent from his tirade, Clinton tried to lighten the mood. "As you can tell, I don't have any strong feelings about this," he said. The partners exhaled again and laughed. No one applauded, however. A sense of hurt and fury lingered on both sides of the room.

Clinton tried to move on to other subjects, but now something in him had been triggered, and he couldn't easily turn it off. A latent resentment had surfaced. He started railing against articles he had been reading about his larger effect on Democratic politics. One piece he brought up, with no prompting, had been written by the writer Michael Barone, who had recently posited that Clintonism had its philosophical roots in the Reagan revolution. "The only people who agree with the Right on that," Clinton scoffed bitterly, "is the far Left of the Democratic Party." There was more uneasy laughter. The far Left he was talking about, after all, was sitting in front of him.

Clinton drew another loud ovation when he stepped off the stage and departed for his next engagement, but everyone in the room was aware that they had just witnessed an extraordinary moment in Democratic politics—an open clash between the party establishment's most exalted figure and the resentful builders of its new progressive movement. Clinton, apparently, understood this too, and immediately tried to minimize the damage. Even before he stepped onstage for his commencement speech across town, he sent an aide back to the resort with a message for Saperstein. Clinton, the aide said, wanted him to relay a heartfelt apology. The former president wasn't really a morning guy, and he had awoken with a headache, and he felt badly for losing his temper. He wanted to set things right.

What Saperstein did with this apology was as significant a statement as anything he had said in the ballroom. Back home in Oakland, he sat down and wrote a long, lecturing letter to Clinton about the inadequacy of his answer on Iraq, pointing out that 148 Democrats in Congress had been prescient and courageous enough to vote against the war. Then he released the letter, which included a reference to Clinton's private apology, to Chris Cillizza, a reporter at the *Washington Post*'s Web site. It was hard to see this as anything other than a deliberate attempt to publicly embarrass the two-term president.

For their part, the other partners of the Democracy Alliance, with the exception of the few who were close Clinton allies, left Austin with a sour feeling about the Democratic first family. Who was Bill Clinton to point fingers and yell at the people who had helped him and his wife get elected? Was that his strategy for 2008— to run around berating Hillary's detractors until they realized the error of their ways? If that was his plan, they grumbled, then she didn't stand a chance. After all, the exchange between Saperstein and Clinton, while nominally about the war, had really been about something much broader. It had been about Clintonism itself and the centrist governing ethos that had led the party to this place in its history. In his comments about the war, Saperstein had only implied what a lot of liberals had long believed—that it had been Clinton's desire to remake the Democratic Party, his insidious argument about modernizing industrial-age government to better serve the middle class, that had stripped the party of its moral authority, and that had, in the end, brought the country itself to the edge of ruin.

CHAPTER TEN

"They're Not Right About That"

Like the citizen-warriors of Rome, American presidents usually retire to idyllic retreats—ranches or farms where flags ripple in the wind and Labradors run free, and where the occasional visitor can sip lemonade on a shaded porch. Bill Clinton, on the other hand, who was just fifty-four when he left the White House, rented a suite of offices in a dreary federal building on 125th Street in Harlem, a few blocks from the legendary Apollo Theater. In a sense, Clinton was taking refuge in what had become the closest thing he had to a political home. He had been, beyond doubt, America's most racially comfortable president, and the resilience he had shown in the face of his enemies' attacks, along with his own emotional frailty, had engendered, in many African Americans, an enduring empathy for the man. In setting up shop in Harlem, a neighborhood he had, as president, designated as a federal empowerment zone, Clinton was also making a statement about the way he viewed his place in history. Let the cynics say that he wasn't liberal enough, that he had abandoned the poor for the favor of Wall Street. Here, on 125th Street, where new chain stores seemed to be popping up every week, was the proof that they were wrong, and it was from here that Clinton planned to continue the fight for economic justice around the world.

When I visited Clinton in Harlem, not long after his performance in Austin, I was surprised by how little appeared to have been done to make the place suitably august. Vagrants loitered outside the main entrance, not far from vendors hawking incense. The elevators looked like they hadn't been touched since the 1970s, and the carpets in Clinton's suite were of the cheap, office-supply variety. Clinton appeared to have taken his own urban legend to heart. About the only obvious sign of presidential power was the hulking Secret Service agents who took up posts near the reception desk, looking bored.

Clinton's meltdown at the Democracy Alliance meeting suggested not only that he understood the current of anti-Clintonism that ran through the new progressive movement, but that he had also spent a fair amount of time privately fuming about it. It also made me think that he understood the threat this new movement could pose— not just to his own legacy and the party he had tried to build, but also to Hillary Clinton's chances of winning the Democratic nomination for president in 2008. I wondered if the greatest politician of his age had a strategy for neutralizing the threat.

I got my answer as soon as I walked through the door. In a glass-walled conference room, I could see Clinton sitting around the table with about twenty men and women, many of whom I recognized instantly. It was a group of some of the most outspoken liberal bloggers, who had been invited here to meet the former president as a group for the first time. Markos and Jerome, who considered themselves above such group events, hadn't shown, but Duncan Black, better known as "Atrios," was there, as were the two main guys from MyDD and the two women who blogged over at the venomous Firedoglake. Some of the bloggers wore suits or sport coats with ties, but many had showed up to meet the former president in open collars and outdoor jackets, as if to underscore their disrespect for everything that was Inside—the presidency included.

This was the first time that most, if not all, of the bloggers in the room had been in Clinton's awesome presence, and while I couldn't make out what was being said in the room from my seat in the reception area, it was clear that Clinton was, as usual, having his way. He wore his customary suit and tie, his thick hair now an icy white, his blue eyes sparkling as they moved like soft stage lights from one rapt listener to the next. It was the arms that always fascinated me about Clinton up close—their span and sweep, the way they spread out and then retracted as he talked, so that one moment he stretched his palms several feet apart to demonstrate his wonder or amazement, and the next he brought them to his chest in a heartfelt gesture of togetherness. The bloggers' eyes rarely left him, even as they chewed on the barbecued chicken and mashed potatoes provided by Clinton's staff. You could see what they were thinking. *We have arrived*.

When it was over, Clinton rose quickly, as if adjourning the Joint Chiefs in the Situation Room, and the bloggers—these people who mercilessly assailed his wife, who pilloried as immoral the Democratic Leadership Council he had helped to found, and who loudly renounced his third-way mantra—ran to have their picture taken with him. They lined up as in a class photo, giggling at jokes and trying to look properly regal for the camera. Then they got their own shots, one at a time, with Clinton's aides pitching in as photographers. A few weeks from now, I knew, they would go to their mailboxes, excitedly rip open the package with the New York address, run to the frame shop, and proudly hang this photo, with its handwritten personal message—"To [blogger name here], with best wishes, Bill Clinton"—somewhere near the desks where they worked.

When at last it was my turn to enter Clinton's inner office, two hours behind schedule, he was standing with his back to me, straightening and rearranging photographs on his bookshelf. It was a habit he had fallen into, as if, in his twilight years, Clinton felt compelled to constantly reshuffle the moments of his life, searching endlessly for the best combination. We sat down around a glass table in his office, but his mind was still back in the conference room. "I really read these blogs," Clinton told me, leaning forward in his chair, which, if true, certainly explained the frustration that had surfaced in Austin. I tried to imagine him sitting in front of his computer late at night, munching on pizza and swearing to himself over some fresh indignity inflicted by someone like Georgia10 or Skippy the Bush Kangaroo. No wonder the man had needed open-heart surgery.

Clinton said that he and the bloggers had agreed on most things, and he had thanked them for defending him during a recent flap over a made-for-TV movie, aired by ABC, that had depicted his administration as weak on terrorists. But he recounted how he had also tried to give the bloggers a short lesson in recent Democratic history. "You know, they had this big resentment toward the DLC," he said. "I said, 'Let me remind you about the DLC. They fought the NRA. They supported the gay rights moves I made. They supported the pro-choice moves I made, including on partial birth abortions. They supported increasing taxes on the wealthy people and cutting them on the working poor.' So we talked about that."

Most of their conversation, though, seemed to have centered on Iraq. Clinton was still trying to convince Hillary's critics in the movement that voting for the war resolution hadn't been a shallow political calculation. "I said, 'I just think that your emphasis on this in this election ought to be on what the differences are with the Republicans and what we do in Iraq, not whether you were for it or against it,'" he said. "'And we shouldn't allow the party to be defined by differences over Iraq, which is a lot of what the party has been fighting about.'"

This was the same ill-fated argument Clinton had made to Guy Saperstein, except that now, after sitting for an hour and a half with the bloggers, his tone was wearier than it was angry. After all, on some basic level, Clinton had been waging this same fight inside the party since the 1980s—a fight against the litmus tests of a party that had become reflexively suspicious of the military and the wealthy. It must have occurred to Clinton, when he was reading those blogs, that these new progressives, these baby boomers who voted for Dean and joined MoveOn.org, were the same people who had opposed his New Democratic ethos in the first place. It was, in some ways, as if the Clinton presidency had never happened.

Bill Clinton had been the first president of postindustrial America, and, more than any Democrat since FDR, he had tried to modernize the party's argument about government. The governing approach of the New Deal and the Great Society, Clinton had argued, had achieved great things, but it was inadequate to the challenges of the information economy, as the era of endless American prosperity was going the way of the textile mills and coal yards. The new world required something different: not the perpetuation of sprawling Democratic government, nor the Republican vision of a docile federal bureaucracy, but a third way—a way that would retool the welfare state without actually dismantling it.

In office, he had realized a few important, if narrow, victories in keeping with this argument. He had given troubled industrial cities the money they needed to reinvent themselves, overhauled the stagnant welfare system, and pushed the country into a new era of free trade. But the cumulative effect of, first, his failed effort to reform health care, followed by the Republican storm of 1994, and finally the sex scandal that nearly drove him from office, had been to transform his presidency from a moment of generational promise to an act of survival. Clinton never got around to restructuring other entitlements or ending employer-based health care; instead, he ended up "triangulating" on more immediate issues, co-opting Republican language and ideas in order to stave off a conservative Congress.

Ultimately, it was this shallower rhetorical legacy, and not the substantive argument, that Washington Democrats had seemed to absorb from Clinton. He had set out to persuade the leaders of his own party that they had to think differently, but all they heard, really, was that they needed to *speak* differently, so they could sound more like conservatives. Clinton's third way became little more than a way of talking, a language of stock, poll-tested phrases to describe those "working families" of the "forgotten middle class" who "worked hard and played by the rules." Coming from Clinton, who had an actual vision, these things had sounded argumentative. Coming from all the lesser Democrats who now imitated his every word and gesture, they sounded like surrender.

Now, sitting in his office, Clinton bristled at the popular notion that his philosophy had always been about tactics and compromise. "It wasn't tactical," he told me. "I always thought the policies should be gotten right, and then if we got the policies right, then we could work to get the politics right, to learn how to talk about it. But I do think there was a tendency to see me as a liberal in moderate clothing and all that kind of stuff. And that just wasn't right."

I asked him why he thought he had been interpreted this way.

"We didn't talk enough and do enough with our own political people—the members of Congress, their staffs, the liberal interest groups, the party apparatus—about why these ideas were important and how they were working," he said. He ticked off a list of bona fide liberal accomplishments: the first rise in real wages since 1973; the biggest land protection measure in the lower forty-eight states since Teddy Roosevelt; taking on the National Rifle Association and the tobacco lobby. This was obviously a well-rehearsed litany, and it seemed likely that Clinton had made this same argument many times—if not to reporters (he rarely granted interviews these days, for fear of upstaging his wife), then maybe to himself. Most of us would readily swap our own insecurities for those of a man who has ruled the free world, and yet it could not have been easy to live with Clinton's anxiety about his own legacy, to wonder if historians of the future, like the bloggers of the present, might dismiss the pinnacle of your life's work as one big nod to political expedience.

"So I don't buy that," Clinton was saying now. "I think that if 'progressive' is defined by results, whether it's in health care, education, incomes, the environment, or the advancement of peace, then we had a very progressive administration. I think that we changed the methods—that we tried also to reflect basic American values, that we tried to do it in a way that appealed to the broad middle class in America. We sure did, and I don't apologize for that. The question is: Were the policies right or not? And I think in terms of the political success I enjoyed, people have given more credit to my political skills than they deserve, and less credit to the weight, the body of the ideas." In fact, Clinton said, many Democrats "thought I was like Michael Jordan and had a four-foot vertical jump." They believed, in other words, that Clinton owed his success to his preternatural charisma, rather than to any prescient vision for the country.

"I think it's very important to the Democrats, at least in their own interest, to spend more than half their time saying what they're for," Clinton told me. "Because I think there is a majority in America now that has reached a judgment that the current approach is not quite right. It's too unilateralist. It's too broad. It has a lot of hubris in it, and it's unfair at home and often ineffective. But they want to know what we're for."

I mentioned that I now heard a lot of skepticism in Washington and online about the power of ideas in politics. Most of the new progressives seemed to think that winning elections was more about machinery and political dexterity. Clinton had been listening with his head down, but, when I said this, his chin jolted upright and he thrust his hands out in front of him.

"Well, first of all, they're not right about that," he said forcefully. "I just think that ideas matter. We still have to be the party of ideas, because otherwise there's no reason to buy us. There's no reason to hire us if we're not going to do anything." He leaned back thoughtfully.

"If I were a young person running for president now," he said, "and I'm telling you this because I have nothing to do with it, although you won't believe it, I would do what Hillary is now doing. Hillary gave a major speech on energy policy. She went to Detroit and gave a major substantive speech on economic policy.

"I would be thinking like I did when I was governor in the eighties," he said. "I would be thinking about every really great challenge I would have to face, and I would force myself to go give a talk on it, so I would have to think it through and come to conclusions. So that if I did ever decide to run for president, I wouldn't have to wake up in the morning and wonder what I was going to believe. And if I did, by accident, get elected, I would not have to wake up in the morning wondering what I was going to do."

Near the end of our hour-long conversation, Clinton talked explicitly about his political legacy. "Teddy Roosevelt was an extraordinary figure who governed at an extraordinary time, and even he saw his legacy rejected until much later," Clinton said. "And I can say, OK, Teddy Roosevelt was a great president, because he was right. And in the long run he was vindicated." Clinton was talking about the judgment of history, but he might just as well have been talking about his place in his own party, which seemed on the verge of being overrun by hostile outsiders.

I rose to leave, and Clinton walked me to the door. I told him that I had been all of twenty-three when he first ran for president, and that, to me, he had been the first politician to talk compellingly about the changed America of the twenty-first century. It was true, and after his long lunch with the bloggers, I had the sense he might appreciate hearing it.

Clinton thanked me and asked if I remembered a specific quote from Machiavelli's *The Prince*. "He says that there's nothing in the world harder than making change," Clinton said. "A lot of people use that part of the quote, but they don't go on from there, and they miss the most important part."

When I got back to Washington, I pulled down my little paperback copy of *The Prince* and found the quote. This is what it said:

It must be considered that there is nothing more difficult to carry out, nor more doubtful of success, nor more dangerous to handle, than to initiate a new order of things. For the reformer has enemies in all those who profit by the old order, and only lukewarm defenders in all those who would profit by the new order, this lukewarmness arriving partly from fear of their adversaries, who have the laws in their favor; and partly from the incredulity of mankind, who do not truly believe in anything new until they have had an actual experience of it. Thus it arises that on every opportunity for attacking the reformer, his opponents do so with the zeal of partisans, the others only defend him half-heartedly, so that between them he runs great danger.

CHAPTER ELEVEN

Into the Abyss

The modern Las Vegas is a shiny, buffed, and polished theme park, the corporate entertainment headquarters for the American nouveau riche. The Riviera Hotel isn't that Las Vegas. The Riv—which was celebrating its fiftieth anniversary in 2006—is the Las Vegas of *The Godfather,* a shabby, sprawling monument to the days when a guy caught trying to cheat the house might have been taken out back and acquainted with a pipe. The saggy-eyed cocktail waitresses at the Riviera are Vegas veterans serving up their last rounds. The customers are largely chain-smoking older women who sit at the slots with tall plastic cups full of change. On the first floor of the swank new Wynn hotel, they sell Italian sports cars; at the Riviera, there's an old coin dealer and a magic shop. Over at the MGM Grand, Cirque du Soleil plays in its own theater; the Riviera's Le Bistro Lounge boasts the best Neil Diamond impersonator in town.

Rooms at the Riv, however, can be had, under the right circumstances, for something like a hundred bucks a night, which is why the bloggers and diarists on Daily Kos selected it for their first-ever annual convention, dubbed "YearlyKos." When I arrived for the opening proceedings on a Thursday in July, I followed the hotel's endless red carpet toward the convention hall. Along the way, I bumped into Markos, who gave me a hug. At the Quiznos in the food court, I found myself reunited with SusanG's son, Jackson, who had made us sandwiches that night months earlier in Santa Barbara.

I was looking for a woman named Gina Cooper—a task made difficult by the fact that I had no idea what she looked like, and neither did most of the other people there. I had first encountered Gina online several months earlier, when a random Google search sent me to the YearlyKos Web page. Back then, virtually no one outside the core Kos community had heard of the convention, so I sent an e-mail to the generic YearlyKos address, asking if maybe they would let me attend. I got an e-mail back from Gina, who had never communicated with a representative of the mainstream media before. She wrote back to me with the caution one might exercise when striking up a correspondence with a murderer at the state penitentiary. Gina said I was more than welcome and asked me for some advice about how to alert other reporters to the existence of the convention, and soon we were exchanging a flurry of candid e-mails about bloggers, the media, and life in general. Gina guided me through the evolving customs and culture of the blogosphere, while trying, at the same time, to draw out what I knew about the imposing world of Washington insiders.

Gina was a thirty-six-year-old Tennessean, and she knew something about what politicians liked to call "real people." Her mom, who had worked as a bartender and then as a clerk at the 7-Eleven, had died of lung cancer when Gina was only ten. Gina had never known her father's identity. She had been raised as a Southern Republican by her sister, who was thirteen years older, and who firmly believed that all politics—let alone blogging—was a waste of time. Gina had been married, divorced, and married again, and for more than a decade she had derived most of her sense of purpose in life from her job as a high school science teacher in Memphis. After the terrorist attacks of September 11, though, and during the subsequent run-up to the invasion of Iraq, another pastime had begun to creep into Gina's little world. She had discovered Daily Kos, and during lunch at school, or in her free time after the students left for the day, she would pore over the latest posts. These were people, she thought, who felt outraged and overlooked, who wanted some control over their world, who wanted to be heard. Gina wanted to be heard, too.

The minutes she spent on Daily Kos turned into hours, and in January 2004, Gina found the courage, sitting at home one night, to post her first diary, under the simple name "Gina." She was furious about a post from a Bay Area Kossack named WalterB, who suggested that Democrats should just abandon the South, because it was full of unsophisticated racists. It turned out that Gina was a sharp and devastating writer. "Is this what I have to look forward to?" she wrote, noting that she and her husband, Rob, who had just taken a buyout at FedEx, were about to pack up their things and move to the California wine country. "You Northern California culture snobs can kiss my Dixie ass. You have the 9th largest economy in the world while your inner cities are in shambles. The middle class can't afford to live there and your poor can't afford to move. . . . Incidentally, the last time I heard the n-word was at a Christmas party in the Bay Area." Markos himself commented favorably on her post. For the first time in her life, Gina felt important in the world, like she had something political to say, and other people were listening.

A few days after the 2004 election, some Kossacks started posting about the idea of a convention. They knew each other only as pseudonyms on the screen, disembodied voices in a virtual salon, so it was only natural that they would want to create an actual community, a way to fulfill the more tactile yearnings that human beings have. Of the three bloggers who volunteered to help organize the thing, though, only Gina, who hadn't gone back to teaching after the move to California and had plenty of discretionary time, stuck with it. She found herself incorporating the business, booking the venue, hiring lawyers and, of course, raising the money. Markos didn't want to get too involved in the convention, but he agreed to let her borrow his brand—or "he didn't say no," as Gina put it—and he hit up Andy and Deborah Rappaport for $25,000 in seed money. MoveOn.org gave twenty-five grand, too. Gina herself was making nothing.

By the spring of 2006, more than a thousand bloggers had paid the attendance fee for YearlyKos. Gina, meanwhile, found herself fending off the same series of attacks that befell virtually anyone who tried to organize a conference in Democratic politics. Women's groups were angry because there wasn't a panel discussion on abortion. Black bloggers complained that their elected leaders were underrepresented. Southerners raged that a panel on the South had been packed with Northerners. Gina tried to accommodate them all as best she could. The allegations of racism made her finally break down and cry as she sat in front of the laptop in her living room.

In the weeks leading up to the convention, Gina told me, she was answering about 150 e-mails a day, on everything from the size of the program to the wiring of the convention hall for wireless routers. "People see me now for more than what I am," she said, with a mixture of pride and self-doubt. She said she wanted people from outside the blog world to come to YearlyKos, too, so they could see what the blogs were really about. ("It's not a bunch of Cheeto-fingered, pajama-clad people banging away on their computers," Gina had assured me.) But she worried that none of the Democratic or media insiders would come.

"Oh, I wouldn't worry," I told her. "I think they'll come."

In fact, YearlyKos had become the political event of the year. Harry Reid and Howard Dean were planning to attend, along with a bevy of presidential hopefuls. The national media—more than 120

reporters in all—had descended on the Riviera like the stifling cloud
of smoke that hovered over the blackjack tables. On the first day of
the convention, there were a bunch of small sessions, the most interesting of which was a training session for bloggers who wanted to
become television pundits, conducted by an operative from the
Center for American Progress. Unfortunately, the session, which
attracted about eight would-be pundits, was overwhelmed by a
dozen big-time political reporters, including Maureen Dowd, the
New York Times columnist, and her assistant. The aspiring talking
heads could hardly get any room to practice amid the throng of actual
talking heads packed into the room. Here at the Riviera, in the
ballroom next to the national billiard championship, two insular,
mutually contemptuous tribes—the twentieth-century media establishment and the new century's citizen bloggers—were about to
collide.

I didn't manage to get a glimpse of Gina until she came
onstage that night, wearing a black pant suit and an orange top,
the video screen overhead beaming her out to the far reaches of
the hall. She had shoulder-length chestnut hair, round cheeks,
and bright brown eyes; she looked like the kind of woman who
would think nothing of climbing a chain-link fence in heels. I
knew she was nervous as hell, having never given a speech like
this before, but as she looked out at the bank of cameras and, beyond
that, the skybox where Air America had unfurled a huge banner,
she was remarkably poised. She gave a short welcoming speech
with lots of smiles and "y'alls," and when she was finished, the
bloggers seated closest to the stage started to chant: "Gina! Gina!
Gina!" The assembled reporters had no idea who Gina was and
seemed generally bored by all this, but for Gina, I knew, it was a
defining moment. I could see her tremble slightly as she acknowledged the crowd.

The night's main event, however, came next. Markos, who had been walking around the Riviera with his very own media coach, burst onto the stage in a black sport jacket and T-shirt, shading his eyes as he peered out at his minions, who were wildly applauding. Word was already buzzing through the convention that, on Sunday, Markos would become the first blogger ever to appear on *Meet the Press*. He strutted past the lectern, nodding toward each corner of the room, before quieting the crowd.

"Hello, my name is Markos," he said at last. "I started a Web site called Daily Kos. Perhaps you've heard of it."

The speech was a declaration of victory, delivered both to the bloggers who idolized him and to the reporters who were now being forced to take down his every word. "There are so many people in the political and media elite who have tried to marginalize us because we dared to be passionate about politics," Markos said. He proclaimed that the bloggers were turning the political universe upside down, and, as proof, he cited a new poll just released in Connecticut. Ned Lamont, the Web-powered political novice I had met at Norman Lear's house with Markos and Jerome, had gained 20 points in the last month against Joe Lieberman. Lamont now trailed by just 15 points among primary voters. "Joe Lieberman's gonna lose this one," Markos boldly predicted, and the hall erupted in cheers.

"The media elite have failed us," Markos said. "The political elite—of both parties—have failed us. Republicans have failed us because they can't govern. Democrats have failed us because they can't win elections. Our issue groups have failed us. Our leaders have failed us. And now it's our turn." If these establishment politicians didn't get on board with the "people-powered movement," Markos warned finally, "they'll be relegated to the dustbin of history."

The reporters in the back of the room exchanged smirks and fidgeted uncomfortably. A thousand bloggers came to their feet and hollered, shaking the Riv to its crumbling core.

Somewhere along the line, as the invitations were going out and the rooms were getting booked, the purpose of YearlyKos seemed to have changed. What was supposed to have been a celebration of the Kos community had become, without anyone ever actually saying so, a demonstration of its power. Gina had noticed it happening. After she had gotten early commitments from Harry Reid and Howard Dean and Mark Warner, Gina had stopped worrying so much about whether anyone important would come to YearlyKos. Instead, she found herself laying down limits and ultimatums to the parade of major politicians who wanted face time with the bloggers. Aides to Tom Vilsack, Iowa's governor, complained that he hadn't been asked to speak. "He's just pissed," Gina told me. "You know what? He didn't ask. He wanted me to ask him." John Edwards couldn't get around a long-planned trip to Israel. "If you're not interested, somebody else is going to be," Gina said she told his scheduler. "Israel's going to be here for the entire year."

It was natural that the undeclared presidential candidates for 2008 would be so eager for a chance to court the bloggers in person. Ever since Dean's shocking rise and fall in 2004, other ambitious Democrats had been trying mightily to ingratiate themselves to the netroots and fill the space that Dean seemed to have vacated. But sucking up to the Kossacks, it turned out, was a dangerous business, fraught with confusion and unintended consequences. Politicians didn't really understand the way the whole thing worked, and they weren't prepared to deal with all the profanity, hyperbole, and conspiracy theories. Take, for instance, the party's two celebrity senators, Hillary Clinton and Barack Obama, both of whom would soon be trailing busloads full of reporters through the snowy roads of Iowa and New Hampshire. Each of them had gamely tried to make their peace with the netroots, and each had come away from the experience profoundly confused.

In the summer of 2005, Clinton had agreed to join forces with her husband's old allies at the Democratic Leadership Council to design a new agenda aimed at middle-class voters. But even Clinton's core advisers, Washington insiders who understood little of the uprising in the states, knew that the DLC was anathema to the bloggers; it had attacked Howard Dean, and it continued to urge a bipartisan, centrist course for the party. To the bloggers, the DLC was the headquarters of the party's wretched establishment. And so Clinton's aides had come up with what seemed to them an elegant way to sidestep this internal rift: In her comments at the DLC conference where the initiative was to be announced, she called for a cease-fire between the DLC and the blogs. Clinton's statement seemed to discomfit the DLC leaders onstage with her, which was exactly its purpose. Her advisers expected the bloggers to see this as a mild rebuke of the DLC and as a sign that she wasn't endorsing one side over the other.

They were stunned when the blogs went ballistic, instead. The bloggers didn't want peace, and if there was one thing they hated in a politician, it was tepid neutrality. "The DLC has always been at the forefront of intra-party mudslinging," Markos ranted. "They're just finally being called on it, and suddenly it's time for peace." Declaring the middle-class agenda "dead on arrival," Markos wrote, "It's truly disappointing that this is the crap Hillary has signed on to. More of the failed corporatist bullshit that has cost our party so dearly the last decade and a half." The online uprising over Clinton's comments found its way into national headlines, where Clinton was portrayed as being out of touch with what was happening in her own party—which, of course, she was. In an unusually blunt appraisal, John Podesta told the *Washington Post* that his friend Hillary had "walked into a crossfire maybe she should have realized was out there."

Obama's encounter with the blogs had been of a more intimate variety, and though it had gone virtually unnoticed in Washington, it had produced an extraordinary dialogue between a Democratic insider and the party's online hecklers. It had started back in September 2005, when the Senate was debating whether to confirm John Roberts, Bush's pick for chief justice. Liberal interest groups and some in the netroots railed vituperatively against those Democratic senators who said they would vote for Roberts, one of whom happened to be Patrick Leahy, the Vermont liberal and the ranking Democrat on the Judiciary Committee. In his comments on the Senate floor, Obama said he would vote against the Roberts nomination, but then he did something remarkable: He went out of his way to scold those in his own party who had attacked Leahy for making the opposite decision. He dismissed their criticisms as "knee-jerk," "unbending," "unfair," and "dogmatic."

Obama was a hero to the new progressives, but now Daily Kos lit up with the first real criticism of Obama from the movement. Who was he to attack the party's activists? Why was he now defending the establishment? "The fact that it has come to the point where they sent out Obama, one of the most popular politicians with the blogosphere and the Democratic base, to tell us to back off, to stop being so unreasonable, is a good sign, because it means we're getting to them," wrote the blogger "wu ming" on Daily Kos. It was a classic netroots view of the world. It wasn't possible that Obama had simply spoken his mind; clearly it had been a nefarious plot by party insiders, who had dispatched the young senator to deliver a warning to the blogs— on C-SPAN.

That would have been the end of it, except that Obama just couldn't let it drop. As he recounted the story to me later during a conversation in his office, his staff had shown him the daily blog clips, and he obsessed over them. It wasn't right what they were saying about him, he thought, and a lot of it wasn't even true. He wondered aloud if he should respond. His aides rejected this idea as insane and urged him not to do it. It was the classic "Lemon Lyman" scenario— so named for an episode of *The West Wing*, Washington's favorite TV show, in which Josh Lyman, the deputy chief of staff, responds to fans on a site called "lemonlyman," only to find himself mocked and insulted by his own admirers. Party operatives were of the opinion that no good could ever come from trying to reason with such people. Obama countered that he viewed it as an experiment. "Let's see what happens if you push back," he told his aides.

Obama, a gifted writer, sat down at his home computer and typed out a two-thousand-plus-word response, which he asked his staff to post for him on Daily Kos. He called his missive "Tone, Truth, and the Democratic Party," and it was easily the most thoughtful and ballsy critique of the netroots offered by a leading Democrat. After a brief introduction, Obama got to his main point, laying out, with accuracy and precision, what he perceived to be the central netroots narrative:

> According to the storyline that drives many advocacy groups and Democratic activists—a storyline often reflected in comments on this blog—we are up against a sharply partisan, radically conservative, take-no-prisoners Republican Party. They have beaten us twice by energizing their base with red meat rhetoric and single-minded devotion and discipline to their agenda. In order to beat them, it is necessary for Democrats to get some backbone, give as good as they get, brook no compromise, drive out Democrats who are interested in "appeasing" the right wing, and enforce a more clearly progressive agenda. The country, finally . . . will rally to our side and thereby usher in a new progressive era.

He continued:

> I think this perspective misreads the American people. From traveling throughout Illinois and more recently around the

country, I can tell you that Americans are suspicious of labels and suspicious of jargon. They don't think George Bush is mean-spirited or prejudiced, but have become aware that his administration is irresponsible and often incompetent. They don't think that corporations are inherently evil (a lot of them work in corporations), but they recognize that big business, unchecked, can fix the game to the detriment of working people and small entrepreneurs. They don't think America is an imperialist brute, but are angry that the case to invade Iraq was exaggerated. . . .

If Democrats really wanted to win the trust of these voters, Obama lectured, they couldn't go around demonizing those who disagreed with them, nor could they impose some kind of purity test on their elected leaders. "To the degree that we brook no dissent within the Democratic Party, and demand fealty to the one, 'true' progressive vision for the country, we risk the very thoughtfulness and openness to new ideas that are required to move this country forward," he said. Citing Abraham Lincoln and Martin Luther King Jr., Obama said the country's most compelling voices had been those who could "speak with the utmost conviction about the great issues of the day without ever belittling those who opposed them, and without denying the limits of their own perspectives."

Obama's post generated an unprecedented number of e-mails to his office. The roughly four-hundred responses that flooded in during the first few hours after the post were almost uniformly positive. But then the tenor of things started to deteriorate quickly. Many of the e-mails stung. The one Obama would remember afterward, when we talked about it, came from a woman who began, "I'm crying as I write this." In all, Obama received about two thousand responses, split more or less evenly between those who appreciated his words and those who thought he was a sell-out or a moron.

Some of these he answered personally; others simply depressed him. Maybe the bloggers were right, he thought. Maybe the only way to build a cohesive party was to tear down Bush and the Republicans at every turn. But he felt certain that such a strategy would transform Democrats, over time, into a permanent minority.

It shouldn't have surprised anyone that neither Hillary Clinton nor Barack Obama wanted much to do with this thing called YearlyKos.

You couldn't have kept Mark Warner away, however. Of all the presidential aspirants who were openly planning for 2008, Warner, the cell-phone millionaire, was the one who most intuitively understood the potential of new technology. He didn't claim to understand the blog world, but, even before the pictures were on the walls of his postgubernatorial office suite in Alexandria, he had gone out and hired the one guy who understood it better than anyone: Jerome Armstrong. The Blogfather got Warner a page on Facebook.com and helped him post on Daily Kos. He designed a Web site that featured a tiny Mark Warner who walked out onto the screen and welcomed you himself. When Jerome heard about YearlyKos, he knew instantly that this was the opportunity of a political lifetime. Don't just go to the convention, Jerome urged the governor—go there and own it. Go there and be the guy that everyone is talking about.

By this time, Warner was emerging among influential Democrats as a strong alternative to Hillary. In a survey of 175 Washington insiders conducted by *National Journal* a month before YearlyKos, Clinton was easily chosen as the most likely nominee, but Warner led the pack of other contenders, beating out Edwards, Gore, Kerry, and Obama. He had a persuasive, business-minded argument, inherited from Bill Clinton and honed during his time in Virginia: Good or bad, globalization was here to stay, Warner said, and the winners in the new economy would be those who had the vision to turn old manufacturing towns into high-tech hubs of the new economy. He had left office in Virginia in January 2006 with approval ratings of around 80 percent, making him the most popular governor in the country, in a state that was—at least until he got there—overwhelmingly Republican.

And yet Warner was a hard sell with the emerging progressive movement and the netroots. He had become governor by appealing to rural conservatives, and he described himself as a probusiness, free-trading centrist and had been active in the Democratic Leadership Council. Warner was also a proud proponent of cutting deals with his opponents; he had reformed the tax code in Virginia by cajoling his Republican legislature.

In the summer of 2005, Warner had attended a dinner of wealthy donors, some of them Democracy Alliance partners, at Mark and Susie Buell's home in Bolinas. He talked about what he called his "Virginia story," about how he had improved schools and raised the living standard in forgotten coal towns, but all the donors seemed to care about were his stands on gay marriage and abortion. At the end of the evening, as one of the women lectured him about abortion, Warner, who did not suffer condescension with a lot of patience to begin with, finally lost his cool. "This is why America hates Democrats," he blurted out before driving away.

This was what Jerome had to work with. He settled on a strategy: Ideology aside, Warner had to show his respect for the netroots. He had to show that he cared what the bloggers had to say, that he understood their influence. And so, while Wesley Clark and Tom Vilsack were sitting on small panels at YearlyKos, and while Bill Richardson was holding an informal breakfast with a small number of bloggers, Warner, at Jerome's urging, had settled in at a posh suite over at the Wynn (you didn't stay at the Riv when you had enough money to buy it), where his full slate of events for the weekend would include hosting a huge party, delivering a keynote address and holding a private sit-down with a group of elite bloggers.

On Friday morning, I met up with Jerome, who was on a hunt for T-shirts. He had ordered more than a thousand of them (black with an artist's rendering of Warner, looking Kennedyesque in profile, against the backdrop of an American flag), and the plan was to leave one on each attendee's chair before Warner's speech on Saturday. The question was, where in the labyrinthine Riviera might they be? Jerome, dressed in a casual button-down and jeans, shuffled from the convention hall to the bell captain and then to the business center, a journey that took the better part of a half hour. It turned out that the business center had them, stuffed into fourteen FedEx boxes in the loading dock.

As we were standing at the counter discussing this with the hotel clerk, a gray-haired Kossack standing next to us turned to Jerome. "Are you progressive?" the man asked.

"Huh?" Jerome looked up.

"Are you progressive?" The guy clearly had no idea who Jerome was.

"Yeah."

"Then you shouldn't use FedEx. They're an anti-union company."

Jerome appeared to consider this for a moment, as he always did. "What should I use?" he asked finally.

"DHL. Or UPS."

"OK," Jerome said agreeably. He shrugged, as if to suggest that you learn something useful every day.

On the way back to the convention hall, he looked at me quizzically. "Am I progressive?" he repeated, shaking his head in wonder. We both broke up laughing.

We passed the billiards tournament being held next to YearlyKos in a cavernous, warehouselike room with makeshift lamps wired above a sea of green felt. Jerome, whose nomadic history had by now become a running joke between us, stopped and took a look inside.

"Did I tell you I used to own a pool hall?" Jerome asked.

"Oh, now, c'mon," I said. "How much of this do you think I'm going to buy?"

"No, really," he said. "It was when I was in college in Arkansas. There was this abandoned place across the street, so this guy and I turned it into a pool hall. This was Arkansas. You only needed a few hundred bucks a month to rent the place."

I threw up my hands in surrender.

"It lasted about six months, I think," he said, ignoring my incredulity. "We did OK."

I t had been Jerome's idea for Warner to host a party at YearlyKos. Warner had been hesitant at first, but then, after a few weeks of mulling it over, he had walked into Jerome's office with a new attitude. "You know that party in Las Vegas?" Warner said. "I want it to be a blowout. Let's do a real blowout party." That was all Jerome had needed to hear. He and Mame Reiley, a veteran organizer, went shopping for venues, but there was never much of a contest. The event planners at the Stratosphere, the aging space needle on the old strip, with a roller coaster snaked around its neck like some errant vine, couldn't believe that a bona fide presidential candidate might actually throw a bash at their place. The cost for the kind of party Jerome was talking about ran to $75,000, but the Stratosphere was willing to throw in a package of extras, like a chocolate fountain and an ice sculpture of a computer.

The kicker was the obvious name for the party, which had seemed to occur to all of them simultaneously while staring out from the top of the needle onto the city below. "Blogosphere in the Stratosphere." Jerome was sold.

On Friday night, the jumbo screen outside the Stratosphere flashed a welcome message: "Governor Mark Warner welcomes the

Blogosphere!" More than a thousand guests meandered through a long line and a metal detector to get to the elevator, which took them to the tire-shaped, glass-walled room at the top of the needle. They drank "Blog-ueritas" and "Kos-mopolitans" and chomped on sushi and coconut crab. Making the rounds, I ran into Joe Trippi, Howard Dean's onetime campaign manager, by one of the drink machines and Tom McMahon, Dean's top aide, at another. He was talking with Penny Lee, who ran the Democratic Governors Association. MoveOn's Tom Matzzie, in his trademark suit, looked sullen, having just lost two grand at the craps tables. Joe Wilson, the former diplomat who had become a famous critic of Bush after his wife, Valerie Plame, was exposed by the White House as a CIA agent, mingled with the nation's most influential bloggers. Had the weathered space needle chosen that moment to teeter in the desert breeze and topple to the ground a thousand feet below (a possibility that did not seem so remote as I felt the floor sway), much of America's new progressive movement would have gone with it.

Warner came in sometime around ten, in an open collar and sport jacket, and was immediately enveloped by a constantly shifting crowd of eager faces and outstretched hands. The bloggers may not have liked the idea of a centrist, bipartisan Democrat, but they were apparently thrilled to get some face time with one. Warner is a tall, gangly man, and I could just make out the top of his extra-large head as he and his throng of admirers circumnavigated the space needle, looking like some organism whose shape kept shifting but whose mass remained constant. An Elvis impersonator was onstage, but he was soon bumped for a would-be Blues Brothers act. I watched poor Elvis wander off to a space by the elevator, where he stood awkwardly against a wall, looking lost and waxen.

The Blues Brothers called Markos, Jerome, and Warner to the stage and played "Hail to the Chief," while Mame and I stood behind them and watched the spectacle unfold. Warner and Markos shared a warm embrace in front of the crowd. For Warner, this alone was worth the seventy-five grand. It was like a kiss from the Godfather at a mob wedding. Jerome spoke first, giving a short plug for the Warner Web site. He had engineered this moment, and he felt carried away. "On your credential, there's just a little typo," he said, pointing to the card around his neck. "It says nine to eleven. But we actually have the place until midnight!" Cheers went up around the room.

Mame looked like she'd just been jolted with an electric current. "No, we don't!" she called out urgently, trying to get Jerome's attention, but I was the only one who heard her over the roar. She stood there looking helpless.

Now Markos had the microphone. "I know you're sick of me," he told the crowd. "*I'm* sick of me after seeing *everything* in this town with my name on it!" He rolled his eyes. "The Kos-mopolitan martini?" Markos didn't sound sick of it. He sounded like he had entered Valhalla. Markos wasn't ready to endorse Warner. All the 2008 candidates, he said, would get a chance to make their cases to the netroots. "I've got to say, though," he added, "as a first date, this is pretty damn cool!"

Warner was clearly loving all this. "This is the new public square!" he proclaimed, taking center stage. "This is the new face of democracy, and the new face of the Democratic Party!" He went on a bit, then stepped down to yet more enthusiastic applause.

"Let's bring back the governor!" one the Blues Brothers called out. And, before any of us knew what was happening, Warner had returned to the stage and donned a pair of Blues Brothers shades and a fedora, and he was shimmying with the band to the driving beat of a guitar. "Bill Clinton ain't got nothing on this guy!" the one who looked like Elwood shouted.

"Let's get out of here," Mame said urgently, making a move to retrieve the governor before things got any more out of hand. She paused, eyeing my notebook, and looked at me pleadingly.

"Be kind," she said.

On Saturday, I visited some of the booths near the convention hall, where you could sign petitions, or buy YearlyKos T-shirts, or pick up leaflets touting some of the potential 2008 candidates. There was a table full of bumper stickers that said things like "Iraq is Arabic for Vietnam" and "I love my country, but I think we should see other people." I noticed that a lot of the bloggers were wearing buttons that showed Bush kissing Joe Lieberman after his State of the Union Address. "The Kiss," they said, and then, underneath: "Bush's favorite Democrat."

I found Gina at one of the round tables in the ballroom. She was never without her laptop, and now she was working on her closing speech for that night. "I'm terrified," she told me. "I'm still trying to wrap my head around what all of this means." Her friends back home were seeing her quoted in the news. She had the sense that all of this was going to change her life in some way, and she worried that some of the other volunteers weren't getting enough credit for their work. She banged on a few keys and scrolled down. "What do you call someone who checks the Web for her own quotes?" Gina asked with a sigh.

After the George W. Bush impersonator had lightened up the ballroom ("Nobody feeds me lines—unless it's Jesus Christ"), and after Howard Dean had electrified the crowd with pointed allusions to his dispute with Rahm Emanuel and other establishment Democrats ("Thank you for coming to my defense every time some Washington politician stands up and says, 'We've got to do it the old way.' You guys are the best!"), Gina and I migrated backstage to watch Warner's speech on a giant video screen. Gina seemed worn out from dealing with politicians and their staffs. "The only guy who hasn't been a problem is this guy," she told me, pointing to Warner's pixilated image.

On stage, Warner went through what was by now his standard personal story, talking about how he had failed in business and had once lived out of his car before getting rich and running for office. He touted his impressive record in Virginia. But then his speech took what was, for him, an unusual turn. I had known Warner since he first ran for governor in 2001, and I knew that, as much as any politician I had met, he was noticeably uncomfortable with partisan attacks. How politicians conduct themselves is largely about their own self-image, and Warner saw himself, fundamentally, as a bridge between factions or cultures, the kind of guy who flattered you into submission; the less inclined you were to agree with Mark Warner, the more inclined he was to have you over to the governor's mansion for a beer. He generally avoided barbs aimed at Bush and his administration, preferring, instead, to criticize the polarized culture of both parties in Washington. He refused to say whether he would have supported the invasion of Iraq, since he hadn't had to make that decision with the facts available at the time.

Now, however, after months of pressure from Jerome and other advisers, and facing an audience full of rage at the president and his party, Warner was apparently ready to try a different approach. He charged that the administration had manipulated intelligence, and he strongly condemned the war in Iraq, asserting, instead, that Iran had been the greater threat all along. For the first time, he called for the resignation of Donald Rumsfeld as defense secretary. He ridiculed the administration for having an "on/off switch" when it came to following the law. He pointed out that two weeks' worth of spending in Iraq could triple the federal budget for research and development. "Of course, that would require an administration that believes in science," Warner said bitingly, eliciting his strongest applause of the afternoon. "It's 2006, and we're redebating evolution!"

Compared with what other Democratic hopefuls were saying about Bush—not to mention Howard Dean, who had already publicly admitted to hating Republicans—Warner's condemnation of the administration hardly qualified as wild-eyed, nor did it ring untrue. For Warner, though, who had never before had to worry about adjusting his demeanor to win over liberal voters, this was closer to the partisan abyss than he had ever been, and he seemed in danger of losing himself in it. From where I sat, Warner sounded like a man playing the role of a politician, his cadence a little stilted and self-conscious. Negative attacks work when the candidates delivering them are having fun; Warner clearly wasn't. The bloggers gave him an appreciative reception, but nothing like the emotional ovations they had showered on Markos and Dean after their remarks.

In fact, there were already rumblings throughout the convention hall that Warner was coming on too strong and too phony. The morning-after hangover from the Stratosphere was setting in. Jerome's guy at the "Draft Warner" table reported that a lot of the bloggers were now complaining that Warner was just trying to buy their support, that the party, with its chocolate fountain, had been absurdly lavish and unseemly. It seemed that in his plan to show the bloggers that Warner respected them, Jerome might have gone too far, to the point where they felt *disrespected* by the transparency of it all.

In the hallway, Warner was accosted by a blogger who went by the name DeanFan84, and who told him his party had been too extravagant. He wanted to know how much it had cost.

"We actually negotiated down the price on that event," Warner stammered, then implied that he'd had nothing to do with the arrangements. "I walked in and saw some of those things and was a little taken aback."

"I don't want our guys to get used to shrimp and martinis, OK?" the blogger said. "We don't want bloggers doing that. I don't want that."

"There seemed to be an awful lot of them last night who liked it," Warner replied.

In a skybox high above the convention floor, about twenty bloggers sat in a circle of vanilla leather furniture around a glass table. All of them had been invited by Jerome to meet Warner because they had their own blogs, or because they were lead writers on Daily Kos. Warner joined their little circle, while, a few feet away, a phalanx of reporters, invited in by his staff, crammed in to watch.

"Fire away. Let's start it off," Warner proclaimed eagerly, rubbing his hands together.

Marcy Wheeler, who blogged as "emptywheel" on Daily Kos, jumped in first. Why, she wanted to know, had Warner pointed to Iran as such a big threat to national security? Wasn't Pakistan a bigger problem? After all, they already had nukes.

Warner had been spending hours in private tutoring sessions on foreign policy, and he talked confidently about Iran's president, Mahmoud Ahmadinejad, and his "whole approach toward regional hegemony." This made him dangerous, Warner said.

"On what grounds?" Marcy demanded. She had short hair and glasses and a serious demeanor. She reminded me, strangely, a little of Marcy from Peanuts. I wondered if she got that a lot.

Warner mentioned Ahmadinejad's explicit threat to Israel.

"I've heard Pakistan described as Iran in 1978, except it's Iran with a nuclear bomb," Marcy retorted, as if she'd just stepped off a plane from the region. There were nods and murmured assents all around. "Maybe I'm crazy."

"I hope you're crazy," Warner said testily. This had caught him completely off guard. He had just given the most confrontational, partisan speech he knew how to give, and he had expected the bloggers to appreciate it. Instead, he was getting hammered on Iran. Why

were they seizing on this one line? What he didn't understand was
that this was the one place in his speech where he had *agreed* with
Bush on something, and thus it had to be probed. To the bloggers, if
Bush said the sky was blue, then it was green. If he said the world was
round, it had to be flat. And if Bush thought Iran was the most serious threat out there, then no Democratic candidate could think that
too. Warner was clearly buying into the right-wing spin.

"But Iran was invaded during the Iran-Iraq war!" another
woman cried. "Can you actually say they're more unstable than Pakistan?" It wasn't clear to me—or, from the looks of it, to Warner—
what one thing had to do with the other. Another blogger said his
"sources" told him that Bush had a plan to invade Iran before the end
of his term. Now it was clear from his body language that Warner
just wanted to try his hand at another topic, like some senior citizen
down in the Riv casino who's gone bust on the slots and figures she'll
move on to Blackjack.

You could tell from the nods and self-aware smiles on the faces of
the bloggers that they were enjoying this immensely. They weren't
used to having an audience with major politicians, and they especially
weren't used to having this audience in front of a pack of national
reporters. For years, they had been lecturing members of the Washington press corps about their lazy, timorous method of interrogating
national figures. Now was their chance to demonstrate how it
was done.

"You said that in Virginia you got a lot done working across the
aisle," a blogger named Hunter said. You could almost see Warner
relax at the mention of his home state, his firmest terrain. "Do you
think that's possible on the national level now?"

Warner proudly ticked off the profound changes he had enacted in
health care and education, working with Republicans. "Even if we take
back Congress," he said, "if you try to ram through transformational
change in a 51–49 way, I don't think it's going to get done. I may be

naive on this, but I think there are still enough people of goodwill in the country and even in Congress. You have to reach out and grab them."

The bloggers shook their heads skeptically. "I think part of what Hunter's asking," said Dave Johnson from the Commonweal Institute, "is, what if they don't? What if, just like with Hillary Clinton's plan, they decide they're just going to block whatever you do?"

"If you don't think there are enough people of goodwill willing to step up and do the right thing regardless of party, then I'm truly worried for the country," Warner said, a little exasperated. But of course, that was precisely what the bloggers thought. It was pretty much the first principle of the blogs. Somehow this seemed to have eluded Warner.

"So are we," Johnson replied. "That's why we're here. The question is, what if they don't? What's plan B?"

"In Virginia, we went around the legislature," Warner answered. "We went straight to the people. I went out in my kind of Ross Perot mode with my PowerPoints, and I did fifty presentations across the state. And I basically said, 'Hey, look, here's where we've cut, here's where we've reformed, and here's where the lines don't meet.' And we took the plan straight to them. This hasn't happened in America in fifty years."

The bloggers were nodding, but Warner wasn't finished. His solicitous, charming mood had drained away. Now he was being forced to defend his core political philosophy, and it was something he believed in strongly. "But full disclosure," he went on. "From day one, I would have Republicans helping." Warner said he had plenty of Republican friends—Republican *friends*!—who wanted to change the status quo too.

"I understand the anger," Warner sighed. "Let me tell you: I understand it. Every group wants me to say what I dislike about the president. 'Tell us what you hate about the president!' But I think we need to do more than that."

Now Warner was done playing around. He fielded a question about whether he would "dismantle the Big Brother state" that was spying on Americans in the name of antiterrorism.

"I fundamentally believe the terrorist threat is real," Warner said.

"But they're not checking out books from our libraries!" the blogger interrupted.

"No, no, but hear me out. Stateless terrorism is a new threat, and it requires new methods." Warner pointed out that Lincoln and Franklin Roosevelt had gone to Congress to ask for additional wartime powers, rather than simply assuming them, and that's what he planned to do. This satisfied no one.

Afterward, Warner was contemplative. YearlyKos had come near the end of an eight-day stretch of speeches and fund-raising, a sort of coming-out week for Warner, and everywhere he went he had seen the same bile directed at the president and his party. It seemed to blind these new progressives to the realities of the world. They reminded him, he would tell me later, of Jane Fonda in the 1960s—activists who believed that the enemy of their enemy had to be their friend, twisted logic that caused them to dismiss the dangers of Iran and al Qaeda while defending a strongman like the Venezuelan dictator Hugo Chavez. Warner came away from these interactions profoundly disturbed and wondering if all this hatred might ultimately consume his party.

Gina and I met for breakfast Sunday morning at Kady's, the '50s-style diner in the Riviera, which, it occurred to me, might actually have been contemporary when it opened. Everyone was packing their bags to leave Vegas. Gina had stopped by that morning's interfaith service for the bloggers, but she said she couldn't stand all that religion, and she was too tired to pretend.

To Gina, when all the posturing and partying were finally past, the convention wasn't really about Warner or the other candidates; it was about the bloggers. Her corps of volunteers had pulled off something truly impressive. They had, with little money and no experience, taken this disparate, virtual phenomenon that Jerome and Markos and other early bloggers had started, and they had turned it into an actual, real-life community. Nowhere else in progressive politics had so many people volunteered so much of their time and abilities to the cause: lawyers, Web technicians, event planners, photographers, graphic designers. Whatever else came out of YearlyKos, it had taken online politics to a whole new phase.

"We've all needed a mission," Gina said, as we stabbed at short-stack pancakes with thawed blueberries inside. "This whole thing with progressivism—" She paused. "I'm trying to find my words here. OK, this is going to sound like I have an ego that I don't have. But people need to know that the things they do every day can make a difference, that the things they do every day can be put to some larger use. Like the sound stage guy. This is what he does for a living. Now he had a way to put it to use on a whole deeper level. He found a way to give it meaning.

"Last night, that's how I got myself to go onstage," she went on. "I said, 'Gina, this is your job.' People need something to believe in. And if they can believe in you, then they can believe in themselves. No one's going to give me permission to just suddenly speak with authority. I just have to do it."

That last bit was, I thought, the best summation I had heard of the ethos behind the online political age.

Leaving Las Vegas, Jerome wasn't bothered by the anti-Warner backlash that had already become an intense topic of online debate. It was mostly coming from a small number of the most vocal and cantankerous bloggers, he figured, the same people who were always whining about something—it was the thing that drew them to the Web in the first place. Let them make pious statements about refusing to be bought off, Jerome thought. The fact was that they had eaten a whole lot of shrimp, and there weren't any spare T-shirts to take back to Virginia, either.

What Jerome didn't anticipate was how soon that same backlash would turn against him. A week after YearlyKos, the Sunday *New York Post* published a story under the headline SHILL TO HACK: CELE-BRATED LIB STRATEGIST HAS SHADY MARKET PAST. It turned out that the Securities and Exchange Commission had lodged a civil complaint against Jerome in 1999, back when he was playing the markets on-line, charging that he had pumped up an Internet "penny stock" in exchange for some cheap shares from the company. The suit had dragged on for years, ending in a confidential settlement under which Jerome, who couldn't afford a costly legal defense, had neither admitted nor denied guilt and had agreed to pay a fine.

Whether Jerome had, in fact, been a willing participant in an Internet scam was hard to discern. But after the *Post* story ran, con-servative bloggers began to draw some unflattering connections. Wasn't Warner kind of like an Internet stock, too? And if this was the way Jerome did business, then how did they know he hadn't paid Markos to pump up Warner to his legion of Kossacks? Perhaps Jerome and Markos had some secret arrangement of their own, this theory went, whereby Jerome was sharing some of his consulting fees with his buddy in exchange for Markos's kind words. The right-wingers even came up with a name for this hypothetical scandal: They called it "Kosola," as in "payola." Soon the allegations found their way into mainstream news outlets like *Newsweek* and the *New Republic* and onto the *New York Times* Web site.

As conspiracy theories go, this wasn't an especially compelling one. But some progressive bloggers soon latched onto it as well. Suddenly, Jerome and Markos were having to defend their reputations not just from conservative attackers, but from some on their side too. In an e-mail to bloggers on the Townhouse list, Markos lashed out at those who were giving life to the pseudoscandal, intimating that operatives for some of the candidates he had criticized—namely Hillary Clinton—might be spreading the Kosola story in an effort to destroy him.

For Jerome, there was yet more indignity to follow. A few days after Kosola hit the news, the conservative blog Riehl World View uncovered another piece of Jerome's eclectic past: his dalliance in astrology. Apparently, during his day-trading phase, Jerome had started predicting finance and politics through the stars. Riehl World View dug up a 2003 blog post from an obscure astrology site:

> Astrologer Jerome Armstrong notes that Ixion and Quaoar are following close in Pluto's wake in early Sagittarius, and connects the rise of the political version of religious fundamentalism with the astronomical exploration of the Kuiper Belt in 1992. He cites incidences as disparate as the rise of Osama bin Laden onto the world stage and the Republican Revolution of 1994, fueled by Christian fundamentalist voters and culminating now with all three branches of government in Republican control.

"I predict," the Riehl World View post concluded, "that Dems will take all fifty states when Venus aligns with Jupiter and kisses Mars' butt. Pardon me if I don't ask the latest Democratic wizard-kid what he has to say about that."

In fact, Jerome had little to say. When I met him for lunch a few weeks later, I expected him to be livid about the things people were saying. Instead, he was typically Zen. He said all that mattered was that Warner hadn't been bothered by the controversy, and he waved away the SEC complaint as ancient history. He made no apologies for having dabbled in astrology, which he said was nothing but another lens through which to see the world. What the whole experience had made clear, Jerome told me, was that he had outgrown the pettiness of the blog world. Whatever he achieved in politics, from here on out, he would achieve in the realm of campaigns, even if it meant having to put on a suit and tie.

As it turned out, Jerome had chosen the wrong vehicle to demonstrate the power of the Internet to realign American politics. In the weeks after YearlyKos, Mark Warner cemented his place as the freshest, most electable alternative to Hillary Clinton. He also continued to take bold chances in the world of online campaigning. At the end of August, Warner became the first politician ever to hold a virtual town meeting in Second Life, an online fantasy world. In what may have been the strangest bit of political correspondence ever recorded, the *Hotline, National Journal*'s respected Washington newsletter, attended the meeting through its own "avatar" and described the scene this way: "Suddenly, Warner turned gray, and then transformed on stage into a nude, buxom woman and flew off. Hamlet Au, the event's host, explained that Warner was 'respawning.' At about 3:40, the real Warner flew in from above the stage."

Just three weeks before the fall elections, however, Warner took himself out of the running for the presidency. In his statement, he said he had come to realize that his three teenage daughters needed their father around during these formative years. Washington Democrats, most of whom would have given both their lungs to have had a legitimate shot at the White House, were stunned by this development, and immediately they began to speculate that maybe Warner was having an affair and was afraid it would surface. Or maybe he had some issue in his past with stock options. No man, they reasoned, walked away from a campaign this promising unless he was taking cover from a political grenade.

I had watched Warner up close, and I took him at his word that he was deeply conflicted about the time he would have spent away from his daughters. But I suspected that his various run-ins with the donors and bloggers of the new progressive movement had also convinced Warner that, in order to succeed, he was going to have to be more angry and divisive than the governor who had won over so many Republicans—and more partisan than the president he hoped to become. Intellectually, Warner knew how to calibrate his rhetoric to adapt to this reality, but, temperamentally, he wasn't really suited to that kind of campaign; he just couldn't locate the burning desire he needed to go out there and sound like Howard Dean. And, no matter how he made it sound, Warner had to know that his bipartisan philosophy was going to make it hard to win the nomination of a party increasingly dominated by an uncompromising progressive movement.

Warner had miscalculated in seeing the Internet as merely another technology in which to invest. He had hired the best talent, spent more cash than anyone else, experimented with different approaches. But the Web wasn't simply a new tool for old politics; the blogs represented their own distinct political culture. They were, in fact, the voices of the new public square, but it was more like the Parisian public square in the days of the Bastille—not a place where townspeople came to carefully consider what their leaders had to say, but where the mob gathered to make its demands and mete out its own kind of justice. As Clinton and Obama had discovered earlier, this was the darker side of the progressive movement that was energizing and democratizing the party. It was also, as Warner himself had put it, the new face of Democratic politics.

CHAPTER TWELVE

The Kiss

A few days after leaving the bloggers at the Riviera, I dropped by the Washington Hilton, where MoveOn.org and Democracy for America were holding a fund-raiser for Ned Lamont. By the time I arrived at the fifth-floor suite, some seventy-five Lamont boosters, most of them in town for the progressive "Take Back America" conference going on downstairs, were crammed into a single oversized hotel room, giving it the feel of a college dorm party. Tom Matzzie from MoveOn was hovering in the far corner, a few feet away from the blogger Atrios. On the way in, I ran into Rob Johnson, the Democracy Alliance partner and onetime economist who had shared my table during Andy Stern's speech in Austin. Rob and Ned, I knew, were neighbors in Greenwich, and their daughters had attended the same exclusive private school.

Ned was standing in the center of the room, allowing himself to be mobbed. It was the first time I had seen him since the night we met at Norman Lear's place, and he had clearly found his comfort zone. He smiled easily and bantered with the guests, expertly gripping hands and elbows. He looked tan and confident, more substantial than he had appeared in Hollywood months before. Groping my way over to where he was standing, I reintroduced myself and asked why he didn't have what politicians call a "body man"—someone to hold his coat and take down names.

"You volunteering?" Ned laughed, as his fans continued to converge on us.

A young guy asked for a picture, and Ned smiled and posed until the bulb flashed, in that frozen, hand-clasped way that experienced politicians can do without so much as interrupting a conversation.

"Where are you from?" Ned asked the kid.

"Young Democrats of Michigan," he replied.

"Oh, Michigan!" Ned cried in surprise, as if the kid had said Greenland or Ulaan Baatar. "All right!"

Ned was a hard guy not to like. At fifty-two, with earnest eyes and a lock of hair dangling boyishly on his forehead, he reminded me of Clark Kent, if Clark had crashed into Kansas with a few hundred million bucks.

When it was time for speeches, Matzzie, in his dark suit, railed against Joe Lieberman's apostasy on the war and other issues. Then he turned the floor over to Jim Dean, Howard's younger brother. Jim Dean was a salesman by trade, but he had taken over Democracy for America, his brother's political action committee, when Howard left to run the party. He looked and sounded exactly like his more famous sibling, except squatter and less charismatic. Establishment Democrats tended to view Jim Dean as the chairman's mischievous alter ego, a political neophyte who carried out Howard's more subversive agenda while the chairman was busy ingratiating himself to the Washington insiders.

"When Ned wins, we'll have a senator who stands up for Democratic values!" the Other Dean thundered. "The battles of the Democratic Party are not battles of ideology, not battles of Left or Right. They're battles of the culture of incumbency versus the culture of activism!" This drew passionate applause and hollers.

Finally, it was Ned's turn. "The Bush administration is wrong," he said, "and if Joe Lieberman doesn't want to stand up to the president, I will!" He was in this race, he said, because he was tired of Lieberman's finding common ground with the White House, mainly on Iraq. "Let people know that this is for real, and we can make a statement. Let people know that Democrats can win by being bold and true and clear about what we stand for!"

Afterward, as the buzzing guests began to trickle out, I talked for a while with Rob Johnson. I asked him why he thought Lamont's primary campaign was so important to so many progressives. He thought for a moment.

"I worked up on the Hill for six years," Rob said, "and I watched good men become alcoholics. We have a system that isn't working. And here we have a guy who's like a real-life *Mr. Smith Goes to Washington*. This is a guy who puts all the pieces together, and he sees that this is a high-leverage play."

"Meaning what?" I asked, a little confused. Rob looked at me gravely.

"Meaning this is bigger than getting elected or not," Rob said. "Ned can change everything."

In a sense, Ned's quixotic campaign against an entrenched senator had solved an election-year problem for the progressive outsiders. Like the Democracy Alliance, the rest of the burgeoning movement was split between two distinct goals: winning back control of Congress, on the one hand, and overhauling the party, on the other. The donors and bloggers liked to pretend that these two things were somehow the same, but they weren't. In Washington, Rahm Emanuel and Chuck Schumer had been careful to recruit candidates who seemed like they could clear a threshold of acceptability with moderate voters who were furious at Bush, candidates chosen more for their unassailable resumes than for any particular attachment to progressive principles. Five House candidates alone were recruited because they were veterans of the Iraq war (Democrats christened them "the fighting Dems"), while in Virginia the winner of the party's Senate primary was Jim Webb, a former Republican navy secretary.

Publicly, the progressives hailed these new recruits as candidates who could actually win, symbols of a pragmatic party that was ready, at last, to do whatever it took to dispatch the Republican majorities. Privately, though, and on the blogs, they wondered whether all these Democrats of convenience would actually make the party establishment any more responsive to them. In hand-picking these candidates, Schumer and Emanuel had also shoved aside some would-be challengers who were championed by the netroots, infuriating some progressives—Rob Johnson was one—who felt that winning might come at too high a cost.

What the progressives needed, then, was a single, galvanizing campaign against the party establishment—a race where they could make a strong statement about the need to cleanse the party of Republican appeasers, then move on to the more pragmatic task of winning back Congress. Movement conservatives had done the same thing back in the 1970s, when unknown challengers had beaten two of the Republican Party's leading moderate senators—New Jersey's Clifford Case and New York's Jacob Javits—in successive primaries. Now, as Democrats looked around for their own Case or Javits, they didn't have to look very far. Joe Lieberman wasn't just off the Democratic reservation. He was living in a whole other zip code.

The disdain for Lieberman among the new progressives went all the way back to Clinton's impeachment, when many of them had first tuned in to politics, and when Lieberman, one of the founders of the Democratic Leadership Council, had been the first Democrat to stand up and publicly rebuke his own party's president. It grew subtly during the 2000 campaign, when, despite his criticism of

affirmative action and other core Democratic policies, he had joined
Gore on the ticket and had behaved so warmly toward Dick Cheney
during their vice presidential debate that it was hard to believe
he was running against him. His religiously tinged rhetoric and his
support for "faith-based" social programs had always endeared him
to evangelicals, even as it rankled the Democratic faithful, including
a lot of his fellow Jews. When, in 2005, congressional Republicans
had intervened in the fight over Terri Schiavo, a Florida woman on
life support whose husband was trying to end her life, Lieberman had
been the only leading Democrat to side with them—even as public
opinion polls showed that voters were appalled by the crusade.
Perhaps Lieberman was, in fact, more principled than a lot of his
colleagues, but there was a reason they called him "Holy Joe" behind
his back.

As with most things in the progressive uprising, however, it was
the Iraq war that finally turned Lieberman's community of critics
into an insurrection. It wasn't just that he had supported the war so
enthusiastically, and that he continued to cheerlead, even as it became
apparent to everyone with a newspaper subscription that the occupa-
tion was a disaster. It was more the way that he degraded critics of the
administration's policy, implying that they were somehow unpatriotic. Returning from a sojourn into Iraq in November 2005, he published what would become an infamous op-ed in the *Wall Street
Journal,* arguing that Democrats needed to support the president's
Iraq policy. A few weeks later, at a news conference, he went even
further. "It's time for Democrats who distrust President Bush to
acknowledge that he will be the commander in chief for three more
critical years," he said, "and that in matters of war we undermine
presidential credibility at our nation's peril." He might as well have
burned Howard Dean in effigy on the Capitol steps.

Lieberman made for a more inviting target in Connecticut,
politically speaking, than most observers assumed. Yes, he was a

three-term senator and former vice presidential candidate with soaring approval ratings in his home state. But it had been eighteen years
since he had faced a serious campaign challenge of any kind (his last
opponent, an obscure mayor whom Lieberman had refused even to
debate, was now in jail for child molestation), and he had made the
classic mistake of taking local relationships for granted. Since
running for vice president, he had behaved as if he were bigger than
any mere state, spending far more time in his Washington townhouse, near Georgetown, than he did in New Haven. Democratic
leaders in the Nutmeg State fumed that their calls to Lieberman went
unreturned.

Naturally, local activists were the first to understand Holy Joe's
vulnerability. Back in February 2005, Keith Crane, a retired truck
driver and Dean supporter, set up the Web site DumpJoe.com,
despite knowing next to nothing about computers. He also printed
up hundreds of buttons and bumper stickers featuring what Lieberman's opponents believed was the crystallizing moment of his
betrayal: that split second after the 2005 State of the Union address
when Bush, apparently carried away by the emotions of the moment,
smooched Lieberman on the cheek. Now that image was all over
Crane's stickers, and, when he stood on the curb outside a major state
Democratic Party dinner and handed them out, people stopped their
cars to offer encouragement.

This latent progressive rebellion was already churning when, in
December 2005, just after Lieberman's *Journal* piece, Tom Matzzie
traveled to Yale to speak to campus progressives. Matzzie commented off-handedly that Lieberman should draw a primary opponent. As it happened, sitting in the audience was Tom Swan, a tough
and impressive organizer who had run campaigns in support of local
ballot initiatives. After the speech, Swan introduced himself to
Matzzie and said he had been trying to recruit a challenger. Was
Matzzie serious about MoveOn supporting a challenge? Matzzie said

the answer was yes—provided, of course, that Swan could come up with a credible candidate.

Before long, it seemed that every liberal millionaire along southern Connecticut's Gold Coast was either considering a run against Lieberman or looking for someone who would. A group led by Tom Swan had tried to recruit a friend of Lamont's in Bridgeport, who had, in turn, sent them to Lamont. He was a good fit. Ned wasn't what you'd call a natural politician, but he was passionate and personable. More important, he was loaded. Lamont's great-grandfather had been a partner of J. P. Morgan, and Ned had built his own little empire in cable television systems. His wife, Annie, was one of the premiere venture capitalists in the country, and, thanks mostly to her, the couple was worth hundreds of millions of dollars. While a lot of Rob Johnson's friends in the Democracy Alliance, including George Soros and Guy Saperstein, would contribute to Ned, the truth was that his campaign would be built on his own personal fortune. (He would spend, all told, more than $12 million.)

Just what Ned's improbable campaign was supposed to be about—aside from taking down Lieberman, a man he had given money to in the past—was never entirely clear. He liked to say that his candidacy wasn't just a protest, but that it was about all the things he was *for*: health care for everyone, improving public schools, good stuff like that. But those were just vague, throwaway lines in a running monologue that always came back to the war or Lieberman's role in the Schiavo case. The truth was that it didn't really matter if Ned had an actual argument for governing the country, because his supporters couldn't have cared less. All that mattered was that he was standing up to Joe Lieberman—and, by extension, to all those establishment Democrats who had blithely joined the parade while the president led the country off a cliff.

"It's like all I have to do is stand up there and say, 'I'm not Joe Lieberman!' and everyone just goes, 'Woo woo woo!'" Ned told me once, waving his arms in the air. "It doesn't even matter what I say. It's all about the war. They don't want to hear about anything else. Even when I point out the other real differences between us, no one's listening."

"Does that bother you?" I asked him. Ned stared at me blankly. "You know, that it's all about the war. I mean, are you comfortable with that?"

"Sure, I'm comfortable with it," Ned said finally, in a tone that suggested I wasn't very smart. "I wouldn't have gotten into this if it weren't for the war."

In the early days, back in those first months of 2006, Ned didn't have a field organization or a staff, and no one knew who he was. The state's newspapers and TV stations wrote him off as a gadfly and paid him little attention. What he did have was the support of a handful of local blogs with names like "My Left Nutmeg." "I discovered the blogs, and the blogs discovered me," Ned told me later. "And they were frank. They said, 'Look, I don't know much about Ned Lamont, but I know a hell of a lot about Joe Lieberman, and we don't like what we see there. So give this guy a shot. Go to Naples Pizza and see what he has to say.' And all of a sudden we would have 150 people hanging from the rafters."

The national bloggers, with their larger readerships and their ability to attract liberal money and volunteers from out of state, were more hesitant. Some in the netroots worried that taking on Lieberman, in a year when Democrats suddenly had a very real chance to recapture the Senate, might alienate allies such as Howard Dean and Harry Reid. Matt Stoller, a blogger on MyDD and the creator of the Townhouse forum, had another concern, which he voiced in a post called "The Risks for the Blogosphere of Taking on Lieberman."

"The progressive blogosphere is right now facing a crisis of legitimacy," Stoller wrote, noting that they were viewed as "disorganized,
immature and incoherent." The problem with backing the Lamont
campaign, Stoller worried, was that it would only heighten this perception. Inevitably, the bloggers would simply be seen as trying to
purge the party of those who disagreed with them, rather than offering up some more positive vision. "In picking this fight against
Lieberman, we're not really running 'on' something," he said. "I see
no thread of articulated principles that would justify a Lieberman
challenge."

Other bloggers responded to Stoller angrily. Lieberman, they
said, was helping the president destroy the country by supporting his
war in Iraq, his ruinous tax cuts, and his penchant for secrecy. (In
fact, Lieberman's voting record wasn't markedly different from a lot
of other leading Democrats', including Hillary Clinton's.) All of this
seemed, more or less, to confirm what Stoller was saying—that the
case for a primary was more about what the bloggers opposed than
about any affirmative argument. But that missed the point. The real
goal here for the netroots wasn't so much about change as it was
about power. If they could take down Lieberman, as Markos himself
liked to say, "then no one will want to be the Joe Lieberman of 2008."
If that happened, Democratic politicians wouldn't simply patronize
the blogs; they would fear them, too.

Stoller declared himself persuaded by his fellow bloggers. In fact,
in the months ahead, he became one of Lamont's main backers online, shuttling back and forth between Washington and Hartford. He
introduced Ned to Tim Tagaris, a sharp former marine who had
blogged about Paul Hackett's Ohio campaign and who was now
doing netroots outreach for Dean at the party headquarters. Tagaris
left the DNC and moved to Connecticut to work full time for Ned's
campaign. Like Dean and Hackett before him, Ned became an Internet candidate. It was true that he couldn't have gained legitimacy

without his millions of dollars, but it was equally true that all his money would have been wasted had the netroots not given him the forum and the base of volunteers he needed to compete.

Markos himself even appeared in one of Lamont's thirty-second spots. Ned told me he had never heard of "this guy Markos" before he decided to run. In fact, the whole online world sounded as foreign to him as it had been to Dean when he first ran for president. "I'm proud of the support we get from the blogs," Ned told me during a conversation in his Greenwich office in July. "People stereotype the blogs. They say they're liberal blogs. Well, it's not that they're liberal blogs. There are conservative blogs, too. There are blogs about stamp collecting. There are blogs about a whole lot of topics."

And yet, if anyone took this to mean that Lamont didn't understand the antiestablishment ethos that had attached itself to his campaign, he was wrong. Ned understood the larger phenomenon of online politics, in fact, about as well as anyone I'd met in my travels—largely because he had come from the fast-changing world of cable television. This gave Ned a unique perspective on monopolies and large institutions, and on the technological advances that were smashing them to pieces. He understood that the Democratic Party was only now experiencing the same upheaval that was already transforming virtually every other area of American society, including the one in which he did business.

"There are more choices everywhere, aren't there?" Ned asked me. "Look at cable TV. We've gone from three channels to three hundred channels. On the Internet, everybody is their own channel. In general, allegiances are just less binding than they used to be." He thought for a moment. "A generation ago, or two generations ago, you joined IBM and, damn it, you held on tight. And you were going to get a good retirement, and you were going to be there forty years later. Today, most people have six or seven different jobs. You're more free as an individual. And I think that's positive. And politics is one of the last things to change.

"So the MoveOns and the Daily Koses, they pick up on that," he said. No longer could the Democratic Party expect its loyal followers to fall in line behind an anointed incumbent like Lieberman, just because they were supposed to. "People have different allegiances now," Ned observed. "They have allegiances to ideas. They have allegiances to passions. And they're developing allegiances to people. Did I anticipate that back in December? No. But I am the happy beneficiary of it now."

If Ned understood, on some deeper level, what was happening in Democratic politics, Joe Lieberman couldn't really have been more clueless. Just six years earlier, he had been the vice presidential nominee of the party, and, other than the fact that it had ended in a defeat he had little to do with, the moment had been everything he might have hoped. The voters had adored him. The reporters on his plane had found him unpretentious and endearingly funny. Joe had assumed that this bravura performance as a supporting actor would make him the leading contender for the starring role four years later. But by 2004, things had changed. It was the war, yes, but something else too—something fundamental in the party that Joe just didn't grasp. Howard Dean, who had been a total nobody when Joe made his improbable leap into history, was breaking all the fund-raising records in the run-up to the primaries, while Joe, surprised and humiliated, lamely predicted a surge of "Joe-mentum" and then bragged about finishing "in a three-way tie for third" in New Hampshire. (In other words, he had come in fifth.) The fall was dizzying.

He came away from the 2004 campaign lost and depressed. He didn't talk to people, not even his closest advisers. When he did, he made it clear that he blamed the consultants who had misled him, and he was determined to follow his own counsel from now on. It seemed that he now aspired to be the Pat Moynihan of the new Senate, a statesman who eschewed doctrine and followed his conscience, somehow rising above the petty political differences between the two parties. The problem was that an intense partisanship now gripped Washington and the country. The day for Pat Moynihans had come and gone.

When I visited him in his Capitol office in December 2005, a few months before Lamont entered the race, Lieberman seemed profoundly confused by what was happening in the party. We talked for an hour about 2004 and what had happened since, and the conversation seemed to literally deflate him, as he receded further and further into his chair. At one point, he remarked that the whole conversation was like therapy, because he hadn't really talked about any of this before.

"The thing that animates our party now is a deep hatred of Bush," he told me. "It's unbelievable." He referenced a poll he had seen, which found that most Democrats thought Hurricane Katrina was a more transformational event than the terrorist attacks of September 11. "That's got to be hatred of Bush," Lieberman said, shaking his head.

He talked about the blogs, which he didn't read. "There's no control," Lieberman said. "There's no editor there." A lot of people said similar things about the Web in a celebratory tone, but when Lieberman said it, he sounded baffled and disappointed. "It's like Hyde Park in London. Anyone who wants to just gets up on the stand and says whatever they want. And it's not like there's an editor who says, 'Hey, wait a minute.'"

I asked him about the Kiss and all the consternation it had caused online. He contended that there had been no actual lip contact.

"It just seems outrageous," Lieberman told me. "If someone wants to disagree with me about the war, that's their right to do that. But there was such an outrageous fuss that went on, and still goes on, when the president came down the aisle at the State of the Union and hugged me. I joked and said, 'He kissed me!' Then there was a Web site in Connecticut for a while where, when you went to it, it showed three photos of his approaching me and allegedly kissing me." He shook his head and slumped back in his chair. "But that's where we are."

You would have thought that Lieberman would understand where all this had to be heading. You would have thought he would understand that a guy like Lamont wasn't a candidate, per se—he was a vehicle. But Joe was living in a bygone political world, where respectable approval ratings meant that an incumbent Democrat could keep his seat for life. He didn't get what was happening out there. After Ned made his fund-raising trip to the West Coast in April, Joe's former chief of staff, Bill Andresen, got wind of it and tried to warn him. "This is going to be a national campaign, and he's going to raise all kinds of money," Andresen told his old boss.

"You really think so?" Joe asked.

Carter Eskew had a similar experience. One of the party's most talented admen and strategists, Eskew had been with Joe since the first campaign in 1988, and although all his work now was corporate, he was willing to help out of loyalty. (Such is the plight of campaign consultants, who, like Al Pacino in *The Godfather: Part III,* are always trying to get out, only to find themselves pulled back in.) Right from the start, though, Eskew could see it coming. This was the Dean campaign all over again, he thought. In order to get his own party's endorsement in a primary, Lieberman was going to have to get through a convention process that was controlled by local activists, and Eskew thought he might lose control of the whole thing right there. Even if he didn't, Lamont had way too much money to be easily dismissed. Plus, Eskew knew Ned—as it happened, they had prepped at Phillips Exeter together—and he knew this wasn't a guy who was going to make an ass of himself. People liked him. He didn't back down.

Not long after Lamont announced his candidacy, Eskew drove over to Hillandale, the Liebermans' gated community. "I know this is going to be an unpleasant conversation," he told Joe and his wife, Hadassah. "But I think you're going to lose the primary, and I think you should run as an independent."

Shocked, Joe asked what his chances were. Eskew put them at 45 percent, if Joe dedicated himself to visiting all those local town committees and the interest groups that had never interested him. In his own mind, Eskew thought he was being unduly kind.

Joe thought it over. Anyone who knew Lieberman knew him to be decent and gentle, but there was something else there, too, a kind of "fuck you" streak when you told him what to do. Joe's favorite song was "My Way." He said he thought Eskew was wrong. He put his own odds of winning the primary at 75 percent.

While Joe spent most of the spring back in Washington, activists in Connecticut were touring the state with a giant, papier-mâché rendering of the Kiss tied to the back of a truck, garnering headlines and whipping up resentment against Bush and the war. Despite Eskew's worst fears, Joe won the majority of delegates at the May convention, which meant that he still had the party's official blessing, but just barely; Lamont came away with a third of the delegates, legitimizing his challenge in the eyes of the local media. In the campaign's only head-to-head debate, Lieberman sounded haughty and petulant, as if he couldn't quite believe he was being forced to share a stage with such a political neophyte. Two weeks later, a new poll showed that Ned had, for the first time, inched into the lead.

Even now, the senator and his wife seemed mystified by the bloggers and the MoveOn volunteers, by all the anti-Joe bumper stickers and the furious activists who stalked him at his campaign appearances. "We don't understand these people," Hadassah told Carter Eskew. "They're from another world."

Nervous Democratic leaders in Washington found themselves transfixed by this intraparty feud, which threatened to split the party between the old establishment and the new, ascendant progressives. "The Lieberman-Lamont race is huge," Donna Brazile, who had close ties to people on both sides of the divide, told me over coffee one afternoon in Washington. "It's huge. Win or lose, it will have ramifications for the party. But if Lieberman loses, it should put the whole party on notice that Dean's people are alive and vibrant and that the old days are gone, when everyone was neutral and gutless. I think the netroots will usher the party into a whole new era."

Normally, the unspoken policy of the national party was to protect its incumbents. But Howard Dean had privately disdained Lieberman since the 2004 campaign, and he was loath to stand in the way of the progressive uprising that considered him its spiritual leader. Lieberman's supporters fumed that Dean refused to rein in his brother, Jim, who lived in southern Connecticut and who was rallying Dean followers to Lamont's cause. For his part, Howard insisted he would remain neutral, as party chairmen must, but that didn't stop him from running around calling Lieberman an "outlier" in the party—until at last Tom Carper, a Delaware senator and a close friend of both men, personally pleaded with Dean to stop.

Most of Joe's colleagues calculated that it was smarter to stay impartial until the matter was decided—a twist that stung the former vice presidential nominee. When Hillary Clinton had run for Senate in 2000 in a state where she was considered an interloper, Lieberman had campaigned hard alongside her in New York City, with its heavy concentration of Jewish voters; now, as he clung to his political fortunes, Hillary was noticeably absent. When rumors circulated around the time of the debate that Joe was considering running as an independent if he lost the primary, Hillary was quick to say that she would support the winner of the primary—no matter what.

Her husband was another story. Despite their problematic history during the impeachment, Bill Clinton and Joe Lieberman had been friends since their law school days at Yale. It was important to the former president, a serious Southern Baptist, to demonstrate that he had forgiven Lieberman for the public assault on his character. More to the point, perhaps, Clinton must have understood that the anti-Lieberman insurrection wasn't just about Joe and the war, but about his own legacy, as well. The campaign against Joe was a campaign against the accommodating, bipartisan ethos of the '90s— against everything, in other words, that the Democracy Alliance donors and the netroots associated with Clintonism.

And so Clinton made a foray across the border into Connecticut. "Don't ever let anybody tell you these guys aren't good Democrats," the former president told a rally in Danbury, referring, presumably, to Lieberman and other centrist Democrats. "Don't say that about Joe Lieberman." Clinton said nothing derogatory about Ned, but, as he did during our conversation in Harlem, he used the occasion to mount a vigorous defense of his own record as a progressive, and he made the case—on Hillary's behalf as much as Joe's—that there was room to have disagreed on the necessity of the war resolution. "Go out and elect Joe Lieberman," Clinton pleaded. "He's earned it. He's been a good Democrat. He's a good man, and he'll do you proud."

Clinton's words disgusted the netroots, who found themselves, for the first time, openly arrayed against the Great Triangulator himself. "I hope this is the final straw for all the remaining Clinton defenders on this board," one diarist commented on Daily Kos. "The guy lives to screw the left." Said another, echoing Markos's speech at YearlyKos, "More proof that the Clintons are obsolete as a political force. Let's dispose of them in the same dustbin we will put the Bush family in."

Lieberman, meanwhile, kept talking about how much he had done for Connecticut, about all the federal money he had brought home and how he had saved the Seawolf submarine built in Groton, but he might as well have been talking about his high school algebra grade, for all the primary electorate seemed to care. By midsummer, he had made a decision that would have seemed, not long before, laughably implausible. He directed the staff to begin gathering the signatures needed to get on the fall ballot as an independent, just in case. That way, if Joe did end up losing the primary, he would get a second shot at Lamont in the general election.

On its face, this move had the look of a longtime incumbent clinging by his fingernails to power, even if it required circumventing the process, but Joe saw it differently. As far as he was concerned, if Ned won the primary, it would be because only a small number of radical activists had bothered to vote. The people of Connecticut, Joe thought, shouldn't lose a senator of such clout and wisdom to the whim of one small, angry throng.

He made a desperate last stand, and it came down to race. Like most establishment Democrats, Joe had long relied on huge majorities of loyal black voters in the cities. And so now, facing catastrophe, his campaign distributed flyers attacking Ned for having belonged to an all-white country club. He brought in a legendary labor organizer from Washington to unleash a massive urban turnout program. The online, outsider movement that was fueling Lamont's campaign was almost entirely white and affluent; if Lieberman could get enough black voters to the polls, he might just be able to survive the wave.

He got an inadvertent boost from one of the leading national bloggers, Jane Hamsher of Firedoglake, who was now spending a lot of time with the Lamont team in Connecticut. A onetime Hollywood producer whose seminal work was *Natural Born Killers,* the movie that set a new standard for senseless violence onscreen, Hamsher now brought that same tasteful sensibility to politics; she posted on her blog a doctored photo of Bill Clinton and Lieberman together, with the candidate inexplicably pictured in blackface, like in one of those old minstrel shows. Lamont was forced to publicly disavow the image, but the whole episode demonstrated the downside of relying on the netroots, and it reinforced the damaging impression that Ned's campaign had been hijacked and hauled away by a bunch of hate-filled quasi-adolescents.

Even so, when it came to courting black voters, Lieberman had again failed to heed the warnings of strategists who understood the changing crosscurrents of Democratic politics. A month earlier, Donna Brazile had urged him to call African American leaders like Jesse Jackson and Al Sharpton and lock down their support. "You've got to reach out to them now," she had said. Lieberman didn't. And so he shouldn't have been surprised when both men, who were against the war and who could see the power shifting inside the party, broke with him and announced they were coming to Connecticut to campaign with Ned.

Joe barely had time to reel before he felt the last, crushing blow: The *New York Times,* the very embodiment of the baby boomer liberal establishment, shocked the political world by endorsing Lamont. The sturdy walls of the party structure seemed now to be falling in.

I n the days leading up to the primary, dozens of bloggers and other volunteers from the online world disembarked at Bradley International Airport, near Hartford, looking to make history. They were on the verge of what could be their first-ever election win, and they wanted to be able to say that they had been there at the moment when the movement finally arrived. "D.C. Democrats should be very afraid," Matt Stoller wrote on MyDD. "If white progressives, disaffected union members, and blacks strengthen the informal alliance that's being created in this campaign, there's not a Democrat anywhere in the country who can't be beaten in a primary."

By day, the bloggers and the MoveOn types milled around Lamont's headquarters in Meriden, or wherever they could get access to wireless networks. At night, they retired to Sullivan's, a tavern near the Yale campus, where Tim Tagaris, Lamont's in-house blogger, happened to know the owner. They stayed on friends' floors or booked the cheapest rooms they could find at budget motels. For many, it was their first taste of a real-life, three-dimensional campaign, and it inspired some exuberant metaphors. "I feel as though this is the quiet before the start of the great battle at the end of a major blockbuster trilogy," Chris Bowers wrote on MyDD, "as though we are about to storm the gates of Mordor or send a tiny fleet out toward the Death Star."

Another blogger, TRex of Firedoglake, described the difference between how the campaign looked online and how it actually looked on the ground: "It's like the difference between watching two people have sex in a movie and actually having sex.... In sex scenes in movies, everything is so choreographed and artful, no one ever falls off the bed, gets hair in their mouth, makes ridiculous noises, or gets a massive cramp in their foot from curling their toes. In fact, watching people have sex in a movie is really nothing like having sex at all. Similarly, watching TV anchors and pundits parse and pontificate about this primary race is absolutely nothing like being here at the white-hot center of the action."

Arriving back at that white-hot center myself, I was glad to find that the sudden influx of bloggers included Gina Cooper. Like the other bloggers, Gina couldn't stand being across the country at such a critical moment, and, since YearlyKos was the closest thing she had to a day job, she bought a last-minute ticket and presented herself at Lamont headquarters as a volunteer. The overwhelmed campaign immediately put her to work entering voter IDs into a computer—

tedious, mindless work that she was all too glad to contribute, even if she felt a little out of place. But then her fortunes turned. A bunch of volunteers from the blogosphere showed up, and they recognized her. "You're Gina?" the other volunteers started saying, loudly. "Oh my God! It's Gina from YearlyKos!" This confused the Lamont staff, who wanted to know what made Gina so special. Before she knew it, she had been given a promotion. They took Gina to the back of the office, where her new job was to take phone messages from reporters.

Then, the day before the primary, Gina accompanied other campaign aides on a tour of the Sheraton Four Points across the street, so they could see where the press would be situated on election night. Having been through all this with YearlyKos, Gina was confused by the setup. Where were the phone lines? she asked. How were they planning to run the TV cables out to the trucks? What bandwidth was their Wi-Fi? The Four Points staff looked at her blankly. They had never hosted this kind of thing. And so now the Lamont team assigned Gina to take care of all the election night logistics, which, she quickly deduced, were a mess.

The hotel manager told her there was no way to set up more phone lines. "Listen," Gina said sternly. "Y'all are going to have 275 accredited journalists here tomorrow. You need to have phone lines." The manager panicked and sent for some regional managers, who saw to it that Gina got dozens of phone lines, TV risers, and a passable, if unreliable, wireless network.

It was Gina, in fact, who figured out how to get Ned and his family from the first-floor suite at the Four Points to the packed ballroom where he would give what they hoped would be a victory speech. No one could find a route through the little hotel that wouldn't subject him to crowds of admirers and reporters. Gina had another idea: Why not bring the Lamont family out the back door and then drive them around the hotel to the kitchen entrance, which would get them to the stage without being mobbed? It was ingenious, and the campaign staff drew it up just that way. They seemed to have forgotten that Gina was a blogger who had just arrived from out of town. It was as if she had been doing this for years.

During her nights in Connecticut, Gina downed a beer or two with the other bloggers at Sullivan's, then drove her rental car back to the Four Points, where she had managed to book a room. She lent some of the bloggers her room key so they could use the bathroom to change and clean up. On primary night, she came back to find Chris Bowers, fully clothed and passed out on her bed, dreaming happily of Mordor.

Lamont's guys set up their primary day headquarters in a series of conference rooms in back of the Four Points, with sliding glass doors leading out to the pool. The space included a separate room just for the bloggers—a first in American campaigns. The bloggers sat at a series of round tables, banging away on their keyboards and sharing dubious bits of information, along with cans of Foster's from a communal cooler.

Tim Tagaris, dressed in his customary Cubs cap and Greg Maddux jersey, with a cigarette dangling from his lips, stalked around the patio all afternoon, cursing angrily into his cell phone. The Lieberman campaign was complaining that one of these bloggers had hacked into their Web site and disabled it, and the local press was all over the story. "If they wanted to, they could have had it back up three hours ago!" Tagaris was shouting. "I will send someone over there to HQ, and we will fix it for them. They don't know what they're talking about. Only thirty people go to the fucking site, anyway."

Actually, Tagaris could think of a few bloggers who might well have torpedoed Joe's site just for the bragging rights—the first thing he did after he heard about it was to call Bob Brigham, one of his blogger buddies from the Hackett campaign, who would have been a natural for such a stunt. Brigham swore up and down that it wasn't him. Now reporters were saying that the state attorney general was going to investigate. "They can have my computer!" Tagaris railed at me, in between calls. "I have other computers. They can take this one and go through my e-mails. There are a few embarrassing ones to ex-girlfriends, maybe, but that's it."

As day turned to dusk, the action moved into the ballroom, where a lot of the progressive activists I had come to know well were now converging in a single moment of much-anticipated triumph. I shared a drink at the bar with Tom Matzzie, who told me that MoveOn's fifty thousand members in Connecticut might well make the difference in the race. Jerome Armstrong showed up late, and he and I talked with an elated Jim Dean over by the pool. Then I ran into Matt Stoller, who had spent the day following Lieberman around and holding up nasty signs. At one event, in a Hartford housing project, some of Joe's supporters—"LieberYouth," as Stoller liked to call them—blocked him from getting near the senator. So Stoller gave his sign, which said "2,600 DEAD," to a little black boy and told him what to do. The boy, holding the sign aloft, did as he was told and walked right up to Lieberman, who stood there awkwardly, not knowing how to escape. Stoller reveled in recounting this story of a little boy used as a political pawn. He found it hilarious.

The night wore on without any sign of a quick resolution. The ballroom speakers blasted out "Born to Run" and "Young Americans." (How did every election night party get the exact same music? Was there a disc somewhere?) Some of the volunteers got bored and decided to mock Alan Colmes, Fox News Channel's sad echo of a liberal commentator. They held up a sign over Colmes's head, where the camera could see it, that said "Fox Sucks Ass." Colmes didn't notice, or maybe he had just grown so inured to indignity that it hardly mattered to him anymore. Either way, his reaction was disappointing.

Ned and his family were holed up in a suite on the first floor, along with Tom Swan and Rob Johnson, two of the guys who had encouraged him to run in the first place. All of them were asking: Where was Joe? Ned wasn't about to go onstage until Joe had conceded the race. But even after the TV anchors had all declared Ned the winner, sending a roar of cheers cascading down the hallways of the Four Points, the phone didn't ring. Swan suspected that Lieberman was going to wait until the last possible minute, to make sure that Ned would have to speak after most of the voters had gone to bed.

Over at the Goodwin Hotel in Hartford, meanwhile, Joe and his aides were assessing the same situation. They knew that the television stations were almost certainly right, that Joe had lost by at least a few points. They knew they were holding up the time-honored procession of speeches. But here was the problem: As the final results trickled in from New Haven and Bridgeport and Stamford, the gap kept closing, and the race kept getting just a little bit tighter. Joe was ready to admit defeat, but Carter Eskew held up a hand. He had been with Gore and Lieberman on that awful night in Nashville six years earlier, when they had been ready to concede the presidential race to Bush and Cheney, only to find out that Florida was still unresolved. "Now, wait a minute," Eskew said. "We've been here before." Everyone laughed. They waited some more.

By about ten twenty, though, it had become apparent that this was no Florida, and Joe's own crowd was starting to dwindle. The moment had come for Joe to go downstairs and admit that he had, in effect, been bounced from his party.

When Joe finally called over to the Four Points, Ned was on the line with John Edwards, who had called to offer his congratulations. (He would be followed, in the next few hours, by Barack Obama, Howard Dean, Hillary Clinton, Chuck Schumer, and Ted

Kennedy). The conversation between Lamont and Lieberman was unusually acid. Joe said he was "conceding this round" but complained that Ned had "smeared" him. He said he would run as an independent. Ned told him he was a citizen of the country and could do whatever he wanted. They hung up abruptly.

"What an asshole," Ned muttered.

I watched Joe's concession speech—and the reaction to it—on a TV in the blogger room. "I am disappointed not just because I lost, but because the old politics of partisan polarization won today," Lieberman said. "For the sake of our state, our country, and my party, I cannot and will not let that result stand."

"Then we'll kick your ass again!" one of the bloggers shouted.

"Fuck you, fuck you, fuck you!" screamed another, brandishing his middle finger at the screen. I couldn't actually hear most of the rest of the speech over all the shouting.

Ned was furious too. Rob Johnson pleaded with him to calm down, not to let his anger show on the podium, in front of all the cameras. They took Ned and his family around back and drove him to the side entrance, exactly as planned.

The entourage felt the building shudder as soon as they walked in. The noise was deafening. It was a primary race decided by three hundred thousand Democratic voters in a small state, a race that hadn't even eliminated either of the candidates from contention—and yet it was much more than that. Through Ned, the new progressives had finally managed to achieve, for the first time, what they had set out to do with Howard Dean three years earlier: They had beaten the establishment. They had served notice to the party and to the assembled national media that none of those sleepless bloggers in the room down the hall, none of the elated volunteers and activists stomping their feet in the ballroom, none of the disenchanted millionaires who had written Ned checks—none of these people were going away anytime soon.

As it happened, this would be the high moment for Ned Lamont, the one he and his supporters would always cherish. Beginning the very next day, the battle between Lamont and Lieberman shifted to the general election, which turned on less partisan, more independent voters, rather than on highly motivated core Democrats. Almost immediately, Ned began to lose control of the campaign. The reasons for this were various and mundane, from his affiliation with Al Sharpton and Jesse Jackson, which alienated a lot of white moderates, to his lack of any discernible agenda, which became more glaring as the months wore on. As his campaign slowly cratered, most of the bloggers abandoned him; they had proved their point, and it was time to move on to the business of beating actual Republicans. By the time the November rematch rolled around, Lieberman cruised easily to victory, and few people outside the state even seemed to notice.

But for these few hours, at least, on the night of that unforgettable primary victory, Ned Lamont, the cable millionaire with the Jimmy Stewart stammer, was the symbol of a movement at the height of its power. Progressives controlled the party now, and Ned was their trophy. As he entered the kitchen on his way to the stage, Ned looked confused for a moment. Then he noticed a woman standing there whom he probably didn't recognize.

"This way, Mr. Lamont," Gina Cooper said, and, as Lamont followed her motion toward the stage, she felt a rush of pride unlike anything she'd ever known.

CHAPTER THIRTEEN

Score!

On election night that November, I decided to visit Democratic Party headquarters in Washington, just to get a sense of the mood. As it happened, Rahm Emanuel had consented to let three or four reporters hang around his office after the polls closed, and by the time I got there at about eight, he seemed even more tightly wound than usual. A soothing Shawn Colvin album was playing on Rahm's iPod, which was docked on his desk, but it was clearly having no effect. Rahm was watching four TVs at once, looking for whatever scraps of information he could get his hands on. Aides kept scurrying in and handing him yellow notes, then fleeing as fast as they could.

"How's Connecticut?" he snapped at one aide. "Any word?" In addition to the Senate race, the state was the site of three pivotal House races. Rahm looked at the group of us leaning against the wall and seated at his conference table. "Nobody knows anything," he complained. "All we've got is anecdotal evidence."

He turned back to the aide, who had almost made it out of his office. "Just find out what Gersh is saying!" he barked, referring to the party's top numbers guy. Rahm feared recounts in several races that might be too close to call by the end of the night. "My gut tells me people will be packing bags and getting on planes tomorrow morning," he said glumly.

The atmosphere in the room was impossibly tense, so I decided to change the subject. I asked Rahm about his day. He glared at me. I ignored it. This was what Rahm almost always did when you asked him a question that didn't interest him. He said that he had woken up in Chicago, swum a mile, and flown with his family to Washington, where his three children had taken their first tour of the Capitol. He was putting his ten-year-old son, Zacharias, to work, having him run the latest election numbers from the war room over to the whiteboard near his office.

"I talked to Bill Daley," Rahm said, referring to the former commerce secretary whose legendary father had ruled Chicago for twenty-one years during the Democratic heyday. "He said, 'When I was a kid, I got my start that way. I used to run district numbers from the Western Union office down to my father at the Bismarck Hotel.' And I said, 'Yeah, well, there you go. Your dad screwed you up, and I'm going to screw up my kids.'"

I laughed. Rahm didn't.

He saw a light flashing on his phone and picked it up. "Yeah," he said, by way of greeting. "Uh-huh. Well, absentees are the key in Baron Hill." Baron Hill was not a place—he was a candidate in Indiana. "You know anything? OK. Stay close." He hung up.

"Isn't this fun for you guys?" he asked the reporters. He looked at us expectantly. "Anything else?"

On one of the TVs, Wolf Blitzer was saying, "Congressman Emanuel was absolutely exhausted two days ago."

"What'd he say?" Rahm said, his head snapping toward the screen. None of us wanted to tell him. He shrugged, glanced at another note, and picked up another flashing line. "Jerry! What do you think? Really? Do you know what's in? Have they gotten the

East End yet?" The East End of what—Cleveland? Dubuque?—he
didn't say. Although it couldn't possibly be true, Rahm seemed to
know the value of every precinct in every congressional district in the
country. I had a feeling that this was what it must have been like
watching machine guys like the elder Daley work the phones back in
the fifties.

Rahm hung up another call, this one from Indiana. Then he
looked at us and exhaled loudly. "OK!" he shouted, by which he
clearly meant that it was time for us to leave. We'd barely said
anything, but he'd had enough, all the same.

Rahm got about two hours of sleep that night, then showed up
for a news conference in the morning, plainly relieved. By then, it
was clear that Democrats had experienced a historic night. They had
gained thirty seats in the House and would end up taking back six in
the Senate without losing a single incumbent—an unprecedented
feat in American politics. Democrats had regained control of both
chambers, albeit by slim margins, for the first time since 1994,
dispatching some of their most despised adversaries on the right, such
as senators George Allen of Virginia and Rick Santorum of Pennsylvania, as well as some of the last surviving Republican moderates,
who simply found themselves in the wrong party at the wrong time.

Two-thirds of the Democratic gains came in states that had voted
for Bush in 2004. In Ohio, where Bush had sealed his reelection and
where every statewide official had been a Republican for the last
decade, Democrats took back a Senate seat and swept the races for
governor, secretary of state, attorney general, and treasurer. In fact,
around the country, Democrats could now claim outright dominance
of fifteen statehouses, compared with only ten for the Republicans.
The once-mighty Democratic Party, having seen its fortunes fall just
two years earlier to the point where its long-term viability no longer
seemed assured, had done more than just rebound. It had been
reborn.

O r had it?

The progressive outsiders who had, over the past two years, waged a campaign to rebuild the party—to make it more confrontational and more tactically adept—now rushed to take credit for the party's remarkable reversal. After battling Rahm and all the other top Democrats over how and where to spend the party's money, Howard Dean asserted that his fifty-state strategy had exceeded his own expectations. MoveOn.org released a memo suggesting that its virtual field program, in which MoveOn members called voters in other states, might well have made the difference. The bloggers, too, declared themselves the force behind the Democratic revival. "No longer will people rely on conventional wisdom to dictate how campaigns are waged," Jerome Armstrong crowed in the *Christian Science Monitor* two days after the votes were cast. "Instead, millions of online activists will guide the campaign strategies of progressives to succeed from this point forward."

There was merit to all of these claims. The new progressives had, at the very least, turned out some additional votes, and they had hammered away relentlessly at Bush's vulnerabilities. But there wasn't much evidence to suggest that the election results had all that much to do with anything that either progressives or Democrats had done, unless you counted not having done something idiotic during the campaign, which was something. Exit polls showed that furious Americans had simply reached their saturation point with Bush— with his calamitous war and his corrupt party and his divisive air of superiority. An analysis of the data conducted by Stan Greenberg's polling firm confirmed that Iraq had played a huge role; 41 percent of voters said that was their most pressing issue, and, of those, three-quarters had voted Democrat. Nearly four in ten Americans said they had cast their votes as a protest against the president personally.

Terrorism ranked fifth among the issues that were most important to voters, suggesting that America had finally and flatly rejected Bush's essential argument—that global terror represented the gravest threat since Hitler and that the only way to eradicate it was to act preemptively. Bush would remain in office for two more years, but his presidency was essentially finished.

What voters had not done was to endorse any Democratic argument—because, of course, there wasn't one. A poll conducted by the Associated Press just after the election found that, while most Americans considered the Iraq war the biggest priority for the new Democratic Congress, 57 percent of them said Democrats didn't have any plan for solving the crisis, compared with only 29 percent who thought they did. In the end, Americans had delivered an emphatic rebuke to Bush and the Republicans by casting their votes for the only available alternative—which, truth be told, was all the Democrats had aspired to be.

The voters had given Democrats in Washington an opportunity to provide some new vision of governance, an invitation to end the tired ideological wars left over from the twentieth century and to begin to think, instead, about modern and ambitious ways to deal with the larger realities facing the country, from global markets to stateless terrorism. But nothing about the new majority screamed "innovation." In fact, the Democratic sweep had returned to power most of the same industrial-age politicians who had governed the last time the party was in control. The average age of the expected committee chairmen in the House was 69.7, with more of them over 70 than under. The new majority—led by Nancy Pelosi, the first woman Speaker in the country's history—vowed to enact a series of mostly worthy measures in their first hundred hours, like raising the long-stagnant minimum wage. What to do when those first four days were over, beyond continuing to attack the administration, remained an open question.

Less than a week after the elections, Simon Rosenberg held a small, salon-style dinner in his conference room, the same room where, in 2004, the Kerry campaign had plotted its strategy. While most of Simon's work at NDN, his political action committee, was now focused on demographics and technology, Simon had also commissioned a series of academic papers on globalization and its ramifications. He wanted to bring together a group of serious-minded progressives to talk about what came next, now that Democrats had a platform from which to lead.

Among those who shoveled Chinese food onto paper plates that night were Andrei Cherny and Kenny Baer of the new journal *Democracy*; Rand Beers, who would likely have been the national security adviser in a Kerry administration and was now running a small foreign policy think tank; Adam Smith, a young and thoughtful congressman from Washington State; the strategists John Lapp and Ali Weise, who had worked closely with Rahm Emanuel on the House campaigns; the progressive political scientist Tom Schaller; the writer and blogger Amy Sullivan; and Jerome Armstrong, who, since Warner's withdrawal, had turned down entreaties from some of the other presidential hopefuls and was now getting ready to attend a two-week Buddhist retreat to clear his head and figure out what to do next.

I took a seat next to Rob Stein, who had also been invited, and started in on some dumplings. For the first half hour or so, the talk around the table centered on how to solidify the party's electoral gains and protect those new House members who would almost certainly face stiff challenges in two years. There was a clear consensus among most of the guests that Democrats had to prove they could pass some kind of legislation in these first few weeks, so that voters would see they were serious about governing, and that they needed to stake out some position on Iraq. "All tactics," Rob whispered to me at one point, shaking his head.

Finally, Rob Shapiro, the Clinton administration economist who was heading up Simon's project on globalization, raised his hand gingerly. He offered that he didn't know much about politics, but it seemed to him that this election hadn't really signaled any structural change in the minds of the electorate. What reason was there to think that Democrats could keep winning if they didn't come up with some kind of serious program? "I heard every kind of argument during the campaign," Shapiro said, "but what I didn't hear was a single new idea."

This prompted Andrei Cherny to make a similar point. "I hate to say something that will get me stoned," Cherny said, "but I think we just won a big election and lost a huge opportunity." They had blown their chance to engage disillusioned voters in a genuine discussion about the future, he said, and they now had, at best, six months to do so, before the voters decided it was all just more of the same.

Congressman Smith waved away these esoteric concerns. Big ideas were overrated, he said, and usually unworkable. What Democrats really had to do was to show they were competent, so they could build on their majorities two years later. Others seconded this. America was watching, they said; this wasn't the time to overstep with big ideas or new paradigms. They needed to maintain party unity and control the media's story line. From the look on his face, Rob Shapiro couldn't have been more confounded by this discussion if the participants had suddenly mounted the conference table and broken into a Gilbert and Sullivan operetta.

It occurred to me to wonder, as I listened, what your average voter, sitting somewhere a thousand miles away, would make of this conversation. Here were some of the leading progressive minds in a party that had just days earlier taken power, at a time of disorienting change, and all they could think about was one thing: keeping power.

It was, to them, an endless game between two teams, one blue and one red, a contest of numbers with a clock that began counting down the moment it was reset. They had scored a big point on election day—nothing more. It wasn't that they didn't care about the problems of contemporary American life; it was more that they seemed to believe those problems would somehow be solved by the simple act of electing more Democrats. So certain were they in this conviction, so convinced were they of its obviousness, that they had completely forgotten to ask themselves why they believed it.

There was, in all of this, a historical irony. Seventy years ago, at the dawn of an age dominated by its towering industrial machines, visionary Democrats had distinguished their party with the force of their intellect. Now the inheritors of that party stood on the threshold of a new economic moment, when the nation seemed likely to rise or fall on the strength of its intellectual capital, and the only thing that seemed to interest them was the machinery of politics.

J ust days after the election, the first of more than a half dozen presidential aspirants began formally entering the Democratic field for 2008, including three with national followings: Hillary Clinton, Barack Obama, and John Edwards. The presence of these three celebrities in the field, along with another group of lesser-known but still credible candidates, set the stage for a dynamic debate about the country's future. It seemed a fair bet that the candidate who could articulate a relevant and convincing argument for change would be the one to rise above the field, just as Bill Clinton had in 1992.

And yet, in that opening phase of the campaign, at least, the candidates seemed strongly disinclined to challenge any of the party's long-held precepts, probably because their donors and activists seemed so disinclined to hear it. Hillary Clinton's slogan, displayed on signs and bumper stickers, proclaimed "I'm in to Win!" as if to suggest that just getting to the White House were a noble enough goal in itself. Not to be outdone, Edwards emblazoned his campaign literature with the nonsensical phrase "Tomorrow Begins Today," and he vowed to eradicate poverty and stop the exploitation of workers— worthy goals, to be sure, but pretty much indistinguishable from what other Democrats had vowed to do one hundred years earlier, at the advent of the assembly line. Obama, meanwhile, declared himself the vanguard of a new generation of leaders, poised to confront a new generation's challenges. He followed this up, however, by asserting that the party already had plenty of big ideas; the only thing Democrats were really lacking, he said, was hope—whatever that meant.

There was plenty of time left for the candidates to develop more compelling themes (at that same early juncture in the 2004 campaign, after all, Howard Dean hadn't yet emerged as the man who would take politics into the Internet age), but there were historical reasons to believe they might not. The story of modern politics was the story of popular movements molding their candidates, not the other way around. Roosevelt didn't create progressive government; the progressives of the early twentieth century created him. Lyndon Johnson and Robert Kennedy, while they despised each other, both derived their essential arguments about social justice from the equality movements of the late fifties and early sixties. Ronald Reagan would not have existed without the movement conservatives who offered him a philosophical anchor. These were great and preternaturally talented leaders, men who had the charisma and the intellect to synthesize the arguments that each of these movements had made, to persuade voters of their urgency, and to adapt them to the realm of policy making. But they were merely conduits for change, and they would never have emerged as public visionaries had others not laid the intellectual foundations for their arguments.

In this way, Clinton, Obama, and Edwards were actually sounding like perfect vehicles for the outsider movement that had come to dominate their party. Their antiwar rhetoric echoed the long-past glory days of Democratic politics. They railed against conservatives and corporations for creating the growing inequities in American life, suggesting, as populist Democrats like William Jennings Bryan had at the turn of the last century, that the march of technology and consolidation might somehow be reversed by executive order. They promised defiance and principle, but they were careful to say nothing that any Democratic activist wouldn't immediately agree with. They didn't sound like FDR or Reagan. They sounded like Ned Lamont.

Even before they hired policy aides, meanwhile, all the Democrats vying for the nomination rushed to hire bloggers who could help ingratiate them to the netroots. It seemed assured, in fact, that, if any of them did win in 2008, America would be introduced to its first official White House blogger. The perils of this cross between virtual politics and the real thing became apparent right away, when two militant bloggers hired by Edwards were criticized by a Catholic group for having said hateful things about religion on their blogs. One had referred to Bush's Christian supporters as "wingnut Christofascists," while the other had mocked the Virgin Mary. Edwards, a thoroughly decent guy who seemed torn between his own sense of propriety and his determined courting of the netroots, denounced the comments but said he intended to keep the bloggers on anyway. After a few more days of turmoil, they did him a favor and resigned.

A little more than a week after the midterm elections, the Democracy Alliance met again, this time at the Mandarin Oriental Hotel in Miami. The mood at this conference was radically improved from the one in Austin, and not only because the Democrats had just taken back Congress. After Austin, several of the largest donors—

including the service employees' union—had decided that the only way to save the alliance was to take over the dysfunctional board of directors, and they had put up a "reform slate" of candidates, all but one of whom were elected. The new board chair and vice chair were Rob McKay, son of the founder of Taco Bell, and Anna Burger, the service employees' secretary-treasurer. The new board featured several professional philanthropists, such as Gara LaMarche, Soros's policy adviser; these were people who ran foundations or managed money for other wealthy investors, and they were determined to straighten out the struggling and chaotic alliance.

The first thing they did was to abruptly fire Judy Wade. They didn't share her ideal of the alliance as a kind of rolling seminar, and they didn't think she could repair her damaged relationships with a lot of the partners. They also scrapped the byzantine grant-making process, with its working groups and project teams, and promised to introduce a simpler, less bureaucratic design in a few months' time. Most significantly, they brought Rob Stein back into the inner circle and asked him to resume his role as the chief visionary and recruiter. Rob had patiently bided his time on the periphery of the alliance, and he had ultimately outlasted most of those who had deposed him in those bitter days after the 2004 election. Now he was also assigned the task of writing yet another iteration of the mission statement, something that might clarify what these progressive investors were actually trying to achieve. After two turbulent years, the Democracy Alliance was, more or less, rebooting.

Gone, too, was much of the ludicrous secrecy. I was surprised when Judy Wade's replacement—Kelly Craighead, a Hillary Clinton loyalist who had been working behind the scenes at the alliance until now—called to invite me to the Miami conference without my even asking. This time, my name tag wasn't black, and there were no shredders or security guards to be found. During the conference, the partners voted overwhelmingly, by an impromptu show of hands, to compile and release to prospective partners a list of members and their contact information, which had to this point remained confidential. It was a small step, but when Rob Stein saw the partners raise their hands, he seemed to physically uncoil, as if these years of skulking around with his PowerPoint, trying not to divulge anything about the alliance or its partners, had caused him to live in a state of constant paranoia. He raised his eyebrows and smiled at me in a gesture of optimism.

For the first time since its inception, the alliance wasn't riven by internal conflicts and melodrama. Even the old soundtrack had been jettisoned. Wade's recordings of the Dixie Chicks were out, replaced by live entertainment in the form of one Malcolm Gets, a onetime actor on the sitcom *Caroline in the City,* who told lifeless jokes and crooned the good morning song while sitting at a grand piano.

There were now 101 partners in the alliance, but Miami was notable mostly for who wasn't there. Rob Reiner and Norman Lear were missing. Steven Gluckstern had a conflict, and most of the other New York partners, including George Soros, hadn't bothered to make the trip. Bernard Schwartz, the octogenarian who had been so instrumental in launching the Phoenix Group in 2004, had quit the alliance altogether in disgust. "They were looking for who they should be when they grow up, and whoever had the latest idea, they went off in that direction," Schwartz had explained to me when we talked just before the elections. "They were bright, intellectual, energetic people who were looking for a mission."

The disengagement of so many of the original partners had changed the nature of the organization, in a way that seemed—oddly—to have brought it closer to Rob Stein's original vision. Most of the partners who had lost enthusiasm for the alliance, and who were likely to follow Schwartz out of it in the months ahead, were those who had been involved in Democratic politics before. The Wall Street guys had advocated a centralized organization, but they had never intended to spend hours of their lives on long e-mail chains and conference calls, trying to micromanage every arcane detail of financing or terminology. Like the Hollywood elite, they already knew the landscape of progressive groups, and they already had entrée to all the Democratic politicians they could ever hope to meet. They didn't need to be part of a club whose members seemed to have nothing but time to waste.

But other original partners, along with some who joined later, the recent tech millionaires and the Aspen vacationers and the apathetic scions who had been galvanized by Bush's war, were eager to connect to people in their own economic world who felt the same way they did. They had never known the best hotels in Washington or which party strategists to trust. They hadn't socialized with other wealthy activists before. For them, the Democracy Alliance wasn't just a vehicle for giving; it was the place where they found camaraderie and reinforcement. Friendships had blossomed and evolved among partners who hadn't even met before Rob Stein had introduced them two years earlier. Rob Johnson told me that he and his wife were even relocating from Greenwich to Bolinas, where Mark and Susie Buell had found them a great place to buy not far from the Buells' own compound.

And so the more buoyant mood in Miami was largely a reflection of people who were genuinely happy to be reunited again, to share stories about their children and their travels. The alliance had become the high rollers' version of YearlyKos or a MoveOn house party. And this, after all, had been the centerpiece of Rob Stein's dream when he had traversed the country in 2004, listening and nodding and relentlessly seeking common ground. He had set out to build a national network of wealthy, progressive activists who felt bound to one another, and who would work in concert. At the time, this part of Rob's pitch had sounded a little too "Kumbaya" for me to take seriously, but now I understood it to be his most impressive achievement. The alliance wasn't the movement of ideas that Rob had hoped it would be—not yet, anyway. But it was, at long last, a genuine community.

"I don't know about the rest of you," Rob McKay told the partners in his opening speech, "but I'm working on day nine of this silly little grin." The alliance partners laughed and cheered the election results once again. And yet, McKay went on to warn, progressives had not yet proven their case to the public and could not be complacent in victory. "The wounded right-wing beast may be more dangerous than ever," he said. In fact, virtually every speaker at the three-day conference stressed this same theme—that Americans hadn't actually voted for Democrats so much as they had voted against Republicans. As Kathleen Sebelius, the newly reelected governor of Kansas, flatly told the assembled partners, "What was done was to fire some people in Washington and give other people a chance. But it's not an endorsement of a policy agenda."

Even Howard Dean, still reveling in the glory of election day, admitted as much during his lunchtime appearance at the Miami meeting. Victory, it seemed, hadn't erased all the bitterness in Washington toward Dean's fifty-state strategy. As it happened, the papers that morning had carried a story about James Carville, the strategist-turned-pundit and close ally of Rahm's, who had informed a group of reporters that Dean was "Rumsfeldian" in his leadership—there was no greater insult to progressives, as Carville surely knew—and that he should be replaced. During a question-and-answer session, Dean declined to comment on Carville's comments—then proceeded, in typical fashion, to do exactly that.

"Let me tell you something about Washington," Dean said, with that tight, I'm-really-not-angry smile plastered on his face. "Washington is basically middle school on steroids." The partners laughed loudly. "It is. It's about your place and who your friends are and all of

that. Real people want to hear about health care and how you're
going to fix the economy and give us clean elections and all of that."
The alliance partners applauded and nodded in knowing agreement,
which was odd, I thought, since not one of them had yet asked Dean
about any of those important issues. John Podesta, who had been surprised to find Dean so tentative back in that first meeting in early
2005, now rose to emphatically declare his unqualified support for
Dean's fifty-state strategy—an important endorsement, given his air
of authority among the donors and his closeness to Carville and the
other Clintonites. Podesta shouted at Dean to keep doing what he
was doing, no matter what anyone in Washington said about it.

Eventually, when one partner did ask Dean about why the party
had seemed to lack a "message" on health care, Dean said that wasn't
true at all, and he blamed the media for ignoring it. As always, however, Dean seemed conflicted about whether he really believed this
or whether the party was, in fact, starved for new ideas. In a moment
of surprising clarity, he seemed to suggest to the partners that what
Democrats needed was an entirely new argument.

"This is a party in evolution," Dean said. "When I did some
thinking, I realized that this is a party of the fifties and sixties. We did
our best work when we did the social safety net stuff. But half the
people we're talking to weren't even alive in the 1960s. We need a
new *idear* of who we are, other than Roosevelt or Johnson."

This question of the progressive identity was the other main
theme that emerged, yet again, in the workshops and panels in
Miami. The donors were thrilled to have humiliated Bush and his
allies in Congress, but even in victory, some of the partners remained
vexed by their inability to articulate what progressives actually stood
for. It was as if a broken-down car had suddenly started up, for no
apparent reason other than the mild weather; they were exhilarated
by the sound of the engine, but haunted by the knowledge that it
would likely sputter again. Podesta gave voice to this nagging feeling

during one of the panels. "We still haven't cracked the übermessage," he said. "We still haven't gotten into people's minds a picture of what a progressive America would look like."

The alliance partners seemed to be wondering just how long that was going to take and how much it was going to cost. During one session, a partner rose to pose a question to Rob McKay. "I wish you'd come back and tell us," he said, "what is the numerical goal to change the country? Is it $150 million? Is it $200 million?" He looked around the room. "How much do we need?"

Andy Stern sat silently through all of these discussions, his mind elsewhere. The way Stern saw it, neither the Washington insiders nor the progressive outsiders were headed in the right direction. Democrats in Congress still had no serious economic agenda for the broad middle class, and the new progressive movement embodied by the alliance seemed mired in the last century's ideology, too obsessed with tactics to embrace any new ideas. He had already decided that he couldn't rely on either of them to figure out what came next.

In the weeks ahead, after months of secret negotiations, Stern would announce that the service employees had formed (along with John Podesta and the Center for American Progress) controversial partnerships with some large American corporations, including the most vilified of them all: Wal-Mart. The idea was to enlist influential businesses in a public campaign for universal health care and for revisiting the social safety net as a whole. At the same time, Stern's team was finalizing the legal details on another ambitious project: the first-ever union for self-employed workers, offering health care and other benefits at a reduced rate to those Americans who were left out of the current, employer-based system and couldn't afford to go it alone. If Democrats weren't going to do something about the country's problems, Stern reasoned, he and his union would.

Stern also joined with Eli Pariser and the guys at MoveOn to create a political action committee called "They Work for Us." The plan was to pick out a few Democratic incumbents in each cycle, congressmen who weren't sufficiently progressive on economic issues, and to finance primary opponents who could beat them. Markos agreed to sit on the board as well. Basically, the progressive movement's most powerful outsiders had now resolved to chisel away at the grottiest corners of the Democratic Party's entrenched establishment, one Joe Lieberman at a time.

For the keynote speech in Miami, the Democracy Alliance had flown in Mario Cuomo. Once, twenty-two years earlier, at Walter Mondale's nominating convention in San Francisco, Cuomo, then in his prime as New York's governor, had delivered one of the great orations in political history, laying waste to Ronald Reagan's mythical "city on a hill"—"There is despair, Mr. President, in the faces that you don't see, in the places that you don't visit in your shining city. . . ."—and closing with that wrenching description of his immigrant father, his feet bleeding at the end of the day from working in his Queens grocery store. They had begged him to run for president four years later, and again four years after that; had he acquiesced, it was possible, if not likely, that the era of Clintonism would never have descended on the Democratic Party. Instead, Cuomo had become the icon of a fading era—the last, along with Ted Kennedy and Jesse Jackson, of the industrial party's great liberal titans.

Now, at seventy-four, he seemed shriveled and more owlish than I remembered from watching him on TV as a kid, and he moved more slowly, but the swagger and the sharpness remained. He had prepared a speech, laced with the unapologetic and expansive liberalism of his time, but, as always, he spoke without a single note. He detoured artfully and with purpose from his text, taking a moment here and there, in that terrific Queens accent, to expound on why you never wanted to go to the beach on Long Island (it took two days to get home), why his mother insisted that God loved Reagan (it was the hair), how Jimmy Carter pronounced Italian ("Eye-talian"), why the Declaration of Independence mattered more than the Constitution (see the Gettysburg Address), and on the meaning of the Hebrew concept of *tzedaka* ("love one another").

The main point of the speech, though, in between all the digressions, was to make these donors understand the transformative power of an argument. Think tanks were all fine and good, Cuomo said dismissively, but the next election wasn't twenty years from now—it was coming right up in 2008—and the country confronted some huge and perplexing realities: terrorism, globalization, an emerging China. The issues in any campaign were too myriad and complex for voters to sort through and weigh, he said. It was simply too much to ask of them.

"So what happens?" Cuomo asked. His answer was not that you build the best voter turnout machine you can afford, or that you bring in a linguist to calibrate your message. "You seize the biggest idea you can," he said, "the biggest idea you can understand. And this is what moves elections."

He then went through, election by election, the larger arguments that had dominated every American presidential campaign since Watergate. Carter won because he made a case for "holiness and cleanliness" in government, Cuomo said. Reagan ran, in succession, on supply-side economics and on forcing a showdown in the cold war. Clinton talked about the fundamental upheaval in the American economy. "It was a big idea," Cuomo said. "It was a very, very big idea.

"In 2000, what was the issue?" he went on. "There was no big idea. Nothing. And what did you get? A dead heat. It was a tie." Some of the partners seemed to wince at this—they still believed the election had been stolen from them—but Cuomo forged on. The last election, he said, had been all about Bush's war on terror. "There was nothing else. What about health care? What about the economy? Forget it," Cuomo said, shaking his head. "No one cared."

Which brought him to the present. "Now it's 2006," he said, "and we're all rejoicing. Why? Because of Iraq. A *gift*. A gift to the Democrats. A lot of whom voted for the war anyway." An uncomfortable silence hung over the ballroom. No one had yet expressed the situation quite that crassly, although everyone knew it was an accurate accounting.

"If Iraq is not an issue, then what issues do we have to talk about?" he asked them. "So far the Democrats have talked about what I think it's fair to say are very timid proposals. The minimum wage? No one in this room would say that's not a good idea. It's a good idea. Lower prices for prescription drugs? Another good idea." And yet, he went on sadly, none of these were grand enough to restore the soul of a party.

"Where does that leave you?" Cuomo asked. "It leaves you in the same position you were in in 2004—without an issue. Because you have no big idea."

Almost two years after their first meeting, the partners of the Democracy Alliance were now more than halfway toward their original goal of spending $100 million on the infrastructure of a new progressive movement, and that money had bought them no end of rapid-response memos and branding sessions and voter files and training programs. But here was this legendary old man—not one of those New Democrats they so disdained, but a giant of the old Left—telling them that ideas really did matter more than the minutiae of electioneering. He stood before them like some apparition from the party's glorious past, come to remind them that political history didn't really turn on the amount of money you spent, but on the courage to think anew.

Afterword:
The Choosing Season

In 2008, for the first time in more than a half century, there would be no incumbent president or vice president on the ballot, leaving the election wide open, and as public faith in the Bush administration continued to plummet (by spring 2008, an astonishing 81 percent of Americans polled would say the country was on the wrong track), Democrats could think of little else but reclaiming the White House. Party insiders and progressive outsiders quickly chose sides among a trio of top-tier candidates, donating and blogging and otherwise hurling themselves fully into a primary season rich with possibility.

Pundits speculated about which of the three leading candidates—Hillary Clinton, Barack Obama, and John Edwards—might inherit the support of what the journalist Ron Brownstein called the "Internet Left," the band of online progressives who had begun to redefine Democratic politics since 2004. Technology, though, had outpaced this conversation; the Internet had already gone mainstream. Four years earlier, the number of Democrats connecting to politics principally through their high-speed modems had been small enough to have rallied progressive support around a single candidate, Howard Dean. But in the time since, millions more Americans of all genera tions had seen their lifestyles transformed by the online revolution, to the point where voters who had never heard of a blog in 2004 were now lurking in the shadows of Daily Kos, and many who had never written a check to a politician were now clicking the "donate" buttons on their candidates' Web sites. Online activism had now matured to the point where there could never be just one "Internet candidate," any more than any one candidate could dominate television.

Presidential politics consumed and divided the donor community as well. By the dawn of the primary season, Democracy Alliance partners had contributed more than $100 million to their portfolio of chosen organizations, but despite all the continuing talk about generating ideas, most of that money was focused in some way on winning back the White House. Not content with that, a select group of Alliance partners, including the ubiquitous George Soros, got together to build a new organization whose sole mandate would be to destroy the eventual Republican nominee with a blitzkrieg of TV ads. They first lured Tom Matzzie away from MoveOn to run it, but when this new effort, like the Democracy Alliance itself, nearly unraveled because of infighting, they instead turned to David Brock, the progressive media critic who had once made his living attacking Democrats. With the wealthiest progressives, it seemed that nothing—not even the straightforward business of mauling Republicans in thirty-second clips—was ever easy.

By the summer of 2007, just about everyone inside Washington, including the reporters whose job it was to cover the campaign, expected Clinton to win her party's nomination with nominal resistance. She had the money, the name, the polish, the endorsements. She was her husband's anointed successor, the validator of his place in history. Edwards and Obama were stalled in national polls and barely holding off Clinton in Iowa, a state only one of them could win but which both of them had to have if they were to have any chance of derailing her in the rest of the country. The Republican candidates were already sparring over which of them would have the best shot at beating Hillary, as if they too deemed her nomination a formality.

When the capital's political class seemed not to understand, however, was just how widely the progressive movement's rejection of Clintonian ideas had permeated the Democratic grassroots. Clinton's campaign didn't seem to get it, either. Mark Penn, the Clintons' longtime pollster and the campaign's chief strategist, insisted that the former First Couple were more beloved by Democratic voters than any other living political figure. He pointed to polls that showed the former president with an approval rating of almost 90 percent among his own party's voters. No wonder Clinton ran her primary campaign on the promise of restoration, the resumption of her husband's sabotaged agenda.

It was true enough, of course, that even Democrats who considered themselves progressives first still adored Bill Clinton personally, and they admired his wife, especially the way she had transcended all the venom and humiliation of the White House years. But had Penn asked those voters what they thought of "Clintonism" as a political philosophy, he would have gotten a markedly different answer. A lot of Democrats in the party's new progressive era seemed to draw a distinction between the Clintons themselves and the political era they represented, and no matter how they swooned over Bill and Hillary in the flesh, they harbored a profound ambivalence about a second Clinton presidency—to a far greater extent than most of the party's leaders seemed able to appreciate.

It was Obama, an untested but singular political talent, who would ultimately emerge as the alternative to the Clinton legacy. He made history by winning in all-white Iowa; she showed her mettle by rebounding in New Hampshire. She won Nevada; he took South Carolina. From there, the two candidates settled into a long and bloody war of attrition that threatened to divide the party along fault lines of class, race, and age. Obama became, in short order, the hope of those new progressives who yearned to break with the Democratic ethos of the '90s. In January 2008 alone, Obama raised more money online— about $28 million—than Dean had during his entire campaign. Obama also received the endorsement of MoveOn.org, prompting Clinton to complain privately that MoveOn members provided her opponent with "a gusher of money" and intimidated her supporters at rural-state caucuses.

The irony here was that Obama had defined his campaign not as an extension of the resurgent progressive movement in Democratic politics, but against it. He was liberal, to be sure, and he was openly contemptuous of the Republican administration, but Obama rejected the confrontational brand of partisanship that so many progressives demanded. Three years after he had written his memorable reproach to members of the Daily Kos community, Obama based his candidacy on the idea that government would only move forward if both parties—and not just the GOP—set aside their outdated orthodoxies and distracting culture wars. To a lot of progressives, this sounded naive and unprincipled. They cringed when Obama said Social Security needed fixing and when he opposed forcing Americans to buy health insurance, arguing that it sounded too much like government telling people how to live their lives. Paul Krugman, the *New York Times* columnist who was an icon for the new progressives, and who openly crusaded against Obama, repeatedly accused him of borrowing Republican talking points. To progressives, there was no graver an indictment.

Even so, Obama continued to rack up money and votes from the party's progressive activists. No, he was not a Dean-like hero to the people who gathered still on the liberal blogs or in MoveOn parties or in privileged cliques within the Democracy Alliance. But he wasn't another Clinton, bent on returning the party to its corporatist heyday, and for many this was enough—at least for now.

As I write this, in the spring of 2008, Obama and Clinton are in the final, wearying stage of a dramatic primary showdown, and the outcome remains in doubt; while Obama retains a slight lead in delegates, either candidate will require the blessing of an exclusive group of the party insiders known as "superdelegates" if he or she is to prevail. Should Obama win the nomination, though, and perhaps even the White House, he will face a choice where the powerful progressives in his own party are concerned: whether to attempt, through the power of his personality and argument, to lead this new movement away from the limited politics of hostility and toward some more modern vision of liberalism, or whether to become, like so many political leaders before him, a reflection of the moment he inherits. If Obama can't change the trajectory of the new progressive movement, then the movement will very likely change him.

Acknowledgments

I am deeply indebted to the hundreds of people in the progressive movement who lent me their time and their trust over these last few years. Rob Stein was never too busy to offer his considerable insights, and I look forward to more meandering conversations. Simon Rosenberg's contribution to my understanding of the progressive world is greater than his presence in the book would suggest, and I'm grateful for it. Andy Stern was unfailingly gracious with his time and sharp in his insights. John Podesta never did let me buy him lunch, but he was a valuable resource. Eli Pariser and Tom Matzzie answered countless queries about MoveOn.org, and Jerome Armstrong and Markos Moulitsas Zúniga taught me about the netroots. Gina Cooper became a friend and an inspiration, as she is to so many in the YearlyKos community.

Many partners in the Democracy Alliance were instrumental in this project, but I wouldn't be doing them any good to name them here. They know who they are. I must, however, mention Mark Buell and Susie Tompkins Buell, whose kindness, at tense moments during the process, will not be forgotten. I also want to thank George Soros, whose commitment to transparency has always extended—in my case, at least—to granting interviews, even when he didn't have to, and even when his fellow philanthropists refused.

Several knowledgeable Democrats have, over the last few years, generously tutored me on various aspects of the party's history and culture. Chief among them are Harold Ickes, Steve Rosenthal, Gina Glantz, Mike McCurry, Pat Caddell, Tina Flournoy, Anita Dunn, Doug Wilson, and Lynne Wasserman. Jay Carson, one of the great young talents in the Democratic Party, was helpful in connecting me to both Andy Stern and President Clinton. Lucky for me he changes jobs so much.

Adam Nagourney and John Harris, two of the finest journalists in Washington, offered critical advice early in the project, and two of my very accomplished colleagues at the *New York Times Magazine,* Jonathan Mahler and Michael Sokolove, helped with writing tips for a first-time author. Another smart journalist, Nick Penniman, acted as a sounding board and often paid for lunch.

Andrei Cherny was a valued source of brilliance, laughter, and thoughtful criticism. Andrei's book, *The Next Deal,* strongly influenced my thinking on politics. Every Democrat should read it.

Wes Kosova and Yahlin Chang read early drafts of the book and encouraged me when I was ready to throw it all away and go work as a batboy. I was also honored to have the assistance of Lucy Shackelford, the best researcher in the business and a great friend. Half the fun of the book was getting to work with Lucy again. If factual errors remain, they are my fault and not hers.

In every aspect of this process, as in so much else, I relied heavily on the unerring judgment of my agent, Sarah Chalfant of the Wylie Agency. This book was Sarah's idea, and she has been a tireless champion. I'm also thankful to Sarah's right-hand man, Edward Orloff, and to Andrew Wylie, who helped shape the concept.

My terrific editor at the Penguin Press, Vanessa Mobley, was creative, unflinching, and unwavering in her faith. She believed in me from the day we met, and I in her—I hope the book does justice to her vision. Vanessa's talented assistant, Lindsay Whalen, was a huge help. I'm grateful, as well, to Ann Godoff, who showed such faith in the project, and the whole outstanding team at The Penguin Press.

It's hard for me to adequately express my gratitude to everyone at *The New York Times Magazine*. Gerry Marzorati is pretty much every writer's ideal editor, and he has given me the opportunity of a lifetime. Gerry also encouraged me to write the book and offered crucial thoughts on the manuscript. Paul Tough, my editor at the magazine, has been a silent but equal partner in everything I've written over the last five years. He is, quite simply, the best story editor there is and a gifted political observer, as well. He also spent an absurd amount of time improving the manuscript, while editing covers and working on his own book. For all of this, I owe Paul a debt I can't repay.

My great friends Debra Rosenberg and David Lipscomb are always patient listeners, and David contributed some important insights to the book that I shamelessly appropriated as my own. Deb's parents, Joan and Paul Rosenberg, made us welcome at their beach house, and I did some of my best writing there. The wonderful Trent Gegax and Samara Minkin let me crash on their couch in Manhattan, and then, when they cleverly thought to get rid of the couch, I thwarted them by sleeping on the floor.

Over the years, I have relied on Jon Cowan's selfless advice on all manner of important topics—this book, career decisions, which *South Park* episodes to watch. Jon is one of the best young minds in Democratic politics, and although he surely knows that our friendship has caused him to be unfairly excluded from my work, he has never once mentioned it.

My mother, Rhea Bai, and my sisters, Dina and Caroline, have always been supportive. So have my wonderful in-laws, George and Nancy Uchimiya. My father never had the chance to read my political writing, but his influence is all over these pages.

And then there's Ellen, my life's editor, who reads every word before anyone else, and who is the best friend and critic and partner imaginable. Coming aboard Bill Bradley's campaign bus in New Hampshire—and sitting behind Ellen—were the two best decisions I ever made. Without her, there would be no book, and no reason.

While I was working on this book, Ellen gave birth to our amazing son, Ichiro. I hope someday he reads this and feels half as proud of me as I am of him. For now, he'll probably just tear out the pages, and that's fine.

Index